GIFTS, TALENTS AND EDUCATION
A LIVING THEORY APPROACH

GIFTS, TALENTS AND EDUCATION

A LIVING THEORY APPROACH

Barry Hymer
University of Newcastle Upon Tyne (Visiting Fellow)

Jack Whitehead
University of Bath (Lecturer)

and

Marie Huxtable
University of Bath (Doctoral student)

A John Wiley & Sons, Ltd., Publication

Wiley-Blackwell is an imprint of John Wiley & Sons, formed by the merger of Wiley's global Scientific, Technical, and Medical business with Blackwell Publishing.

Registered Office
John Wiley & Sons Ltd, The Atrium, Southern Gate, Chichester, West Sussex, PO19 8SQ, UK

Editorial Offices
The Atrium, Southern Gate, Chichester, West Sussex, PO19 8SQ, UK
9600 Garsington Road, Oxford, OX4 2DQ, UK
350 Main Street, Malden, MA 02148-5020, USA

For details of our global editorial offices, for customer services and for information about how to apply for permission to reuse the copyright material in this book, please see our web site at www.wiley.com/wiley-blackwell.

Library of Congress Cataloging-in-Publication Data
Hymer, Barry.
  Gifts, talents and education : a living theory approach / by Barry Hymer, Jack Whitehead and Marie Huxtable.
    p. cm.
  Includes bibliographical references and index.
  ISBN 978-0-470-72539-9 (cloth : alk. paper)
  1. Gifted children–Education. 2. Gifted children–Education–Research. I. Whitehead, Jack.
II. Huxtable, Marie. III. Title.
  LC3993.H96 2008
  371.95–dc22

                                                                    2008022822

A catalogue record for this book is available from the British Library

ISBN 978-0-470-72539-9 (hbk)

Typeset in 10/12pt Palatino by SNP Best-set Typesetter Ltd., Hong Kong
Printed in Singapore by Fabulous Printers Pte Ltd

CONTENTS

ABOUT THE AUTHORS

Dr Barry Hymer is a freelance educator, chartered psychologist and Visiting Fellow at Newcastle University's Centre for Learning and Teaching. Barry has written widely in the fields of learning, teaching and gifted education and he actively champions inclusive and holistic approaches to knowledge-creation and personal growth in his work with children, young people and adults – especially through such approaches as Philosophy for Children (P4C) and Dilemma-Based Learning. Barry received the 2003 Award for Excellence from ICPIC – The International Council for Philosophical Inquiry with Children. www.barryhymer.co.uk

Dr Jack Whitehead is a Lecturer in Education at the University of Bath where he began his research programme in 1973 into the nature of educational theory. He is a former President of the British Educational Research Association and a Visiting Professor at Ningxia Teachers University in China. He originated the idea of living educational theory to support the academic legitimation of practitioner-knowledge in the Academy and has pioneered multimedia representations of explanations of educational influence in learning. His website, www.actionresearch.net, is an internationally used resource for developing living educational theories.

Marie Huxtable is a senior educational psychologist, working within an English local authority where she coordinates and develops the inclusive gifts, talents and education project. Her work rests on the belief that all learners have the capacity for extraordinary achievement. Her responsibility as an educator is to contribute to improving educational contexts that inform the aspirations of children and young people as they learn what it is to live a satisfying and productive life that enhances their well-being and well-becoming. She is working to develop her inclusive and inclusional practice through living theory research to reflect her growing understanding of what she means by extraordinary achievement and the educational environment in which it can flourish. www.spanglefish.com/mariessite

ABOUT THE CONTRIBUTORS

Gillie Bolton is the author and editor of five books and many academic papers on how writing can enable powerfully beneficial illuminative insight personally and professionally. Her *Reflective Practice Writing and Professional Development* (Sage Publications) will be in its third edition early in 2010. Gillie is the Literature and Medicine editor of *Medical Ethics: Medical Humanities* (BMJ Publications) and is a freelance consultant, award-winning poet, Quaker and now nearing her 40th wedding anniversary and the birth of her first grandchild.

Professor Dona Matthews has been teaching, writing, counselling, consulting and conducting research on gifted development and education since 1985. From 2003 to 2007 she was Director of the Center for Gifted Studies and Education at Hunter College, City University of New York. Co-author of *Being Smart About Gifted Children*, she now teaches at the University of Toronto, is engaged in several writing projects and is working with families and schools on issues relating to gifted education.

Dr Moira Laidlaw went into teaching in 1978, without ever having had a thought about doing anything else. She taught in comprehensive schools for 18 years and at Bath University for four years. She has a passion for democratising the learning process and finds the greatest pleasure when someone learns something of value for themselves, and whose world as a result becomes a more interesting place. She spent five years in China as an educational volunteer and became a Visiting Professor at Ningxia Teachers University.

Dr Alan Rayner was born in Nairobi, Kenya in 1950. He obtained BA and PhD degrees in Natural Sciences at King's College, Cambridge and is currently a Reader in Biology at the University of Bath. He is a biological scientist, ecological philosopher, artist and writer. He has published around 150 scientific articles, six formal scientific books (including *Degrees of Freedom – Living in Dynamic Boundaries*, Imperial College Press, 1997), a three-volume multi-author e-book and three Internet-downloadable books (*Inclusional Nature and Natural Inclusion*, 2006, Natural Communion, 2008).

Andrew Leggett is a teacher with 19 years' experience of working in comprehensive schools in London and South Yorkshire. He is currently an Advanced Skills Teacher in Doncaster where he works with others to improve teaching and help students learn through innovative practice. He describes himself as "a reflective and practical teacher with a true love of learning".

Belle Wallace is the immediate past-President of the National Association for Able, Gifted and Talented Children (NACE), Editor of *Gifted Education International* (AB Academic Publishers) and a well-known national and international consultant on all aspects of inclusive provision for gifted and talented children. Belle has been a member of the Executive Committee for the World Council for Gifted and Talented Children (WCGTC) and has published extensively in the field. Her particular interest lies in the development of problem-solving curricula across multiple capacities for all levels of students and the educational needs of gifted disadvantaged learners. She has recently been elected a Fellow of the Royal Society for Arts (FRSA) for her services to education.

Chris Reck has been teaching for seven years. He is currently an Advanced Skills Teacher in English at Belfairs High School, Leigh-on-Sea, Essex. He is highly respected at local and national level and is a leading practitioner in both English and Learning to Learn strategies.

INTRODUCTION

Why do we expect someone to say "thank you" when we give them something? Shouldn't we give it to them for free? (Towan, 2004, aged 10, comment during a philosophical enquiry)

This book represents a shared, three-way passion, which runs on twin-track lines: we hope that it will serve both our purpose in helping to generate a cultural transformation in ideas about gifts and talents in education (through living educational theories), and will serve your purpose in enhancing your possibilities for living a worthwhile and productive life.

The book has been some years in gestation and represents an outcome of our various collaborations. Marie and Barry have worked together for several years in developing their practices and understandings of gifts and talents in education. Marie encouraged Jack to attend one of Barry's philosophical workshops with infant school children in 2006, and Jack was inspired by Barry's ability to support the generation of a creative space with teachers and their pupils, in which the pupils contributed as experts in their own learning and questioning. Jack has been influenced by the ideas of Martin Buber and felt that Barry expressed a dynamic loving energy in his educational relationships with both teachers and pupils that distinguished his special humility as an educator:

> If this educator should ever believe that for the sake of education he has to practise selection and arrangement, then he will be guided by another criterion than that of inclination, however legitimate this may be in its own sphere; he will be guided by the recognition of values which is in his glance as an educator. But even then his selection remains suspended, under constant correction by the special humility of the educator for whom the life and particular being of all his pupils is the decisive factor to which his "hierarchical" recognition is subordinated. (Buber, 1947, p. 122)

In bringing Barry and Jack together, Marie believed that both would benefit. Jack would experience the presence and practice of a professional educator

Gifts, Talents and Education By Barry Hymer, Jack Whitehead and Marie Huxtable
© 2008 Wiley-Blackwell

who had the talent of expressing values Jack believed in. Barry at the time was disengaged from his doctoral studies, having become disenchanted with the capacity of the positivist method to address his areas of interest and unable to connect the data he had accumulated with his passions as an educator. Marie believed that Jack, originator of an approach to action research that is now practised and valued internationally, might be able to excite Barry about the possibilities of generating his own living educational theory of gifts and talents in education.

This is indeed what happened. Barry successfully completed his living theory doctorate in educational psychology at the University of Newcastle, graduating in July 2007. By coincidence, Jack had attended the initial teacher education programme in the Department of Education at the University of Newcastle in the 1966–1976 academic year. Some 40 years later, Jack returned for Barry's graduation and was able to offer a gift to the Department in the form of a seminar and a presentation on his learning from 40 years' professional engagement with education (Appendix 1). This presentation emphasised the idea of a gift being something that is produced from one's developed talents and freely given. It was also offered as a celebration of three living theory doctoral graduations: Barry's from the University of Newcastle, Eden Charles' from the University of Bath and Margaret Follows' from the University of Plymouth. Each of these educators, Jack believes, has expressed a passion for education and a willingness to account for their learning and influence in terms of the energy and values that give meaning and purpose to their lives. They have expressed, developed and used their unique talents in their particular contexts to produce the gifts of their living theories that are now flowing freely through web space.

Our approach to producing the book collaboratively has been for each to take the lead in writing the initial draft of certain chapters and then for each of us to participate in the redrafting of all the chapters until we feel a sense of joint ownership and participation.

Barry took the lead in the first two chapters, describing our dissatisfactions with traditional routes to 'giftedness' and outlining a non-deterministic, fluid and inclusional framework for understanding the processes of talent development and gift creation – a framework which emerged from his own living theory research. Marie and Jack identified with Barry's story of the transformation in his understandings of gifts and talents in education and have helped to refine and develop his thinking further.

Jack took the lead in the third chapter, exploring giftedness as a living concept. Barry and Marie have both embraced Jack's idea of the significance of individuals generating their unique living educational theories as an explanation of their educational influences in learning. The three of us have transformed our own thinking from ideas about 'gifted and talented children', as in 2007 Government policy, to the view that everyone has the capacity to develop and express talents, from wildly different starting points, that they can manifest in the production of gifts that are freely given.

Marie, with Jack's support, took the lead in the fourth and fifth chapters, in which she draws on Barry's idea of developing a generative-transformational approach to gifts and then extends it – making connections with the possibilities in Jack's seminal work on living theory. In these ideas, she embraces the potential for young people to engage in the generation of their own living theories. This work offers the possibility of enabling individuals, irrespective of age, to recognise the living values that give meaning and purpose to their lives and to develop, express and use their unique talents to create and offer gifts to the benefit of themselves and society. This approach takes the three of us beyond the boundaries of economic rationalism into the recognition of the importance for human beings and societies of freely offering gifts. We are aware of how easy it is to ritualise the giving and receiving of gifts. A true gift asks for nothing in return. We focus instead on the human desire to produce something from one's talents that can be freely given.

In producing this book together, we seek to recognise, and offer a generative response to, a mistake in ideas about gifts and talents in education as they have been traditionally understood in our Northern European context. We are also aware of seeing in each other's professional practices, relationships and understandings that we have learnt from understanding this mistake in a way that offers possibilities for an educational transformation in the dominant culture. For this transformation to move from our particular workplace contexts into a general cultural influence, many others are needed to understand the mistake and to engage in a cultural transformation of understanding.

What we are hoping is that you feel that we have produced and shared ideas that are worthwhile with our own unique talents that are being amplified through our collaborative working together. We hope that you will feel this collaboration and that our way of working has also enabled the readers to feel that their own unique contribution is being recognised as of value. We recognise that there is a tension between offering ideas about gifts in a book that is sold in a marketplace. We also recognise that the marketplace in which books are sold and circulated can help to communicate ideas widely. We have also included in the text the URLs for web-based resources that have been freely given, by these authors, as gifts.

We wish also to acknowledge the generosity of the outstanding educators whose personal stories, introducing each chapter in the book, illuminate and vivify theoretical considerations. These accounts are, we hope you'll agree, rare gifts: deeply reflective, authentic and searingly, sometimes painfully, honest tales of their lives and the values that inform those lives. The occasional pain is part of the gift, invoking the poet Auden:

> (Auden) was always moving on to the next task, suffering failure sometimes, and aware of a widespread rejection of his later work. He had a private, even secret, generosity to match the public generosity, the copiousness of his achievement. An enviable gift, then, although not always an enviable life – unless we say that in some cases the gift is indeed the life, and that the suffering is all part of the gift. (*The Guardian* Review, 3 February 2007, p. 12)

CHAPTER 1

WHAT'S IMPLICIT IN 20TH CENTURY NOTIONS OF GIFTEDNESS? WHY ARE THESE NOTIONS UNFIT FOR PURPOSE IN THE 21ST CENTURY?

**Natural Inclusion – from Adversity with Love
by Alan Rayner**

My struggle has been based in a simple longing to be included in the common space of natural human neighbourhood, from which my upbringing and education singled me out. I have needed to uncover a way of thinking that does not alienate reason from emotion, and does not disparage ordinary human qualities in the quest for exceptional performance. I wanted to discover the extraordinariness of the mundane and express this in a common sense and obvious way that isn't necessarily obvious to the highbrow, but is deeply embedded in our everyday experience of living, loving, fear and death.

From an early age, I was brought up with the expectation that I *ought* to be faultless, both morally and intellectually. Never mind that this was an unrealistic and ultimately meaningless aspiration for any human being, my duty as a privileged child of the British Empire was to try as hard as I could to achieve it. The message was that my family and I would suffer greatly if I failed in this endeavour. I would succeed by becoming a scrupulously honest and dutiful paragon of virtue who always put others' interests and welfare before his own needs, whilst paradoxically being supremely competitive when it came to the kind of performance deemed important by those in my vicinity.

Spurred on by this pressure to excel and a need for my father's approval, I came through my early education with all the A and S Levels he could

Gifts, Talents and Education By Barry Hymer, Jack Whitehead and Marie Huxtable
© 2008 Wiley-Blackwell

have wanted. They got me to King's College, Cambridge, where I studied for six years, gaining a triple first in Natural Sciences, followed by a PhD in fungal ecology. I soon moved to Bath University as a lecturer and at the age of 35 was promoted directly to a Readership.

By the time I became President of the British Mycological Society at the age of 47, I had published six books and over 120 scientific papers. My academic colleagues, however, did not see this as good enough reason for further promotion or celebration. My research by then was producing findings that challenged orthodox schools of thought concerning the fundamental nature of evolutionary creativity and the legitimacy of scientific method and was therefore becoming neither publishable nor fundable through channels acceptable to the mainstream.

I felt unsupported and unvalued. Ever-present tensions and anxieties suddenly exploded to overwhelming proportions. Long-suppressed self-destructive and self-reclaiming processes took over my life. I had to take six months sick leave. Later I managed to return to work, but I was a changed man and an embarrassment to my colleagues. I set about radically changing the course of my teaching and research to include artistic and philosophical themes relevant to the global social, environmental and psychological crises that I now saw as paramount.

I had never got over my childhood feeling that there was something fundamentally *wrong* with me, some *gap* in my make-up, which, when exposed, would prove both catastrophic and profoundly humiliating. My experiences of school and university education, with its many cruelties, iniquities, absurdities and pretences, did nothing to alleviate and much to reinforce this feeling. I never felt more than temporary relief from my academic successes. They only served to cover up and delay recognition of my underlying deep inadequacy, until the next fearful test came along that could finally show me to be the dreadful fraud I really am. This sense of being a fraud also infected my personal life; loving and caring for others felt like a dangerous charade.

Yet at the same time I had the feeling of being possessed by an exceptionally inspiring, creative, knowledgeable, perceptive and empathic spirit, capable of seeing through the obstructions that everywhere block our human understanding and enjoyment of the flow of nature. This feeling would fill my heart with enormous enthusiasm and joy in sharing my experience and learning whenever I could just let go of my fears and not be painfully reminded of them.

My quest to understand and heal the seeming contradiction within myself began with the supposition, in line with much modern thinking, that my childhood perception was correct: there is indeed something fundamentally *wrong with* me. But I had great difficulty identifying what this something was.

Recently, my wife, Marion, brought home *The Achilles Syndrome – Overcoming the Secret Fear of Failure* by Petruska Clarkson (Element Books, 1994). Reading it was a revelation. I had already vaguely heard about and related my experience to what has been called the Impostor Syndrome, but Clarkson's book goes further and deeper in identifying a psychological archetype, epitomised by the myth of Achilles. If ever a character combined exceptional prowess with exceptional vulnerability arising from a *gap* in his upbringing, here is the one. Moreover, this character was not only a great warrior (and worrier – like me, he would doubtless have been diagnosed these days as suffering from obsessive-compulsive disorder), but he also expressed enormous creativity, compassion and healing power.

In identifying the origin of this syndrome, Clarkson had no hesitation in pointing to over-expectant forms of upbringing and education in a competitive culture, which neglect human needs for love and respect in the quest for fast-tracked superiority. The result is what she calls pseudocompetence – apparently advanced skill built on fragile foundations: in another word, bullshit.

Conventional rationalistic thinking regards individual behaviour as a definable product of internal brain structure and chemistry (genetic "nature") and external environmental influences including education and upbringing ("nurture"). A hard line is drawn between inner world and outer world, notwithstanding that there is no modern scientific evidence for the existence of such discrete boundaries and much evidence to the contrary, implicit in relativity, quantum mechanics and non-linear theory.

I think it is just this kind of objective rationality, however, which creates the divisive cultural context in which the sense of vulnerability underlying Achilles Syndrome can grow out of all proportion. It makes this vulnerability seem like something wrong *with* individuals – a failing that needs to be surmounted, not a vital and inescapable source of human and evolutionary creativity.

Objective rationality also fails to appreciate how viewing vulnerability as a failing contributes to global crisis. It underlies the human propensity to try to remove doubt by imposing unrealistic definitions of things. We embed such definition deep within our philosophical, mathematical, scientific, linguistic, educational and governmental foundations. We strive to be complete and perfect individuals who will be preserved (if not pickled!) in the Darwinian struggle for life, whilst not appreciating that any form of completion rings the death knell for evolutionary creativity. We render ourselves into discrete subjects and objects capable only of transactional, competitive or co-operative interaction rather than being lovingly receptive and responsive inclusions of one and another. We don't recognise that evolutionary perfection can only be a property of *all* in dynamic relationship, not *one* in isolation, and so try to live out our lives as paradoxical singularities, alienated from our natural neighbourhood.

But the gaps in our individual make up are *not* the problem. The *pretence* that these gaps can be eliminated or covered up is what makes us pseudocompetent. We cannot breathe or move or love or live without gaps in our bodily boundaries. These boundaries are necessarily *incomplete*, distinct and dynamic, not discrete and fixed. As William Wordsworth said, in nature everything is distinct, yet nothing defined into absolute, independent singleness.

There is therefore very good intellectual reason for compassion. What we might deem, in a perfectionist framework, to be a flaw in human nature, our vulnerability and proneness to error, is actually vital. It is the source of our creative spirit. It is an aspect of our nature that enables us to love and feel love and so work co-creatively in dynamic relational neighbourhood, celebrating and respecting rather than decrying our diversity of competencies and appearances.

Correspondingly, my personal response through adversity has been to develop and explore a form of awareness called "inclusionality." This does not replace objective rationality but utterly transforms it into a far deeper and more encompassing appreciation of all form as *flow-form*, a dynamic inclusion, not an occupier of space. With this awareness, seemingly opposing external forces are transformed into complementary influences within the limitless immanence of Natural Inclusion – the co-creative, fluid dynamic reconfiguration of all through all in receptive spatial context. The local, "to be *or* not to be" objective logic of the excluded middle is transformed into the fluid dynamic "to be *in* not to be", of the included middle. The possessive sovereignty of the individual, "I alone", self is transformed into the complex identity of self as neighbourhood with both local (particular) and non-local (everywhere) aspects. The occupation and fractionation of territory is transformed into a *natural communion* of pooled togetherness. The exploitation of other by one is transformed into sustainable attunement of one with other. The imposed box of three-dimensional geometry – with space and time abstracted – is transformed into an infinite, dynamically nested, holeyness.

> To view our human vulnerability as an Achilles Heel allows us to arrive at a naturally creative solution for adversity, a gap that opens the possibility of *agape* (spiritual love).

What we are seeking to do in this book and in our practice is to restore a focus on the idea of a gift as something freely created and offered with the intention of contributing to the possibilities for well-being and well-becoming. We eschew the obsession with objective rationality that can lead to a dead-end drive for 'pseudocompetence' – identified in Alan's story, above – in favour of true educational journeying.

In a world that emphasises economic rationality, the value of what we produce is often understood in terms of the price for which it can be sold. In this book, we are emphasising the importance of expressing a life-affirming energy as we express and develop our talents in producing something that is offered freely as a gift. This is not to deny the importance of our economic activity in meeting basic needs for food, shelter and productive work, or to disguise the fact that this book may have cost you, the reader, something to buy! It is to highlight the importance of the flows of life-affirming energy that carry hope for the future of humanity in the expression and development of our talents, in the production and offering of gifts.

Whilst this book as a whole is avowedly a story of enchantment with the concept of gifted education, this particular chapter is a story of disenchantment, not with 'giftedness' per se, but with the ways in which giftedness has traditionally been conceptualised, interpreted and applied in educational settings. It seeks to set the scene for the later descriptions which we offer of inclusive and inclusional (Rayner, above) understandings of gifts and talents, rooted in values of humanity such as love, justice, respect and egalitarianism. We see these descriptions as contributing to the endeavours of educators working in progressive 21st century classrooms and schools where practice can be recognised as non-normative, truly personalised, growth-oriented and enquiry-centred.

In our view of education, history is important for the way that it can show that many of our beliefs and ways of thinking are socially constructed and developed through cultural influences in our families, schools, peers, media, universities, colleges and workplaces. Present ideas of giftedness, which we wish to transcend, have such historical and cultural antecedents, and they are considered below. They are sustained by what people do, and whatever individuals do requires power and energy. Such expressions of energy are only weakly conceptualised in educational and social research, and we are aware of the need to recognise the influence of such power and energy in offering our generative transformational approach to giftedness.

This chapter is also a story of Barry's expression and development of his drive to extend and deepen his understanding of gifts and talents in education. He is creating and offering his story of the transformations in his learning as a gift, a living example, of the new conceptualisation of gifts and talents we are offering through this book. It carries his life-affirming energy and passion for education – the qualities that attracted Marie and Jack to work with Barry on this text. They have both seen Barry working with teachers and pupils in workshops on philosophy for/with children (P4C). They have been inspired by his expression of a dynamic, loving energy in his educational relationships. In expressing this loving energy, they believe that he seeks to avoid violating the integrity of the other, and this is expressed as the 'special humility of the educator' (Buber, 1947, in the work cited).

The three of us have studied the growth of our educational knowledge in masters and doctoral research programmes. We recognise that some transformations in the way we think have been disturbing because they involve a change of mind. It hasn't been easy to respond creatively to the recognition that the kind of knowledge that dominated the pedagogies and curricula of our school, college and university teachers did not address the embodied knowledge for living a loving and productive life. The knowledge most highly valued in the pedagogies and curricula was theoretical knowledge of a particular kind. This is still the case. It is a propositional knowledge, a 'knowledge that', communicated in relationships between abstract statements that can lose a feeling of connection with lived experience.

In the story below, Barry demonstrates a level of scholarly engagement with abstract conceptualisations at a level appropriate for a doctoral programme. This is expressed in the movement from his grasp of abstract conceptualisations of gifted and talented education into our shared educational enquiry into gifts and talents in education. In the story that follows, Barry deconstructs the field and explains its limitations as he moves us into our shared enquiry, starting with the socially constructed concept of 'giftedness' and moving on into 'definition' and 'identification'.

The motivation for Barry's changing perception of gifts and talents in education developed from his feeling of being a living contradiction in holding certain values and being aware that these were being denied in what he was doing. The tension in this contradiction stimulated his imagination and creativity to work on ways of changing his actions and understandings to bring them more in line with his values. This tension is felt by many practitioners in their daily practice, as instanced in an email by a deeply committed (and increasingly dispirited), gifted and talented coordinator in an English local authority (sent to Barry on 10 March 2008):

I find I'm being systematically boxed – which is anathema to me – very stress-ful. I had a review of my job description last week. I will have primary work removed, and be labelled a secondary strategy consultant, which means I will deliver "the word" of National Strategy G&T, based on measurement and progress in levels. I'm told that the whole school ethos is not what I should be concentrating on – just a class of level 7's – since when I've gone down with a severe case of allergic conjunctivitis and am off work today. They listen, but they don't hear. My motivation has hiccupped – I'm more set on retirement. However, I'm sure I'll manage to do my own thing in schools for the next 6 months, though they've removed my central budget, and effectively downgraded my post.

This educator's sense of being asked to live a professional life far removed from her core beliefs and values is, alas, far from exceptional. Her tacit, embodied knowledge is ignored or rejected. Her skills, professionalism and competence as an educator are considered subservient to what the 2008 Primary Review of Education in England characterises as 'the state theory of education'. Her sense of disempowerment stands in marked contrast to the words below, emailed on 16 March 2008 to Barry by Anna Grayson, a former head teacher, long retired, who has found a way to continue to work with passion, engagement and moral purpose as a teaching assistant in a small, rural school:

Having spent a lifetime in education I am still humbled by the thoughts that children share and feel that we are truly privileged to be able to enter their world and be part of their learning and thinking. Having had a life threatening illness three years ago, namely complete kidney failure in the space of three days, the one thought that kept me going during the dark days for nearly a year was that I still felt that I had something to contribute to children's thinking and learning in a small way and I feel so humbled to think that I can still do this.

What now follows is in the language of abstract concepts. We have found that much formal assessment in education is focused on being able to demonstrate a grasp of such abstract concepts. In transforming our ways of thinking to emphasise the importance of embodied knowledge in educa-tion, we have needed to move within such abstract concepts, to feel our-selves as living contradictions, and to allow our imaginations and creativity to move us into a different way of thinking that does not separate our minds from our bodies as we express and develop our own talents and craft our gifts.

The concept of 'giftedness' is closely related to the study of such equally abstract concepts as 'ability', 'intelligence' and, in more recent years, 'creativ-ity' (cf. Perkins, 1995 for an overview). Borland (1997) draws particular parallels between the concepts of 'giftedness' and 'intelligence'. Both con-cepts can be viewed as being historically recent, reified social constructs, representing not some objective, discoverable reality 'out there', but concepts constructed to meet the needs of 19th and early 20th century social structures in the Western world. These centuries were predicated on industrial metaphors, on expanding education for the masses, and on norm-referenced procedures for measurement and standardisation. These beliefs continue to exist in the imagination even when contradicted in experience. England's addiction to 'testing' is a case in point. The Primary Education Review of 2007/2008, the first for 40 years, is showing evidence of the damage of too much 'high-stakes' testing, and thereby poses challenges to a test-insistent culture.

We know that many people who are recognised as leading the thinking in their fields of expertise do not reach that point in their journeys by following neat, linear paths – and yet it is just these neat paths that are so often created for children who fit a particular category. Examples of this can be seen in the personal stories in this book – e.g. Alan Rayner's story at the start of this chapter. In real life, some people take an apparently straight path, whereas other journeys are far more obviously diverse and diffuse. Traditional approaches have specifically sought to predetermine the end points of individuals' journeys as early as possible, without reference to their evolving awareness of who they are and who they want to be. Traditional approaches are intended to create a smooth career path to carry the individual over the years, ignoring the experiences that contribute to that person's determination of a point they identify in their careers as desirable, fulfilling or satisfying, an indicator amongst many of a life well lived.

Borland (1997) writes as a critical friend of the field, asking awkward questions yet anxious for an education for people designated as gifted to retain a central role in broader and more inclusive debates around education, learning and teaching. But the shifting nature of the socially constructed sands that focus our professional energies is acknowledged when he notes that even 'Gallagher (1996), one of the more conservative writers in the field, wrote "We should admit that 'gifted' is a constructed concept"' (Borland, 1997, p. 7).

As might be expected of a socially constructed concept, the world of gifted and talented education has been, and still remains, a world riven by competing perspectives, internal dissensions and contradictions. This is apparent at the macro-political level (national policies in 'gifted education'), as much as it is at the micro-personal level (specific practices in relation to individuals). At the macro level, in many countries, there have been high and low points of interest in and commitment to 'gifted and talented' education, and this ebbing and flowing can be related to cultural ambivalences, even to the point of national crises of identity and ethics (see Balchin, Hymer & Matthews,

2008 for many examples of such cultural ambivalences in countries across the world):

> Gallagher described the struggle between support and apathy for special programs for gifted and talented students as having roots in historical tradition – the battle between an aristocratic elite and our concomitant belief in egalitarianism. (Reis, 2004, p. ix)

Tied in with the notion of provision and 'special programmes' are the related notions of definition and identification – who are 'the gifted', and who says they are gifted? These are contentious, ethical, socio-political issues as much as they are issues of social science and educational research, and as a result, they remain culture- and context-dependent.

Despite its socially constructed provenance, in the Western world at least, education for learners classified as gifted and talented is traditionally approached dichotomously, as if giftedness is a state, not a construct. It is therefore associated with the mental (or physical, as in many understandings of 'talent') *attributes* of 'gifted and talented' learners, with the processes of *identifying* these largely pre-existent gifts or talents, and then with *providing* for these individuals' particular needs (e.g. Eyre, 1997; Ross, 1993; Terman, 1925, ff.; Winstanley, 2004). This response has its antecedents in a quasi-deterministic, largely genetically determined and *neural processing* model of learning where giftedness exists across the lifespan – although its adherents hold to this model to varying degrees. Winstanley, for instance, offers a partial critique, as well as a partial endorsement – as do Hymer with Michel (2002), whereas Simonton (2008) seems to hold quite rigidly to a linear-sequential, 'gifted zygote' line: 'A gifted child was probably a gifted infant, even zygote, and may later become a gifted adolescent and adult, and may even die being gifted'.

As a result of locating giftedness individually and intra-vidually *inside the head*, the burden of identifying gifted and talented learners is commonly placed on the results of standardised tests of other reified concepts – e.g. 'ability', 'potential' or 'aptitude' [variously quantified in the form of intelligence quotients (IQs), Cognitive Abilities Test (CAT) scores or scholastic aptitude test scores] or standardised measures of scholastic attainments (e.g. tests of proficiency in literacy or numeracy, Standard Attainment Test (SAT) Levels), albeit often in association with behavioural checklists and teacher or parent observations (e.g. DfEE, 1999). Historically, less attention has been given to the role of the learning environment and of meta-cognitive tools in providing opportunities for students to 'create' or (to use the language of constructivism, as in Adams, 2003 or Watkins, Carnell & Lodge, 2007) *to make* their unique profiles of gifts and talents – although there is now a burgeoning interest and literature in these areas (e.g. Fisher, 2003; Hart *et al.*, 2004; Jeffrey & Woods, 2003; Matthews & Foster, 2006; Perkins, 1995; Shore & Dover, 2004).

In an overview of the research literature, Sternberg (2004a, pp. xxiv, xxv), whilst recognising the difficulties inherent in achieving a consensus on all the issues associated with giftedness, identifies what he perceives to be several points of broad agreement:

- Giftedness involves more than just high IQ.
- Giftedness has non-cognitive components as well as cognitive ones.
- Environment is crucial in terms of whether potentials for gifted performance will be realised.
- Giftedness is not a single thing – there are multiple forms. Hence, one-size-fits-all assessments or programmes are likely to be too narrow.
- Measures for identifying or evaluating gifted individuals need to be proposed to operationalise theories, and then they need to be evaluated rather than merely being assumed to be valid.

However, despite the recognition in the academic literature of the limitations of traditional, 'actuarial', neural processing definitions of giftedness, and the challenges these pose especially in communities of cultural diversity (e.g. LGT, 2007), in practice, such formulations still predominate within applied educational fields. The UK's Excellence in Cities and Excellence Cluster initiatives, for instance, have had a gifted and talented strand, which bifurcates the field into *gifts* (seen as relating to the core academic areas) and *talents* (seen as relating to sports and the expressive arts), and which then adds an actuarial element and an invocation of segregated provision (DfEE, 1999):

- Giftedness relates to high-level ability (or potential) in one or more statutory subjects other than art, music and Physical Education (PE).
- Talent relates to ability (or potential) in art, music, PE or any sport or creative art.
- At least two-thirds of the cohort are to be gifted.
- The cohort should comprise 5–10% of the school roll.
- The cohort should have access to a distinct teaching and learning programme.

This definition meets almost perfectly the specification many people cautioned against before a House of Commons Education Committee Inquiry in 1998/1999 (House of Commons, 1999). Concerns over this definition, and doubts over its potential for making a significant difference in the educational opportunities for our nation's children are several and multifaceted. These include moral and ethical concerns over the rationalist, exclusive and discriminatory philosophies of the sort embodied in the phrase 'distinct teaching and learning programme', which assumes neat delineations of human characteristics at an abstract level, in the belief that these correspond to the *truth* of individual people. There are also practical and pragmatic reservations over a *test-and-place* methodology which are outlined in more detail below. Moreover, the synthetic distinction being made between *gifts* and *talents*, and the implicit hierarchy established, can be seen to be troubling. We are aware, for instance, of Winner:

> While children who are precocious in those kinds of scholastic skills assessed by an IQ test are called gifted, children who show exceptional ability in an art form such as the visual arts, music, or dance or in an athletic area such as skating, tennis, or diving are called talented. Two different labels suggest two different classes of children. But there is no justification for such a distinction. (Winner, 1996, p. 7)

The dominant conceptualisation continues to draw substantially on fixed-state factors, and a rigid, entity theory of intelligence (Dweck, 1999) – albeit overlaid, sometimes, with social-emotional considerations. Moreover, there is an implied suggestion that the two classes of children require two different routes to meeting their needs. Dweck, amongst others, finds no such distinctions – dispositions such as persistence, risk taking, seeking out challenges, etc. apply as much to maths as to music, to biology as to business, to physics as to PE, to astronomy as to art.

The provision of enriched, extended or accelerated learning opportunities for the identified few, as in current formulations within the UK and many other countries, is a model that is located substantially within a modernist, actuarial view of giftedness which places little emphasis on gift creation through relational activity, and much more on gift identification leading to instrumental provision. Within this model, the mantra is *test and place* – identify the cohort of students who are likely to conform to some definition of 'gifted or talented' – then do something special with them. There are often accompanying exhortations to seek to raise the achievement of all by adequately responding to the needs of the 'most able' (encouraging their 'slipstreaming' in the wake of the gifted and talented, cf. LGT, 2007), but the gifted/non-gifted dualism remains ever present. It's the approach that dominated gifted and talented education in the 20th century – and which still does.

White (2006) proposes that the beliefs about intelligence and a subject-based curriculum, which underpin so many of the national strategies and implementation plans, and so much of the practice in schools, are rooted in values of a bygone era. He asserts that, '. . . if you look for sound supporting arguments behind them, you will be disappointed. There are no solid grounds for innate differences in IQ; and there are none for the traditional subject-based curriculum' (p. 1).

White goes on to explore the sources of these influential but flawed driving forces and provides well-reasoned arguments for those frustrated by dominant practices that feel to be negations of our educational values of egalitarianism and a love of humanity. He asks why, despite the philosophical doubts about the justifiability of these core beliefs, they have persisted and have been so powerful. He turns for his answers to socio-cultural history and the lives of the individuals that embodied the theories which have been systemically influential. White's story of intelligence starts in 1865 when Francis Galton first put forward his notion of intelligence. No one before Galton had posited that we all possess different degrees of an ability which is innate, intellectual, general and limited. The theory clearly reflects the beliefs of a man living the values of empire, class and preordained destinies, who had the Victorians' enthusiasm for measurement and statistics. Despite modern values being those of egalitarianism, inclusion and self-determinism, Galton's theory has made an invisible transformation from a hypothetical construct to accepted 'fact' which significantly influences policy and practice in education in much of the world today. 'Test and place' has a long history:

> It will be an important though subsidiary object of the School to discover individual children who show promise of exceptional capacity, and to develop their special gifts (so far as this can be done without sacrificing the interests of the majority of the children), so that they may be qualified to pass at the proper age into Secondary Schools, and be able to derive the maximum of benefit from the education there offered them. (The 1904 Elementary Code, Board of Education, 1929, p. 9) (White, 2006, p. 8)

Traditional routes to 'identification' follow traditional test-and-place practices. Schools invest in a range of standardised tests of ability or performance, combine these with more qualitative measures of achievement or potential (e.g. judicious use of checklists, parental, peer or self-nominations), identify the highest performers, then do something special with them – implement a 'distinct teaching and learning programme' (DfEE, 1999; DfES, 2005), for instance. Given the time and financial resources, it's relatively easy to do, and it can be dressed up as an 'inclusive' approach through the application of circular logic – because it includes the most 'able' in its considerations, and often takes place in the mainstream classroom (ibidem)!

There are a number of problems with 'test and place' though, even from a modernist perspective, and it is these that in recent years have initially provoked our own senses of being 'living contradictions' (Ilyenkov, 1977; Whitehead, 1993) when operating as researchers or consultants in gifted education. Here are just a few:

- To link provision and resourcing decisions to test outcomes is questionable, when the validity and reliability of tests is highly variable, and none is perfectly reliable and valid. No test can claim accurately to predict future performance because no test can adequately 'measure' the full range of cognitive, contextual and dispositional factors that combine inseparably to give rise to performance. To pretend otherwise is optimistic at best, dishonest at worst. Many of the standardised tests in use in schools today are notoriously weak at discriminating between high-level performances, a criticism which is also commonly levelled by university tutors at A-grade A-level examinations. The most statistically 'reliable' of intelligence tests, individually administered tests of IQ or cognitive abilities (e.g. *Wechsler Intelligence Scale for Children – 4th edition* or the NFER-Nelson *British Ability Scales*, Elliott, 1997), are widely regarded nowadays as measuring only one type of 'analytical' intelligence (Gardner, 1983, 1999; Sternberg, 2004b, 2008), not the full range of abilities represented in the school-age population (e.g. Denton & Postlethwaite, 1984; Renzulli, 2004; Sternberg, 2008).

- Ability and performance are demonstrably neither fixed nor predetermined. Both are amenable to high-quality teaching. Intelligence as described by test scores is far more malleable than had been thought and taught, and certain methodologies, especially those drawing heavily on the application of meta-cognitive processes, can lead to gains both in measured intelligence and in school attainment outcomes (e.g. Adey *et al.*, 2007; Baumfield *et al.*, 2005; Claxton, 1999; Dweck, 1999; Trickey, 2007; Trickey & Topping, 2004). In essence, abilities and performances that are valued in school are not just discovered through identification strategies – they can be developed through access to rich, challenging learning experiences.
- Test and place has in itself little or no effect on general classroom provision (OfSTED, 2001).
- Test and place, especially when configured around the concept of ability, can be disempowering both for students left behind and their teachers (Hart *et al.*, 2004).
- Many teachers feel their role is to teach, not to judge. Test and place invites judgement (Hart *et al.*, 2004; Leyden, 1990). It invites judgement of the person – it does not invite a shared appreciation of learning to inform an educational process. The purpose is to 'prove', not to 'improve'. Judgement is also made against standards of attainment not against values and the progression to living them as fully as you can through the development of talents or the creation, valuing and offering of gifts.
- Test and place implies the existence of an evidence base which supports the notion of two classes of children – the 'gifted or talented' who need access to a specialised 'curriculum plus', and the rest – for whom a bog standard, early 20th century skills – and knowledge-based curriculum – is more appropriate. We are aware of no such evidence base. The evidence we have seen suggests, on the contrary, that students classified as 'gifted and talented' are a non-homogeneous sample from a non-homogeneous

population (e.g. Feldhusen, Asher & Hoover, 2004; Winstanley, 2004), with as diverse a range of needs and learning styles as the group labelled 'non-gifted'. Moreover, all students respond positively to focused enrichment and extension opportunities and opportunities to construct their own meanings – and to the high-quality, well-differentiated teaching which allows this to happen (e.g. Lipman, 2003; Sharron, 1996).

Unsurprisingly from the contemporary perspective and given the problematic issues associated with *test and place*, in Excellence in Cities schools, the issue of identification has been the most problematic aspect of this and related initiatives (OfSTED, 2001; White, Fletcher-Campbell, & Ridley, 2003), as has its failure to bring about significant changes to the usual classroom practices (OfSTED, 2001) – although it *has* given rise to many innovative and well-received experiences for those students accessing the 'distinct teaching and learning programmes' (ibidem), in response to creative and dedicated teaching and support.

Test and place is not, however, the only route to identification. As observed earlier in this section, the limitations of 'within-child', fixed-state or entity theory, conceptualisations of giftedness, and the fundamental relationship between gifts and talents and the environment (social, emotional and physical) in which these gifts and talents emerge, have become increasingly apparent in the academic literature (e.g. Csikszentmihalyi, Rathunde & Whalen, 1997; Gardner, 1983, 1993, 1999; Passow, 1979; Sternberg, 2004b, 2004c; Tannenbaum, 1979; Walberg *et al.*, 2004). Like Borland at the start of this chapter, Sternberg exposes further the foundations of cultural relativism in the concept with the observation that 'Giftedness is something we invent, not something we discover: It is what one society or another wants it to be, and hence its conceptualisation can change over time and place' (Sternberg & Davidson, 1986, pp. 3, 4). In Japan, for instance, Western preoccupations with concepts such as intelligence can cause bewilderment.[1] Within wider society in the Western world, too, there is evidence of a realisation that the concept is more problematic than we once believed, and that great intellectual breakthroughs often have as much to do with context, collaboration and good fortune as they do with the person as a unique individual:

> If Einstein had not existed, physics would sooner or later have invented him. I am sure of that. His theory of relativity was an understanding of nature. It

---

[1] In a conversation with Prof. Lauren Resnick of Pittsburgh University (27 April 2006), she described to Barry a mealtime encounter with a group of Japanese academics, in which they struggled to provide an equivalent term for the Western concept of *intelligence* within their own culture. In the end, they suggested the term *niceness* as the closest approximation!

lay over the cosmic horizon, awaiting discovery by the first genius to pass its way. (Simon Jenkins, *The Times*, 21 January 2005)

The discovery of Viagra came in 1985, after thirteen years of intense teamwork. I was one member of a 1000-strong team, and we didn't set out to invent it. (Dr Gill Samuels, Director of Vascular Biology at Pfizer, *The Independent*, 9 June 2005)

Contemporary approaches to identification take greater account of *extra-neural* factors, and rely more on *identification through provision* – an approach which sees the challenge of identification as being contiguous with the challenge of educational provision (e.g. Freeman's 'Sports Approach', 1998). Such an approach is thought to be more compatible with inclusive educational principles, since it is grounded in the basic premise that enriched learning experiences should be made available in the first instance to *all* children (not just to some pre-identified gifted group). It is anticipated, however, that individual children will respond with varying degrees of commitment, enthusiasm and interest to these experiences, and that these experiences can then be adapted, developed or extended to suit the needs of the strongest responders – who might then form a 'more able' group *in that domain of enquiry*. The approach can therefore be seen to take the form of *provide and place*, rather than *test and place* (Hymer with Michel, 2002).

This shift to identification through provision signifies a move towards the construction of more inclusive gifted and talented educational theory and practice which begins to connect with the inclusive, egalitarian and humanitarian values we believe are essential in the 21st century. However, because there has been no understanding that the traditional approaches have been created as expression of values that we have evolved beyond, there are still tensions which are experienced but which cannot be resolved.

Whilst it is generally accepted as being more inclusive, more fluid and more context-dependent than traditional test-and-place models, most formulations of the identification-through-provision model conform in at least two significant respects to traditional approaches:

(i) It is usually the teacher or other authoritative adult who is the agent of identification, and the self-knowledge of individual students is often underused or even barely tapped into at all.

(ii) The terms 'gifted' and 'talented' remain wedded to a comparative, norm-referenced framework in which a student's gifts and/or talents are identified only in relation to his or her peers' relatively inferior abilities in any particular domain, not in relation to his or her own unique array of skills, qualities, abilities and dispositions across the broad field of human achievement.

Albeit to a lesser extent than *test and place*, the shortcomings of *identification through provision* remain a challenge to our values and beliefs. A few years ago, Barry set out his broad personal educational beliefs, values and principles in the following way (Hymer with Michel, 2002, p. 3):

- All children have a right to a high-quality education.
- The primary aim of education is to excite in children and young people a passion for learning, and to facilitate the acquisition of skills and dispositions which will permit this passion for learning to be satisfied and sustained.
- The primary role of the school is to maximise opportunities for all children to reach their educational goals.
- Children's educational goals will differ.

To these (relatively) uncontroversial principles, he added the following:

- No one – not even the person himself or herself – is ever fully aware of an individual's potential for learning.
- A fixed concept of 'ability' is an unhelpful descriptor or predictor of performance.
- Children's educational goals are best reached by the setting and answering of questions. These questions are best set by the children themselves.
- Deep learning takes place collaboratively rather than competitively.

Barry felt at that time the implications of the above would include recognising that:

- Giftedness and talent are best seen as relative rather than as absolute terms, within the context both of an individual child's profile of strengths and weaknesses and his or her wider learning environment.
- The school has an important role in helping *every* child to identify his or her gift/s or talent/s.
- The most effective form of assessment is formative (assessment for learning) rather than summative or normative (assessment for showing or comparing). Relatedly, promoting learning orientation (concern for improving one's learning) is more likely to lead to effective learning than promoting performance orientation (concern for grade success).
- A genuinely inclusive policy for gifted and talented education is the only model consistent with these principles. We can't have non-inclusional theory and practice underpinned by inclusional values. The standards by which improving practice is judged is against evidence of the underpinning values being lived.

- The school should take steps actively to implement teaching and learning procedures and methods which will accommodate the principles set out above.

Of course many, if not all, of the principles and implications set out above were (and remain) open to challenge from a variety of standpoints, but where values, principles and core beliefs can escape the constraints of subjectivity, a battery of supportive evidence could be cited. This included, by way of illustration

- Joan Freeman's comprehensive survey of international research into the education of able children and young people, in which she concluded that 'The dominant current concern of research into the education of the very able is *the interaction between the child's potential and the provision to develop it* [italics added]. Without that dynamic element, we return to the old idea of fixed abilities, most notably intelligence' (Freeman, 1998, p. 56). In addition to differentiation, Freeman saw individualisation as the other route to the development of potential – 'Where the pupil has greater responsibility for the content and pace of his or her own educational progress. In this, children would be required to monitor their own learning' (ibidem, p. 56).
- Stephen Ceci's (1990, 1996), Michael Howe's (1990) and Carol Dweck's (1999, 2006) robust refutation of the idea that people who excel in certain fields do so because of their special gifts or talents: commitment and practice have been shown to be stronger determinants of exceptional performances than underlying ability. 'Potential' needs to be seen not in Galtonian terms as a ceiling on performance, but as an opening for further development.
- Paul Black & Dylan Wiliam's (1998) highly influential account into the key role of formative assessment (or 'assessment for learning') in raising standards in schools.
- Chris Watkins' (2001, 2005) and Watkins, Carnell & Lodge's (2007) extensive reviews of research evidence suggesting that preoccupation with grade attainment can actually *lower* the quality of performance.
- The growing recognition that thinking and learning are socially regulated activities; social interactions are seen to be essential to such learning processes as voluntary attention, logical memory, concept formation and internalisation. Research in these domains owes a great deal to the writings of the Russian psychologist Lev Vygotsky, but more recent applications in the UK educational arena include Paul Light & Karen Littleton's (1999) demonstration of the significant social and relational bases of learning – even in an age of 'standardised assessment tests' (which are designed to drive up educational standards through the illumination of individual successes and failures).

- The educational implications of the burgeoning body of evidence from cognitive neuroscience. In his review of this area, Geake noted that 'There are educational implications here for the measurement of school success as a function of students' perceived individual successes, regardless of their level of achievement. This is not a call for dumbing-down – in fact, quite the opposite. It is a call for school organisation to even further recognise neurobiologically-driven individual differences in responses to school learning, in order to break the cycle of low competence generating low confidence generating low competence, as well as to minimise under-achievement by children designated as academically gifted through boredom with an underchallenging age-normed curriculum' (Geake, 2002, p. 7).
- Diane Montgomery's conclusions to the book she edited on *Able Under-achievers* (2000), in which she observed that 'All learners need to experience an education which is supportive and valuing, whatever their differences. To achieve this, general education needs to be made more flexible. Access to special provision where it is useful should be based on the principles of inclusion and self-referral and use authentic or performance-based assessment to provide feedback to both learners and teachers. Learners need opportunities to contribute their own views on the value and appropriateness of the education they are receiving' (ibidem, p. 202).

At the time, Hymer and Michel's book expressed explicit doubts about the direction in which national policy was moving. An example (Hymer with Michel, 2002, p. 8) relating to the emerging and rather short-lived National Academy for Gifted and Talented Youth, which was still in gestation in 2002 follows:

> The challenge of true inclusion is a stiff challenge, which can make the relative ease of providing something different for the few very alluring. This is not a new insight. In her thoughtful account of Clever Children in Comprehensive Schools, Auriol Stevens (1980) foreshadows the attractions of separate and different educational experiences that are embodied in, for instance, the UK's emerging Academy for Gifted and Talented Youth: 'The task is hard. It is made infinitely harder by setting up alternative systems to "save" the clever by taking them out of the common schools. The problem may appear to have been solved by such means, but it will not have been. Attention will simply have been diverted from undertaking the detailed, painstaking work that raising standards for all requires' (ibidem, p. 164).

Given a dominant modernist and positivist framework in which 'giftedness' is embedded, it is all too easy to habituate to that domain, and to orient one's practices accordingly. Personal values and beliefs can be overridden by the demands of hard-pressed professional groups (teachers, local authority

advisers and coordinators) for ready-made 'solutions' to the needs of traditionally identified cohorts of 'gifted children'.

It might be helpful at this point to recount in more detail Barry's story of
involvement in the field of gifted and talented education, as an illustration
of the disconnect that can exist between values and practice, and as an explanation for our felt need to construct giftedness differently – a construction
which forms the substance of this book.

When reflecting on his own practice as a consultant in the field, Barry
realised that he tended to habituate to the prevailing orthodoxy of gifted and
talented education in the UK. His in-service training sessions were usually
modelled on a three-part *test-and-place* formula: establish definitions, illuminate identification strategies and promote appropriate provision for the
identified few. As part of this, he constructed and offered up for use plausible checklists of giftedness, from which teachers and parents could identify
gifted pupils in their classes (Hymer, 1998, 2001b). In essence, he provided
material and advice in pre-masticated form and eschewed opportunities to
get participants to think for themselves and, in particular, to question the
assumptions and orthodoxies lying at the heart of dominant Western
approaches to gifted and talented education.

Moreover, Barry constructed and advocated definitions of giftedness which
had operational advantages, but which were couched in traditional,
attainment-oriented conventions – cf. the definition first adopted by the
Cumbria LEA Policy for the more able child or young person (1997): 'The
term "more able pupil" is taken to apply to that individual who is consis-
tently functioning at a level two or more years in advance of the majority of
his or her same-age peers – in at least one area of the school curriculum'.
This definition's weaknesses include its failure to include within it the needs
of the underachieving student, its failure to take account of age-within-grade
effects (is a 16-year-old performing at the level of an 'average' 18-year-old
really as able as a 3-year-old performing at the level of an 'average' 5-year-
old?) and its limp acceptance of the knowledge-based formal curriculum
(and the attendant forms of assessment) as being the *only* legitimate domain
for the expression of exceptional achievement. It is at heart a complacent
definition that sets few incentives and offers no real signposts to a school
wishing to walk that bit further, to move beyond a recognition of existing
high-level performances and to work towards the demonstration of high
achievement in its many forms for all its students.

In June 1998, 2 years into his work as coordinator of Cumbria LEA's Able
Pupil Project, Barry was invited to submit evidence to the House of Commons
Education and Employment Committee Inquiry into Highly Able Children.
At that time, Cumbria had just adopted the operational, readily measurable
and traditionally achievement-oriented definition cited above. Yet in his

submission to the Inquiry, reinforced verbally before the Committee in December 1998, the definition he advocated was already very different, drawing as it did much more on a multiple intelligence (Gardner, 1983, 1999) perspective:

> I would define a highly able child as that child who, given access to a wide and stimulating environment, creates products (which could be recorded in a range of forms) which demonstrate originality, depth of understanding and high levels of expertise. This definition resists quantitative measurement. I believe it is counter-productive to set out to identify that sample of children who meet the requirements of an operationalised definition, which will be largely arbitrary, and then to provide that sample with a qualitatively or quantitatively enriched educational experience. If all children are given access to an enriched curriculum, the most able will identify themselves. This is not – in my view – an idealistic or precious position to adopt – it is a necessary one. (Hymer, in House of Commons, 1999, p. 136)

Even ignoring the *naivete* of the penultimate sentence,[2] it is possible to attribute the substantial inconsistencies between the views identified above and the definition actually implemented, as evidence in part of the living contradiction between Barry's values and his practice, and in part to his reflecting over time on the inadequacies of the 'operational' definition as it was being applied in schools with children. The yawning gap between social science and social policy becomes a chasm when social policy is considered in relation to the individual person. Looking back now on the definition recommended to the Inquiry, it is possible to see that this, too, was couched in a Western, modernist and un-deconstructed (let alone reconstructed) understanding of the term 'gifted and talented' – although it took a more obviously liberal and less reductionist line.

Shifts in definition continued. In September 2001, in conversation with a colleague in the Barrow Education Action Zone (EAZ), Deborah Michel and Barry asked the question, 'What would be different if we spoke about *gifts* and *talents*, rather than *gifted* and *talented*?' Reflecting on that question permitted a re-framing of the concept from one representing a static *within-person* state to one allowing a separation between the concept (giftedness) and its embodiment (the 'owner' of the 'gift'). At the time, this distinction was attractive, despite the reification implied in the concept of 'gift'. In the co-creation of Barrow EAZ's definition, Barry was more concerned to give

---

[2] The suggestion that, given access to an enriched curriculum, 'the most able will identify themselves' is ignorant of the literature on institutional racism – children who have 'ability' but who lack cultural or social capital in certain contexts and who are typically under-represented in traditionally identified gifted and talented populations – cf. Lidz & Macrine (2001), Chaffey & Bailey (2003), Lidz & Elliott (2006), Warwick & Matthews (2008).

due regard to the complexities underpinning the terms gifted or talented, and to frame the definition of individual gifts and talents in relative terms, rather than as absolute 'abilities' measured against set 'norms'. This would be a departure even from the more inclusive – but still performance-based – definition he'd provided to the House of Commons Inquiry. He wanted factors giving rise to giftedness and talent to be seen as inextricably interrelated and, wherever possible, he was anxious to reject false dualisms – e.g. *intellect–body, gift–talent, knower–known, identifier–identified*. Looking back on this period, it appears that these ambitions were only partly realised, and attempts to liberalise conceptions of giftedness were nonetheless framed within a traditional psychological epistemology: the complexity would embrace, for instance, both within-child factors (e.g. inherited or acquired predispositions, aptitudes and intelligences, learning dispositions) as well as situational and motivational factors (e.g. levels of opportunity, encouragement and learning challenge). Moreover, the *concept–embodiment* dualism was retained.

Barry was, however, also anxious for the evolving definition to draw heavily on a meta-cognitive component – i.e. the awareness of and control over one's own mind or thinking (Claxton, 1999; Flavell, 1979). This would offer increased scope for the creation and self-identification of gifts and talents over time (as revealed in any single domain of knowledge or experience), not just a snapshot identification drawing on the usual *test-and-place* criteria – with learners seen as the passive recipients of a label awarded on the basis of a test score, exceptional performance or similar criterion.

Whilst the job of identification should lie, he felt, substantially with the individual learner, the educational provider (in this instance seen as the teacher/s and school) had a responsibility to ensure a broad, balanced, enriched and truly challenging curriculum for all, as opposed to a distinct teaching and learning programme for the few. The identification of personal gifts and talents should represent an opportunity open to all learners, irrespective of 'ability', 'potential' or prior achievements. A definition which it was thought could go some way to achieving these intentions, yet without becoming unhelpfully complex and over-nuanced, was the following:

A gifted or talented student is regarded as one who has

(i) experienced a degree of facilitated self-reflection on his or her pattern of learning strengths and preferences, *and*
(ii) identified his or her area(s) of greatest strength(s) within the framework of an enriched or extended learning environment.

Strengths would include gifts and talents as identified by the Department for Education and Skills Excellence in Cities initiative, G&T Strand (DfEE,

1999), and also less easily measurable 'soft' skills and qualities such as inter-personal and intra-personal skills and other elements crucial to thinking for learning (e.g. resilience, analysis, wise judgement and discernment, intuition and imagination, etc.).

Such a definition defied any capping of the numbers of children identified (e.g. by an arbitrary figure of, say, 5–10%), or a narrow understanding of who might be gifted or talented, yet it also avoided, it was hoped, a woolly, 'All children are gifted, so let's not talk further about it' response. Without being prescriptive about means of implementation, implicit in the definition is a clear requirement for schools rigorously to discharge their responsibilities – e.g. to provide meta-cognitive learning opportunities to support the child's self-reflection (stilling activities, guided visualisation, learning logs and thought journals, peer mentoring, etc. – cf. Fogarty, 1994) and to focus their energies on creating enriched, challenging, stimulating learning environments. There was the potential (never fully realised during Barry's association with the EAZ) for 100% of a school's roll to be identified as gifted or talented – but only through the rejection of a norm-referenced, comparative understanding of the term, in which a child is gifted because she is objectively 'better', 'brighter', 'more successful' than another, in any given domain – the 'competition game' described by Holzman (1997). Instead, there is the potential for the term to be conceived in ontogenetic terms, in which a child (any child) is seen to have a gift in a domain, because *relative to her other interests, aptitudes or performances*, this domain emerges as a relative strength or focus of energies. With this latter interpretation, it is clearly possible for a special school to engage fully, genuinely and unapologetically in the 'gifted and talented' agenda.[3]

This definition was subsequently adopted without revision by the EAZ and was promoted in its schools. Alongside the definition, we advocated an identification strategy based on *identification through provision* (Freeman, 1998), characterised by the following features:

- seeing identification as process-based and continuous;
- basing identification on multiple criteria, including provision for learning and outcome;
- validating indicators for each course of action and provision;
- presenting students' abilities as profiles rather than as unitary figures;
- adopting increasingly sharp criteria at subsequent learning stages;
- recognition that attitudes may be affected by outside influences such as culture and gender;

---

[3] As indeed was the case within the Barrow EAZ, which included support for a special school for children with severe, profound and multiple learning difficulties, and a pupil referral unit for children and young people with emotional, social and behavioural difficulties.

- involving students in their own educational decision making, especially in areas of their own interest.

In promotion of this approach, supportive procedures and tools were recommended – those which might probe and illuminate from multiple angles – e.g.

- self-reflection exercises;
- evidence-based checklists (e.g. Freeman, 1998, pp. 12, 13);
- teacher nomination based on a combination of structured observation, instinct and intuition, and inspection of classwork performance;
- peer nomination through games and affirmative activities;
- parental nomination;
- self-nomination through the process of self-reflection, communicated to teaching staff;
- standardised and unstandardised test results, including national curriculum tests, tests of attainment and aptitude available through commercial publishers and tests of creativity.

To promote identification and provision contiguity, consideration of general principles underpinning decisions in relation to organisational responses was encouraged, with an emphasis on maximising

- effective learning for all students (including self-knowledge and meta-cognitive awareness, currently emphasised in the Department for Children, Schools and Families (DCSF) material on 'Thinking Skills', as well as the acquisition of facts and concepts);
- the delivery of an enriched curriculum to all students;
- the active participation, engagement and inclusion of all students.

It was believed that these principles were incompatible with a policy of blanket student streaming or even setting. That said, it was considered that there would be times where teachers might feel that significant alterations to the usual inclusive arrangements were appropriate, without violating the general principles above. These alterations would best, we felt, be related to the time, context and groupings needed for the learning objectives to be met or realised. An example was the formation of an editorial board for the construction of a school magazine or prospectus, drawing on students with appropriate gifts and talents from across the school. Similarly, the option of pursuing forms of acceleration in particular content areas was retained, but it was expected that this would be appropriate for only a small minority of students, and only after

- The introduction and outcomes of sustained high-quality enrichment and extension activities had been critically evaluated.

- Full consideration had been given to the likely short, medium and longer-term impact of the acceleration on the whole child; this would include reference to the perspectives of the child and his or her parents.

Realisation of these considerations would involve, it was thought, the use of a wide variety of class and student groupings in order to promote effective learning. This included

- collaborative learning groupings;
- groupings arising from curriculum compacting processes (Reis *et al.*, 1992);
- the use of mentors, including peer mentors;
- cross-age interest groupings and clusters;
- a degree of informed experimentation with groupings (with evaluation and review);
- where appropriate to the learning needs of the students, occasional opportunities for advanced enrichment work in withdrawal groups.

The tracking of the evolutionary shift in definitional stances outlined above provides some insight into Barry's conceptual journeying towards living his values and beliefs in his practice, but it reveals also, we feel, a residual drive to 'contain' and to 'control' the educational process from the 'outside', and to keep a strong focus on the issue of identification, rather than on gift creation. This may not be coincidental. Whilst allowing himself to be designated as an 'expert' in meeting the needs of gifted and talented learners, and benefiting from the professional recognition that this designation afforded him, Barry felt at times like one of '. . . those seductive story tellers . . . on the speaker's circuit (who) would lose a good part of their consulting fees if they couldn't assure audiences that they know with certainty who is *truly gifted'* (Renzulli, 2004, p. xxvii).

The more he read, communicated and practised in the field, the more he realised that far from moving forward in the direction of his values, he was retreating – assuming a technocratic, mastery-oriented role. At the level of content, his practices and his values felt incongruent – he was a living contradiction.

When engaged in formally researching his practice (Hymer, 2007a), Barry ultimately attempted to move his practice in the direction of his values as a constructivist, enquiry-oriented, inclusive educator, but he had begun more confidently, with the intention to find out something 'worthwhile' in the area of gifted and talented education – something *out there*, something empirically verifiable, replicable and generalisable, and which might contribute to the canon of established orthodoxy in the field.

During the early, taught years of his involvement in the field of 'high ability', he directed his energies accordingly. He read widely around the field of underachievement and synthesised his findings (e.g. Hymer, 2000); he undertook small-scale studies involving traditional hypothetico-deductive methods (e.g. Hymer & Harbron, 1998) and busied himself with the administrative requirements of managing a countywide project on a financially tight budget. This latter role included establishing the operational definition of giftedness cited earlier. More flexibly, he also sought ways of integrating his learning from his role as a coordinator of able pupil provision in a local authority with his part-time role as an educational psychologist in that authority (e.g. Hymer, Michel & Todd, 2002).

Over time, Barry saw his interests and energies shift from the identification and appropriate 'management' of 'gifted learners' (the *given state*) to the exploration and advocacy of approaches to 'creating' gifts and talents in learners – i.e. to nurturing and developing the dispositions, attitudes, skills and motivations required to realise achievements in any domain. However, this stopped short, for the most part, of exploring in any overt way the relational, non-individualistic nature of gift creation. The shift in focus was gradual, and not entirely linear in its chronology. It can though be traced in the subject matter of his thinking and writing from 2001 ff. – attempts at embracing holistic conceptions of giftedness (Hymer, 2001a, 2002); constructivist methodologies (but with modernist origins) such as P4C (Hymer, 2003a, 2004; Hymer & Jenkins, 2005) or more recent, less well-evaluated thinking skill approaches such as dilemma-based learning (Wood, Hymer & Michel, 2007), *MTa-PASS* materials (Davies, Hymer & Lawson, 2005) or *logo-visual thinking* (Best, Blake & Varney, 2005).

His early critiques of traditional, non-inclusive ways of understanding and responding to 'giftedness' were mildly expressed (e.g. Hymer, 2003b), whereas later attempts were more passionate and personal, and bordering on the polemical (Hymer, 2006, and below):

> We should certainly continue to invest heavily in the pursuit of excellence and achievement, confront anti-intellectual bigotry, and seek ways of raising aspirations within and without areas of deprivation. We need also, however, to remain open to radical reformulations of what we mean by intelligence, achievement, and potential, to the evidence of how achievement arises, and to non-normative, non-deterministic conceptions of what we mean by gifts and talents. We can learn a great deal from abroad and also from within the UK – e.g. the work of Guy Claxton, Susan Hart, Belle Wallace, and others. This may – perhaps should – lead us to question the structures and strictures currently embedded in national policy, and to suggest alternative formulations. The risk otherwise is that we end up with "gifted" students who avoid challenges, risk, uncertainty and lifelong learning, and opt instead for easy successes and validation through performance – the very opposite of what we intend. Gifted and talented policy should be the last area of education to be exempt from

challenge. If we have learned anything about exceptional achievement in the past, it has been about the value of asking new questions, and seeking new answers. And so it shall be in the future. (Hymer, 2005, p. 7)

The shift in focus and thinking which is represented in these writings was rarely arrived at in isolation, or through any single epiphany. Barry was fortunate in having enjoyed (and sometimes having been challenged, even disturbed by) many conversations with critically (and open-) minded friends and colleagues, some of whom are listed as co-authors in his publications, and all of whom contributed in some way to the evolution in his thinking. These conversations, and the resultant shift in his thinking, meant, however, that data collected through the experimental method never kept up with the journeying, nor represented anything fresh enough to be truly meaningful to him. These data missed the easily dismissable: 'the ineffable', that domain so dominated by tacit knowledge that articulation becomes impossible. The ineffable is captured in Chesterton's wry observation that you can only find truth with logic if you've already found truth without it, and also by Polanyi:

> ... what I call "ineffable" may simply mean something that I know and can describe even less precisely than usual, or even only very vaguely. It is not difficult to recall such ineffable experiences, and philosophic objections to doing so invoke quixotic standards of valid meaning which, if rigorously practised, would reduce us all to voluntary imbecility. (Polanyi, 1958, p. 88)

Having made a number of half-hearted and rather timorous attempts to orient his research around the experimental method with which he was familiar, he experienced two critical, at the time unnerving and as it turned out, deeply generative conversations during a working visit to Bath and North East Somerset. The first of these, on 12 July 2005, was with Marie. The second, the following day, was with Jack, originator of the living theory approach to action research. These conversations were good-natured and disinterested, but they challenged Barry to confront his qualitative demons, and to consider carefully his intentions and purposes in completing his doctoral studies. In an email to Jack, he wrote the following:

> Marie and I had had a super conversation the day before – variously wide-ranging and focused. . . . Marie challenged me (gently, kindly, as is her and I suspect your way) about having been stuck on my doctoral write-up for around four years now. I've given her legions of excuses for failing to start the write-up, these mostly involving lack of time, but that conversation seemed to unearth deeper reasons, confirmed in my brief meeting with yourself: I had failed to find a way of connecting my research questions with a methodology capable of doing the job authentically. Whilst I've been aware of action research approaches for some years, I've never really shaken myself free from my background training (interesting word that – from the Latin traho – "to drag") as

an experimental psychologist, steeped in things positivist, and my insecurities about bringing myself into my studies. As of today, I think my doctorate is taking a very different direction. Your work helps me connect my passions with my writing, and validates an account which will, I hope, involve me not as a trainer but as an educator (educere – "to draw out, to bring out, to lead"), and which can draw I think on the core educational beliefs and principles set out in my 2002 book. (email to Jack Whitehead, 18 July 2005)

This email dates the moment he resolved finally to abandon the experimental method, and to use instead the data which had arrived almost unnoticed over many years, and which lay untidily all around him. These data were neither obviously connected to each other nor did they conform easily to the types of scale (Stevens, 1968) that his background training as a psychologist had taught him to collect and work on. They weren't neutral, and they were most definitely self-referential – the enemy of traditional research accounts. They held though, he now realised, a potentially rich and fruitful source of evidence. They also revealed gaps in his self-knowledge which suggested that he needed to collect further data, much more systematically and self-consciously than hitherto. The analysis of these collective data in search of evidence[4] became the focus of his research, and over time, a central question emerged: 'How do I understand and communicate my values and beliefs in my work as an educator in the field of giftedness?'

Whilst the form of action research that Barry used is described in more detail in Chapter 3, for present purposes, it suffices to say that it helped Barry to integrate the contradictions between his values and his practice in his claim *to know* his educational practice, so that he could go on to construct descriptions and explanations that would empower and vivify his educational development as a person, and through improved self-knowledge, to influence also the learning of others, and of social formations. In this claim to knowledge, he asserted his ambition to create new theory, not just to improve his practice as an educator.

We are all three of us aware that practitioner research enquiries are often seen to enhance practice, but not theory, and both are often disconnected from underpinning values. The originators of theory are traditionally located within a social science model, applying hypothetico-deductive methods as uninterested lookers-on, from a high vantage point. This is as true in the field of gifted and talented education as it is elsewhere in educational

---

[4] We draw on the distinction between data and evidence provided by Whitehead & McNiff (2006), Chapter 5, whereby archived data (e.g. notes, journal records, video footage, reflective writing, etc.), collected during the enquiry are sifted, sorted, analysed, categorised and interpreted in search of evidence (those pieces of data carrying special meaning and significance – 'the good in action') which might be used to justify, test and hopefully support a claim to knowledge.

research. As evidence, we offer the following passage, in which the perceived hierarchy of research status is strongly implied (our italics added):

> The literature reviewed indicated that there have been relatively few empirical studies of gifted and talented education and, consequently, evidence-based policy and practice are scarce. Instead, much of the literature reflects practitioner experience. Whilst this is important and valuable, *it is different from rigorously conducted research studies*. (White, Fletcher-Campbell & Ridley, 2003, p. 1)

Whilst recognising that research models which take on board the perspective of the interested insider (as opposed to the disinterested outsider) are vulnerable to critiques which assume Aristotelian, *knowing-that* epistemologies, we contend that an 'insider' approach is best suited to an enquiry which has as a fundamental premise a sense that 'oranges might not be the only fruit' – that giftedness need not be seen as a reified 'thing', germane to an individual person and quantifiable as one might quantify the amount of liquid in a glass. As a rationale for our decision to use and to advocate a living theory action research model, with ourselves as the insider–enquirers, we offer two tables which attempt to make explicit the nature and implications of insider–outsider stances (Tables 1.1 and 1.2). They draw initially on distinctions suggested by Whitehead & McNiff (2006), but then relate specifically to the field of gifted education.

Table 1.1   Ontology: a theory of being – how you perceive yourself in relation to your environment

	Separate from others	*Part of others' lives*
Frequently held tenets	Neutrality, objectivity, task efficiency, the veracity of externally set targets, 'generalisable truth', respect for the truth	Involvement, participation, open relationships, the power of intrinsic targets, 'individual truth', respect for others' truths
Preferred research orientation (Freire, 1993, p. 64: 'The form of action they adopt is to a large extent a function of how they perceive themselves in the world'.)	'Outsider' approach – observing others and offering descriptions and explanations of their actions, social science research	'Insider' approach – offering descriptions and explanations for how you and others were involved in relationships of influence, action research

Table 1.2 Epistemology: a theory of knowledge – what is known and how it comes to be known

	Separate from others	*Part of others' lives*
Beliefs	Knowledge is objective, explicit, reified, and it tends to be discovered, acquired and transmitted.	Knowledge is personal, tacit, fluid, and it tends to be created, transformed and communicated.
Preferred approach to the field of giftedness	Concern for accurate identification of G&T cohorts, faith in psychometric data, external target setting, knowledge *acceleration* and specialised provision	Concern for the creation of gifts and the authenticity of personalised targets, knowledge *extension*, suspicion of labels and standardised data

The 'separate from others' column of Table 1.2 captures, we believe, the dominant paradigm of gifted education in most Western countries. This normative model, to which there has been surprisingly little dissent, is couched unambiguously in the language of propositional 'truth', through which educators' energies are focused not on conceptual, holistic, ethical or moral exploration of the terms involved, but on the circular, self-perpetuating, technocratic, proceduralist concerns of identification, provision and 'product outcome'. We have *national academies* and *registers* to populate, cohorts to 'track' and 'monitor', records to keep, Key Stage 2 SAT Level 5s and General Certificate in Secondary Education (GCSE) A and A* grades to work towards and to count. Little wonder, perhaps, that many teachers feel there is a gulf between their practice and their values – as evidenced by this teacher's comments: 'I have to get results based on objectives. I am paid to do the opposite of what I believe – how sad is that?' (reported in Hymer, 2007a).

This is a situation familiar to Whitehead & McNiff (2006, p. 26):

> ... we are deeply concerned with how teachers and other practitioners are systematically bullied by dominant forms of research and theory, and are persuaded to think that they cannot think for themselves or participate in public debates about education and the future of professional endeavours.

There are concerns shared within and outside the field of *giftedness* – that many children are bored, unchallenged and unexcited by their educational diet, and that many teachers do not know how best to stimulate a passion for learning and discovery – especially within a system that seems to put performance before learning (Watkins, Carnell & Lodge, 2007; Watkins,

2001). But to move from this shared recognition to a conviction that the answer lies in identification strategies, labels, cohorts and the apparatus of data gathering, tracking and monitoring is, we believe, questionable. There is a dominant story that one has to identify/label a child as 'G&T' before one can adequately meet his/her needs. There is an alternative story: we would suggest that many excellent schools and teachers (for example, the nine teachers whose practice was studied in depth by Hart *et al.*, 2004, or the practice of Hannaford, 2005) have been meeting the needs of their students for years, and without needing cohorts, labels or performance-led approaches such as acceleration in order to do this. You can access a range of such alternative stories from teachers at http://www.actionresearch.net/mastermod.shtml.

These teachers dispense with a priori identification procedures, and instead invest their energies in creating challenging, enriching, extending, enquiry-friendly learning environments for all their students – and being led by the unique student responses these conditions elicit. They know that for students identified as gifted and receiving the resources that become their due, you will always be able to find another, equally deserving and able to benefit from the same provision, but who lacks the high-status but double-edged 'gifted' designation (Freeman, 1980, 1991, 2001). This, however, is not an argument for identifying more thoroughly or widening access to such institutions as the Student Academy. On the contrary, it's an argument we believe for questioning a preoccupation with 'identification', burying the labels, and putting the considerable resources saved into teacher continuing professional development and inclusive, high-quality opportunities for learning, enquiry and knowledge creation.

In this alternative story, we wish to surrender an obsession with quantitative systems, summative record keeping and number crunching, and instead invest our efforts in understanding and improving the quality of educational provision. What we are offering is a different way of understanding quality. This will involve the amplification of the educational stories of educators who are developing their talents and creating and offering gifts and doing the same for the educational stories of pupils. We believe that the amplification of such stories, with the help of the Internet, will spread their influence. We think that such an approach is suited to the creation of a curriculum for all, one which allows us to be continually surprised by who responds to truly inclusive *gifted education* and by how the response is made and contributes to the education of a critically engaged citizenry in a 21st century democracy.

If we need the term, perhaps it's the education, not the children who are best seen as *gifted* (Borland, 2003). The argument is that the label gifted is as damaging to those who have it as to those who haven't (Rayner, this chapter).

When it's their education, we can touch the hard-to-reach and the disadvantaged. This is not an idealistic story, based on a belief that all children are the same, or a call for dumbing-down education – it's the very opposite. There are a growing number of people who have documented the advantages of responding radically and inspirationally to the needs of their students, such as Susan Hart *et al.* (2004), Sapon-Shevin (2003) and others, but being outside established conventions, the new understandings, the unknown species and the robust hybrids are easily missed. Closed systems like the field of gifted education need critical voices and fresh ideas to grow. We exclude them at our peril.

We are struggling to find a suitable language to communicate standards of judgement – viz., the extent to which we live in and practice the values and dispositions we hold as central to our being. Traditional terminology can be seen to be inappropriate where it has arisen from incongruous values, theories and practices, and our reservations follow from this – for instance,

- our personal values which hold that 'Labels are for jam jars, not children' (Leyden, 2000);
- our awareness of the evidence that 'Intelligence labels, good or bad, have undermining effects. Both teach children that their underlying intelligence can be readily judged from their performance' (Dweck, 1999, p. 121);
- our knowledge of the anti-psychiatric, anti-pathogenic critique offered by Illich (1976): the label once applied becomes the only 'reality', and all perception is filtered through it and all action directed towards it, not the person or the 'truth' of the person's condition;
- within the postmodernist perspective of narrative therapy (e.g. Crocket, 2004; Ingram & Perlesz, 2004; White & Epston, 1990), our sense that the invisible social 'controls' of linguistic terms have the potential to subjugate and oppress: '. . . if family members, friends, neighbours, co-workers, and professionals think of a person as "having" a certain characteristic or problem, they exercise "power" over him or her by "performing" this knowledge with respect to that person. Thus, in the social domain, knowledge and power are inextricably interrelated.' (Tomm, 1990, p. viii)

Within the field of giftedness, the *power-over* stance illuminated in narrative therapeutic understandings is as much an issue for the child 'having' *giftedness* as it is for the child 'lacking' it. For this reason, in response to a well-intended invitation to all parents of children attending one parent's secondary school to 'nominate' their children (with 'evidence') for inclusion on the school's 'G&T Register', this parent replied as honestly as he could – requesting an opportunity to meet with the school's G&T coordinators in order to discuss alternative models for supporting high levels of challenge for students and, relatedly, to request that his daughter be excluded from any existing register:

> We are as anxious about [our daughter] being labelled as "gifted" as we are about her being implicitly labelled "ungifted." In some situations she excels, in others she doesn't – much like any child or adult anywhere. The flaw is with the concept of ability in itself – terms like "bright," "clever," "G&T," and "intelligent," or euphemisms such as "smart cookie" are usually well-intentioned, but they act insidiously to reinforce the belief that an individual's exceptional achievements are explained by "her intelligence" – when there is no evidence for this belief. We are alert to the dangers of a child being identified (or even identifying herself) as "gifted" – invariably on dodgy and sometimes spurious grounds, and innumerable pieces of research document the dangers of children being judged "ungifted" relative to their peers. Does this happen at [her school]? You bet: it happened just yesterday. I have no idea what the criteria for being selected to take part in the Enterprising Activities Day were ("G&T" cohort? Excellent life and enterprise skills? Poor life and enterprise skills?) – and, I would suggest, neither do the students. What I do know, is that [our daughter] told me when I picked her up from school yesterday, that "All the brainiest kids are doing an Enterprising Activities Day tomorrow. I'm not doing it, so I guess I'm not that brainy." When I asked her how she knew it was the "brainy" ones who'd been selected, she said, "Because it's all the brightest kids, and [the teacher] told [two friends who'd been selected] that 'It's because you're all the bright cookies.'" This may be reality or it may be children-talk, but apparently her French set was talking about little else – and in the absence of clear criteria for admission, children, like adults, will create their own explanations.

> Please forgive the length of this piece – it in no way is intended to devalue the admirable efforts of yourselves and your colleagues in making [the school] the outstanding school that it is, and to creating the extension and enrichment opportunities that can make education magical. It is, however, intended to ask challenging questions about practices in a school I believe has the reputation, confidence and skills to transcend 20th century formulations of intelligence or giftedness (enshrined in NAGTY's constitution), and to explore 21st century routes to excellence and achievement. In so many ways, [the school] already manages this. Just one example from our own daughter's case: we know how much ... has benefited from the opt-in opportunities she's had in music – none of which has needed her to be judged as "musically gifted". (ibidem)

These concerns may well represent a minority view, and they are easily dismissed by a dominant paradigm as being woolly, unhelpful, unrealistic, even pernicious concerns over 'elitism', or as setting back the 'cause' of gifted education, in much the same way as Sapon-Shevin was attacked for questioning the concept of giftedness from a sociological perspective (Sapon-Shevin, 2003). But in asking the question 'Whose interests does the term *giftedness* serve?' the likely answer is, 'many', but at its worst, it can damage the interests of many more: it might be seen to benefit all those for whom the term denotes positivistically some 'direct knowledge of the world', and those whose livelihood, status and sense of self-worth is, at least to some considerable extent, caught up in its supposed 'reality' and veracity. We could, of course, include ourselves in the latter list, but in choosing to reject a global renunciation of the field, we seek also to offer a way forward which we believe brings the best of giftedness along with it.

In choosing to reject a global renunciation of the field, we must ask what our reluctance to repudiate is founded upon: sincere ontological and epistemo-logical reservations, or rationalisations, pragmatism, compromise and craven self-interest? Whilst recognising that renunciation of 'G&T education' is in many ways distinctly attractive, we are aware that there are many things that would, for us, be lost in so doing. These are picked up again in later chapters of this book.

How then, do we reconcile our present and future practice with our values? We attempt to do so in this book, in which we provide evidence of the extent to which our values can be lived through our practice, and in which we eschew an affiliation to orthodox conceptualisations of giftedness in favour of those elements which are rooted in values of a loving, just society and are germane to non-deterministic, inclusive conceptualisations in the field – concepts such as *challenge, personal enquiry, extension* and *enrichment*, for instance.

In integrating these elements in our approach to giftedness, we are using a living theory approach in which we express and develop our talents in the production of gifts that are freely given. This living theory approach to gift-edness, an approach that is generative and transformational, has required a transformation in the way we make sense of the world.

CHAPTER 2

BEYOND DEFINITIONS AND IDENTIFICATION – A GENERATIVE-TRANSFORMATIONAL FRAMEWORK FOR GIFT CREATION

A Professional Life – on Reflection by Dona Matthews

What values motivate me in my work? At heart, I am driven to do what I can to make the world a better place for children growing up. This comes from troubles and advantages I've experienced and observed, resulting in a deep desire to make things work for children as well as possible, and putting my professional focus on helping each child to find and develop her gifts and passions as far as she can. This translates in practice to a strong belief in the importance of respect, meaning that I do my best actively to respect each educator as a caring and dedicated professional, each parent doing the best he can for his children, each child as a capable and enthusiastic learner, and myself as a thoughtful educational psychologist. If there is one value that weaves its way through everything I've done and am doing, it is the need to respect the light of love, competence, and wisdom as it flows through each one of us. This translates into many ancillary and deeply-held values: authenticity, integrity, honesty, kindness, empathy, and courage come most readily to mind. These are the values that drive my daily practice and that I do my best to live out in my research, writing, teaching, and consulting.

If I can lay claim to having done any original work in gifted education, it would be my observation that we are in the midst of a paradigm shift in the field. For many years, I conducted a private psycho-

Gifts, Talents and Education By Barry Hymer, Jack Whitehead and Marie Huxtable
© 2008 Wiley-Blackwell

educational practice, specialising in issues related to giftedness. I came to see that traditional approaches make the idea of giftedness mysterious, by postulating, for example, the innate and permanent intellectual superiority of certain individuals – "the gifted" – over others – by default, the "non-gifted". Parents, children, and educators all talked to me about finding this categorical dualism hard to fit into their lived realities, causing problems with family and school relationships, as well as being thorny to implement educationally. At the same time as I was seeing up close the problems with a mysterious IQ-based notion of giftedness, I was identifying a serious disconnection between this model and emerging findings in a number of research directions, findings that demonstrated the domain-specificity of cognitive development, the enormous implications of neural plasticity across the lifespan, and individual developmental differences in maturational timing, among others.

I became increasingly concerned about the popular misconceptions of what intelligence is and how it develops, and how these misconceptions were damaging children and their learning. But I was simultaneously heartened in my observations that the field was gradually shifting paradigms to a model that took the evolving evidence-based understandings into account, a model that I've called a "mastery" model to describe its focus very simply on giftedness as incremental learning, and to distinguish it from the traditional "mystery" model. The two defensible agendas of gifted education, as conceived from a mastery model perspective, are (1) to address the special learning needs of those students who are so advanced at a certain time and in a certain subject that they require special educational adaptations at that time and in that subject area, and (2) to use what we learn about gifted development to foster giftedness more broadly. This mastery approach is simpler, more transparent, more accessible, and more inclusive. It is much easier to explain to people, and to implement educationally. It is harmonious with emerging findings in cognitive development, neuropsychology, and education. And it works really well to support gifted-level learning in all kinds of students.

Although this approach has been informed by the work of many people, including Michael Howe, Maria Montessori, Howard Gardner, Dan Keating, David Lohman, Lev Vygotsky, Jim Borland, Mihalyi Csikszentmihalyi, Joe Renzulli, Frances Horowitz, Julian Stanley, and many others, I see Carol Dweck's distinction between fixed and growth mindsets to be the most important and exciting idea in psychology and education today. In its affirmation of all learning as incremental, and intelligence as domain-specific and dynamically responsive to hard work over time, it validates a mastery approach to gifted education, and provides powerfully effective tools for teachers to foster high-level development more broadly and inclusively across the population.

Where this takes me by way of practical ideas for the teaching-learning process is that we need to respect individual developmental differences, and make sure there are opportunities in children's education both for individual learning tasks and projects, and for meaningful collaboration with peers they may well find challenging. This does not mean the dualistic categorisation of some kids as "gifted" (and others therefore as "not-gifted"), but it does mean thinking about children's individual learning needs, by subject area, and within subject areas too, making sure that what we're asking of them in their hours at school is meaningful, that it is sufficiently challenging, that they are actively engaged in their learning, and thereby creating their own giftedness. I can't say it better than Barry Hymer did in his doctoral thesis (Hymer, 2007a, Abstract), where he proposed and described ". . . an inclusional, non-dualistic alternative to the identification or discovery of an individual's gifts and talents by arguing that activity- and development-centred (not knowing-centred) learning-leading-development (Vygotsky) environments lead not to the identification of gifts and talents but to their creation."

In a recent essay, Jack Whitehead talks about the "creative space in which to read, think and write" that he experienced as a student at Newcastle University. I find this startling, because I am finding and making for myself now, for the first time really at age 56, such a space. As a child growing up in a busy household, I yearned inchoately for such a space, and the time in which to savour it. In my 20s, when I read Virginia Woolf's *A Room of One's Own*, this dream was validated in a way that allowed me to affirm it and continue to hold it aloft as a possibility, but it has taken me all these intervening decades of raising a family, getting an education, and earning a living, before I could finally create some real space in which to read, think, and write. Sadly, "getting an education" and "earning a living" – even though these were both academic pursuits purportedly focused on teaching and learning – did not provide such spaces. They were too filled with administrative and hurdle-jumping tasks to afford the luxury of time for reflection, for contemplation, for thoughtful digestion of all I was "learning".

One thing I would change for children in their schooling, then, would be to give them the time and space they need for thinking, for reflection, for contemplation, and for productive collaboration. I would slow down the clock, add in more time for optional, unplanned, unorganised, physical play, and similarly, lots more time for contemplation, optional reading, and unplanned, unorganised, intellectual play. I would give them time to figure out what they don't know yet, what they want to learn more about, what's troubling and interesting to them about the world. And then of course, I would want them to have the good teacherly guidance they need to use that time and space effectively, to support them in finding and creating and building on their giftedness.

So far in this book, we have attempted to disturb the contours of traditional understandings of the concept of 'giftedness'. In addition, we have tried to show how and why the core values which comprise the lived truths of educators must necessarily impact upon their practice in the school and classroom, and why the concept of 'giftedness' cannot be left to the mercies of a 20th century 'mystery' model (Matthews & Foster, 2006) – which remains shrouded in deterministic aetiological explanations, instrumental approaches to definition, and complacent and uninclusional stances towards provision. We are telling a different story, a counter-narrative to the 'hegemonic narrative' (Richardson, 2002) which is commonly told and listened to in our society.

Stories are, of course, old truths, but they have the power to create new realities. They are, in Ben Okri's (1996) words, '. . . the secret reservoir of values: change the stories individuals and nations live by and tell themselves and you change the individuals and nations . . . If they tell themselves stories that are lies, they will suffer the future consequences of those lies. If they tell themselves stories that face their own truths, they will free their histories for future flowerings'. In his book *Induction and Intuition in Scientific Thought*, Medawar (1969) proposes that scientific enquiries constitute, at least initially, stories about possible worlds that are created, critiqued and reconstructed in the process of living: stories, in other words, of real life practices. These 'possible worlds' throw other, more dominant worlds into stark relief. In Pace Marshall's words (in Abbott & Ryan, 2000, pp. 230, 231):

> We have to draw a sharp comparison between the current story that underpins educational assumptions as being a story I call the Culture of Acquisition, Independence and Competition, and a new story. I call this new story the Culture of Inquiry, Interdependence and Collaboration. These stories are grounded in very different ways of knowing and discovering who we are. It is in how we come to understand ourselves that we shape particular kinds of learning environments, and these shape the way our minds work . . . and that of course shapes our futures. It is my belief that the ultimate purpose of education is to liberate the goodness and genius of all children in the world. Learners of all ages need to be engaged fully, and in an interconnected way, around significant questions that matter to them, to the community, and concerns the

most significant issues of our time. This would create a new mind for the new millennium (and of course this new mind also includes a new heart, soul and spirit).

We call therefore in this book for an emphasis on old truths and new logics. In advancing a very different, 'living theory' approach to the field of giftedness, it is incumbent on us to tell a *plausible* story, one which resonates with you, the reader, and which makes explicit how a unique model of gift creation (not gift identification) has itself emerged through lived experience, and moreover, how this model advances and is answerable to its own standards of judgement. This is the job of the present chapter, in which we draw substantially on Barry's research into his own practice as an educator in the field of giftedness (Hymer, 2007).

In researching his own practice, Barry found it helpful and necessary to call upon the evidence of those individuals who had come to know something of his ontological values, of his related epistemological values and of his revealed methodological values in practice, either over time or through their one-off engagements with him during workshops and conference presentations – engagements which for the most part form the raw material of his work as a freelance educator in the field of giftedness. In the latter instance, he drew occasionally on transcripts of video footage from presentations and workshop facilitation, and heavily on the written evaluative reflections made by delegates at the end of inservice education and training opportunities (INSET) sessions or presentations, especially the written reflections made in response to three specific questions, each located around educational and personal values. These questions asked

- Do you feel Barry's values were in evidence in his presentation/course? If so, what do you understand these values to be?
- Do you feel that Barry's values connect with your own? Please state why/why not.
- To what extent do you feel your own educational values can be lived out in your own professional practice?

These questions were created when he realised that the usual evaluation forms distributed and collected by course organisers focused on the more visible, familiar, technical aspects of presentation skills and style, on issues of knowledge or skills *transmission*, and on a *tips-for-teachers* understanding of the course's immediate usefulness, but very little on alternative epistemologies: how, for instance, do delegates/participants 'read' the course leader's values? What congruence is there between these values and how she/he 'lives' these values in practice? How do perceptions of these values connect with their own felt ontological values? And how are they best able to translate their own values into practice in their own unique circumstances?

In reflecting on the nature of the evaluative feedback described above, we have been interested to see the emergence of five core themes, described below. None is neatly distinguishable from the others – they overlap in multiple ways – but they have been the categories we have found most meaningful in 'carrying' the collected data into evidential form. We acknowledge that the themes may not reveal any universally generalisable 'truth', as they must necessarily arise from individually unique histories and onto-logical and epistemological stances, but they do offer the framework for a model that constructs conditions for talent development.

By way of illustration, we call in the first instance on Marie's observations (Huxtable, 2005) when she wrote in relation to her presence at a conference at which Barry spoke:

> Barry introduced the audience of educators to the work of Carol Dweck (1999) focusing on the entity and incremental theories of intelligence and invited them to reflect on the implications of which theory they and their pupils, probably unconsciously, held. You can hear and see Barry's response to one member of the audience who had spoken about how she could see the reflections of her embodied educational theories through her grandchildren's stories as learners. The very personal resonance in professional life of this understanding for another member of the audience can be heard when she says how deeply depressed she felt now she recognised (to coin Jack Whitehead's words) the "living contradictions" in her own practice. I hear the audience laughter as an expression of the shared recognition, and empathy with, the irony and the emotional consequences that needed a supportive response in a public (and very English) arena. The damage of yardsticks provided by the establishment which berate, rather than scaffold, is acknowledged in that laughter.

Barry was heartened that Marie sensed that he had managed, at least for these two participants, both to challenge them to see themselves as living contradictions (with all the pain that this sometimes involves), but also to respond with warm respect to their open and very public acknowledgement of their emergent insights. Her observation allowed him to propose, for the first time and initially only very tentatively, that two values were here simultaneously being recognised (as already being) and germinated (coming into being): Marie saw evidence of individual intellectual respect for the experiences and unique meanings created by the speakers, but more than this, she describes through the articulation of the thought/insight and the reaction of the audience/peers the co-creation of something deeper – what we term here 'generative-transformational giftedness'.

We introduce the term tentatively because we prefer to see it not as some fixed, predictable capacity, as with traditional understandings of such (socially constructed) concepts as 'intelligence' or 'giftedness', but rather as a dynamically fluid dispositional quality, occasionally mercurial and always simultaneously both a value in and of itself, and a relational outcome. 'Giftedness' is understood therefore in a non-psychometric sense of 'gifted disposition' – a tendency to think creatively, clearly and analytically in certain contexts. This draws on but also extends the term as used by Perkins, Jay & Tishman (1993), who define a disposition as a 'tendency to think or behave in certain ways under certain conditions'. What are the 'ways' and the 'conditions' specifically in relation to generative-transformational giftedness? We suggest that these can be described under the following five emergent themes:

GENERATIVE-TRANSFORMATIONAL (G-T)

This 'signature' theme is instanced, in Marie's account above, in the suggestion that at least one member of the audience might be disposed to change her practice in some way – or multiple ways (e.g. her engagements with her grandchildren, her classroom interactions, etc.), not through acceptance of 'research evidence' or authoritative pronouncement, but through a critical reflection of her own practice in the light of newly created (not received) knowledge and through her sense of empowerment as a lifelong learner, capable of transforming herself into an infinitude of new forms. The term is borrowed from McNiff *et al.*, who note: 'This idea of generative power acts as the basic unit of energy whereby each thing may transform itself endlessly in the process of its own realisation of potential' (McNiff, Whitehead & Laidlaw, 1992, p. 35). It is expressed equally succinctly by the Academy Award-winning actor Daniel Day-Lewis in the words, 'The thing about performance, even if it's only an illusion, is that it's a celebration of the fact that we do contain within ourselves infinite possibilities'. In my own research, exploring my practice as a trainer and educator in the field of gifted education, I found that I 'grew' in my own learning not in presentation mode *to* my audience, but in dialogue mode *with* them: it is at these moments that I can inform and develop my own grasp of the subject matter, refining, cultivating, pruning – *growing* it, and an 'audience' can do the same. I have come to see myself as *performing* when delivering a well-rehearsed 'script' (past learning), but as *performing above myself* when in true dialogue with others (new, two-way learning). In the Vygotskyan sense, this performatory function is associated with learning, not ego, and betrays no sense of inauthenticity or deception. We wear a mask without inhibition or guilt – to 'act up', to play the 'role' of learner and through this play, to habituate to and advance within the learning role. In the words of Kelemen (2001, p. 95), 'In the facades we put on for others we demonstrate our potential'.

The generative-transformational element makes the transition from theory to practice in its connection with Freire's notion of *praxis* (Freire, 1993, p. 68)

– the generative combination of reflection and action which exist '… in such radical interaction that if one is sacrificed – even in part – the other immediately suffers. There is no true word that is not at the same time a praxis. Thus, to speak a true word is to transform the world'.

It is our belief that the generative-transformational element is present as a latency in all situations that carry learning potentialities, but that it requires activation through the creation of meaning and knowledge – and these are in turn created at moments of recognition, connection, insight and inspiration. Data collected from educators' responses to the evaluative prompts described earlier in this chapter provide further evidence of this generative-transformational element. Can you feel, for instance, the sense of impatient vitality contained in these reflections?

- 'My current job is not about teaching and learning – IT HAS GOT TO CHANGE!'
- 'Can't wait to get involved. I feel like I've found my own strength in the education world'.
- 'The best is yet to come'.
- 'My own personal history is as an "entity" [seeing abilities as fixed, after Dweck, 1999] – and sadly this is still so – but I will try to change – ICT here I come!'
- 'Inspired me to make changes to my own practice and indeed the whole school'.

or the related sense of resolute intention contained in these?

- 'Have decided that I'll start to do some "proper" reading after today'.
- 'I will further encourage questioning in my classroom and set up an interactive display where children can ask and view these questions'.
- 'I will be sure to put all I've learnt today into practice'.
- 'This course will give me the impetus to change and adapt'.
- 'The reason I became a head was my passion to be able to do just that [live my educational values in my own practice] – the power to impact on change – to lead a learning-centred rather than performance-driven school'.

or the growthful recognition of shared beliefs in the power of intellectual development and generative learning experiences?

- 'Yes! Yes! Yes! I have long believed that children can outstrip my own narrow education. Children do not see restrictions – they believe anything is possible, and we should never restrict this fantastic gift'.

- 'Creating intelligence is not just G&T. Children have different gifts and talents which can be both found and created'.
- 'Really encouraging creative questioning of my philosophy of education and life. Who I am is not what I am capable of doing'.
- 'I only learned my subject when I had to teach and I was resolved to come out of all lessons knowing more. This is what happened in [this] talk. I am different in significant ways'.
- 'I believe you value the whole child and want every child to be the best they can be'.
- 'Socrates' dialogues change you; so did [this] INSET today'.

and the suggestions offered by these educators as to how generative intentions might be realised in present and future practice:

- 'I will listen to children's ideas more'.
- 'All staff are really fired up about philosophy now and every teacher has already planned their first activity for next week. Two classes have already done their first session and the feedback has been fantastic!'
- 'I enjoyed the training immensely and couldn't wait to try it out. [After Day 1] (J)ust seeing children's responses to constructive praise is amazing. Seeing how children listen to others and are able to agree/disagree without prejudice'.
- 'Growth of the intellect/senses/making of meaning depends on encouraging questioning/searching'.
- 'I will be more determined to live [my values] out after today than before. I have often taught as though the content is more important than the process'.
- 'I realize that some of the things I've felt tentative about doing in the past I can now really "go for" in my lessons'.

and, finally, the honest recognition of work invited, accepted and still to be undertaken:

- 'I am still learning where I would like to place my values. However, I do share his passion to promote human creativity in every way and person'.
- '. . . it is hard to change the way you praise children when you've used/ heard the same style for years. I'm in my NQT year and am adapting my teaching every day'.
- 'Given that I am more of an entity learner/personality, I am having to try much harder at not imposing this view on others. But I must be turning more incremental because I view this as a challenge now!'
- 'Believes in the process rather than the product. To sow a seed, engender a love of learning'.

CONTRADICTORY/DIALECTICAL (C)

This second theme is predicated on the observation that knowledge is more likely to be created through the felicitous convergence of opposing or apparently contradictory views, beliefs, experiences or 'facts' than through the comfortable receipt of accepted (already 'known') views, beliefs, etc. Learning happens when these apparently contradictory and distinct units of knowledge can be seen as existing in inclusional flow form (Rayner, this book, Chapter 1), rather than as competing warriors. With a disposition of openness to new learning, contradictory information can be reconciled or rejected within schema, and these schema then re-calibrated to accommodate new learning. In Piagetian terms, therefore, this theme is understood in terms of the creation of new mental schema, arising through the experience of disequilibrium.

Within a Platonic, non-propositional understanding which does not require the proving of one truth and the disproving of another contradictory truth, but which is able to accommodate the legitimacies of apparently competing truths, we argue that the meanings generated consist of a dialectical unity, not a relationship of cause or tool (e.g. an isolated or contextualised comment or a full presentation to an audience) and effect or result (e.g. a consequent 'understanding' *transmitted* to the audience). '(T)he dialectical unity rather than metaphysical duality was central [to the totality of Vygotsky's enterprise]' (Holzman, 1997, p. 59). The author Mark Haddon (2004), for instance, recalls his time at Oxford: 'I remember . . . discovering a view of the world very contrary to the one I had been given at school. It can be very exciting to discover that everything you've been taught might be wrong'.

As with the generative-transformational and temporal-social themes, we see the constructivist and co-constructivist learning environments being the natural homes of the contradictory/dialectical theme, with knowledge residing not as it does in an objectivist model in the transmission of inert 'good knowledge', and not even (as it does in traditional conceptions of 'the intelligent person') within individual heads, but in the living spaces occupied by the dynamic interactivity and dialogical sense creation of multiple heads – what we term the 'exo-brain':

> So you will search in vain for any semblance of a self within the structures of the brain: there is no ghost in the machine. It is time to grow up and accept this fact. But, somehow, we are the product of the operation of this machinery and its progress through the physical and social world. Minds emerge from process and interaction, not substance. In a sense, we inhabit the spaces between things. (Broks, 2003, p. 55)

This is a process well described by J., aged 11, reflecting meta-cognitively on the experience of doing philosophy with his peers: 'You can't think by just sitting in your room, because you've only got . . . what's inside your noggin. But these other people, they've also got noggins, and you've got to get all these noggins together . . .' (video transcript, 2003), and also by Hannah Arendt: '. . . but if the wind of thinking . . . has shaken you from sleep and made you fully awake and alive, then you will see that you have nothing in your grasp but perplexities, and the best we can do with them is share them with each other . . .' (Arendt, 1978, p. 175).

We see the contradictory/dialectical theme played out in the following evaluative observations, again provided by educators. Can you sense the open-minded valuing of challenge to existing views and mindsets in these reflections?

- 'You put forward provocative views that had the desired effect of making teachers question what they do and challenge their current practice'.
- 'I felt challenged by ideas, but enjoyed the challenge . . . to look at more exciting ways to teach'.
- 'You have to come out of your comfort zone, be brave and challenge your own way of teaching/engaging with learners'.
- 'I learn best when I'm intellectually uncomfortable – that's what really stretches me'.
- 'This has been a totally fantastic, reflective day – really encouraging creative questioning of my philosophy of education AND LIFE'.

or the attempts to synthesise externally imposed objectives with internally derived principles and beliefs?

- 'It is easy to get swept up with standards and generic targets in teaching. I will encourage self-target setting and evaluation of [pupils'] own work and effort'.
- 'I have to get results based on objectives. I am paid to do the opposite of what I believe – how sad is that?'
- 'My values change as I learn more about education as opposed to teaching'.
- 'Bringing together thoughts and feelings – they don't have to be separate'.
- 'I believe in the needs of the 3Rs. I also believe in fostering creative writing, drawing and PE, to produce more rounded educational opportunity'.
- 'A commitment to enabling teachers to feel "whole" in the job they do, rather than just doing what they can'.

or the recognition that multiple truths (including core values) need not be overridden by the dominant imperatives?

- 'Answers trump answer'.
- 'Encouraging that we ARE allowed to think – and so are CHILDREN!'
- 'I feel most of my values come from life experiences rather than education – I draw on these constantly'.
- 'Each teacher knows the joy of a lesson gone well and the guilt of principles not adhered to. Values are ever-present and should be lived out in the classroom – marvellous!'
- 'How children learn is more important than how I teach. Teaching is time-based, learning is not!'

RELATIONAL (RE)

Where is the love? Within traditional *test-and-place* 'capacity' models of giftedness, very little significance is attributed to the gift-creating power of enriched, respectful and life-affirming teacher–student and student–student relationships. Far more important in these dominant conceptualisations are the instrumental, semi-linear assumptions that underlie considerations of definitions, identification and provision. For illustrative purposes, we cite just the chapter titles of one of the most popular British resources in the field, written for teachers – Deborah Eyre's *Able Children in Ordinary Schools* (1997):

1. Defining Able Children
2. Identification
3. A Differentiated Approach to Classroom Planning
4. Classroom Provision
5. Issues for Secondary Schools
6. Issues for Primary Schools
7. Appendices – Policy Documents

Even in what might be assumed to be the 'natural home' of the relational element – books focusing on the social-emotional needs of gifted children – this dimension often seems to play second fiddle to curricular considerations or to the particular needs of 'special populations'. Consider, again for illustrative purposes, the chapter titles of Michael Stopper's *Meeting the Social and Emotional Needs of Gifted and Talented Children* (2000):

1. Introduction
2. Curriculum Development and Process in Mainstream Classrooms
3. Extension and Enrichment Programmes: "A Place I Could Fit in"
4. The Role of the Family
5. Gifted and Talented Children with Dyslexia
6. Culturally Diverse Gifted Students

7. Able and Talented Learners from Socio-economically Disadvantaged Communities
8. Conclusion

Conceptualisations which minimise, ignore or deny the relational provenance of gifts and talents are ignorant of the lived realities of people – including both teachers and pupils – who are in our collective experience almost always able to talk with passion and at length about the significant 'other' who connected with them, within school or outside of it. The *Times Educational Supplement*'s long-running 'My Best Teacher' column catalogues the stories of high-achieving ('gifted'?) figures in all disciplines, and it is rare in these stories to find instrumental attributions – the teacher who inspired and invigorated through her impressive efficiencies of knowledge transmission, her adherence to the rules of the dominant order, her ability to gain control over others or her omniscience. These people tell other tales, of trust, mutual respect and recognition, of sharing, reciprocity and friendship, and of unconditional support at times of adversity – tales of *relationships*.

Just a few examples of these tales of relationship, from hundreds of possible stories: the author and scriptwriter Anthony Horowitz (*Times Educational Supplement*, 5 October 2001), for instance, speaks of a man, Harry Thompson, who stood out for his humanity in an environment of terror: 'You had the feeling that he understood, which is often all that children are looking for'. The actress Saffron Burrows (28 September 2001) speaks of her mother, a Hackney teacher, whose pupils '. . . trust her. She treats them as young people who have the potential to be anyone'. The Channel 4 newsreader, Jon Snow (6 October 2000), recalls Bob Thomas, his A-level teacher (and former lorry driver from the Welsh valleys), who redeemed for him the most inauspicious of educational beginnings: 'What made him special . . . was that he had infinite respect for us as students. He really thought we were worth something, which no one had ever made me feel at public school. . . . [Y]oung people respond best to being treated with respect'.

These memories of the relational, growth-creating 'we' are played out repeatedly in non-fiction (e.g. Albom, 1997), in fiction (e.g. Spark, 1961) and in film (e.g. Ashby, 1971). All describe a *power-with* or *power-through* rather than *power-over* relationship between people – a relationship which is respectful of the differentness of the *other*, yet also secure in one's own integrity and open to the creation of something new – 'All real living is meeting' (Buber, 2002, p. xiv). The relational 'between' is the ontological reality – as explored not only in educational terms [the concept of inclusionality developed by Alan Rayner, the Buberian play of I~thou, I~we which lies at the heart of much of Jack's writing and that of his students, cf. http://www.actionresearch.net, Whitehead & Huxtable (2006) and Farren's 'web of betweenness' (2006)], but also theologically (Buber, 1958, 2002), and in Sandy Eisenberg Sasso's children's picture book, *God in Between* (Sasso, 1998).

Very recently (February 2008), Barry received an email from a teacher who'd attended one of his courses a year previously. She felt that her subsequent engagements with her students had '. . . immediate and significant effects on learning and, something I did not predict, greatly improved my relationships with students. I know them so much better because they communicate their ideas to me – rather than the other way round – and they inform me about what they learn and how they learn it. This is true of all ages and all abilities. It's truly inspiring to have such stimulating relationships with my students. We are all so motivated in our joint learning. It's fantastic!'

We provide further evidence of the significance of the relational by referring to the transcript of a reflective observation made by a participant towards the end of a (videoed) workshop facilitated by Barry in Harrogate, on 24 November 2005. Earlier that morning, he had made a keynote presentation to open the conference; the workshop group was much smaller. Here is the observation in full:

> One of the things you haven't mentioned, even in the work of Bruner there, is the notion of the relationship between that significant adult in the room, teacher, facilitator, whatever, and the children. You alluded to it. If the relationship hasn't been built effectively [pause] . . . and if I can talk about a real example: this morning I came because I have an interest in G&T but interestingly trying to avoid filling in this 5-10% form this LEA will send me and I wanted to try to find a justification for saying, "Sorry, I haven't identified them for this particular problem because I don't know what your problem is that you're going to solve, and so there's the justification and you've paid for him to come and tell me that," and . . . but interestingly I was signed up for a totally different workshop this morning and the relationship and the credibility of you as a presenter hooked me into this session because "dilemma-based learning" was just another title to me, was another bandwagon coming past my school and I didn't want to hook to it because it might divert my school from what we were doing; so the relationship part of it for me as a learner was very important and I think it's probably the most important factor in anything we do with children – with regard to how we hook them into their learning.

We use this head teacher's observation to instance the creation of relationally dynamic epistemological standards of judgement – created in the process of living, clarifying and communicating the values used to give meaning and purpose to one's life. This participant focuses on the salience of 'the relationship part of it' as being, for him, 'the most important factor' in what we do as educators.

Thayer-Bacon also focuses on the relational:

> In Relational "(e)pistemologies," I seek to offer a feminist (e)pistemological theory that insists that knowers/subjects are fallible, that our criteria are

corrigible (capable of being corrected), and that our standards are socially constructed, and thus continually in need of critique and reconstruction. I offer a self-conscious and reflective (e)pistemological theory, one that attempts to be adjustable and adaptable as people gain further in understanding. This (e)pistemology must be inclusive and open to others, because of its assumption of fallible knowers. And this (e)pistemology must be capable of being corrected because of its assumption that our criteria and standards are of this world, ones we, as fallible knowers, socially construct. (Thayer-Bacon, 2003, p. 7)

The fallible knower is well known to practitioners of philosophy for children (P4C) (Lipman, 1993, 2003; Lipman, Sharp & Oscanyan, 1980), who are aware, as Socrates himself was, of the value of ignorance. It diverts agency from the assumed 'omniscient knower' (traditional understandings of the teacher) to the seeker of knowledge. The fallible knower finds further traction in the notion of *caring thinking* (one of P4C's core elements, alongside *critical, creative* and *collaborative*). Sharp (2007, p. 249), one of Matthew Lipman's key colleagues, enters explicitly into the inclusional domain in acknowledging that

Caring thinking expresses itself in prizing, esteeming, cherishing, healing, consoling, taking care of, nurturing, empathizing, sympathizing, valuing, appreciating, celebrating, responding to the other. . . . It tends to approach the "other" (person or object or river or animal, etc.) from the inside . . . It is caring thinking that is responsible for the fostering of a "relational consciousness" in children – rather than viewing things atomistically, the caring thinker tends to focus on the relationships between things – and this results in a deep understanding. . . . Relational consciousness is knowing and feeling oneself intimately connected with and part of everything that is, and coming to act and relate out of that awareness. It is experiencing oneself not as an atomistic ego, but as a self in relationship to the other. Some have called this consciousness the "we-consciousness." . . . For a long time we have lived under an illusion of separateness. We've lived as detached egos, unaware that we are part of a vast fabric of being, and communal oneness. Now we are learning from the new sciences that the universe has actually to be constructed as a "we." Everything in creation – oceans, whales, mountains, human, eagles, roses, giraffes, and viruses – is a dance of sub-atomic particles. Fields of energy flow and mingle together. They are all stitched into the cosmic quilt, which underlies and gives rise to everything.

This understanding of the relational 'we' is described by Rayner's (2005) notion of inclusionality, identified as '. . . an awareness of space and the variably permeable boundaries . . . that inseparably line it, as connective, reflective and co-creative, rather than divisive'. Within an inclusional understanding, it is possible to see the power of fallibility in places where, hitherto, we might have seen only weaknesses. Invited by Jack to have a look at and to comment on a series of video clips of educators in interaction with others, in support of his own research into his own and others' practice, he posted the clips on YouTube. In an email dated 18 December 2006, Barry responded to a particular clip of Alan Rayner expanding on the implications of his concept of *inclusionality* as follows:

> Dear Jack – Thank you for this posting, which I have just opened and found surprisingly affecting … The effect was slow and cumulative, but by the time I looked at the exchange between Eden and Alan, it seemed that something surprising was taking place … – Alan was living out inclusionality in his reflections on it (meta-inclusionality?): I was struck by how Alan began with a comment about human frailty being at the heart of human creativity – and then proceeded to speak falteringly, painfully, and fallibilistically about inclusionality (in response to Eden's gentle probes and provocations) in a way which mirrored beautifully his opening comment, and in a way that I haven't seen before. I see inclusionality made real in that exchange, and the creativity that isn't inhibited but is cultivated in that "frailty". "There is no conflict." [Alan's summary of his core message.] I see the gift of frailty there as a world-leading living standard in itself, and hope for ourselves in our imperfections. Thank you for sharing it.

A valuing of frailty in the relational 'we' often finds itself embodied in the tacit knowledge of educators, however minimised they might be in the usual bureaucracies of many teachers' institutional lives. From the evaluation returns previously described, can you see the relational 'we' in evidence at an abstract level?

- 'Education is not purely about academic achievements but getting to know children as individuals'.
- 'Teachers' connections with children are more important than curriculum'.
- 'I try to connect with and inspire my children. The positive relationships I develop help my pupils achieve excellence'.
- 'My personal relationships with children are always important to me'.
- 'I have been saying for the last 24 years that good teaching is about relationships between teacher and child'.
- 'Respect and challenge – two core ingredients for a good teacher'.

and can you see it in the lived, concrete experience of participants in in-service training sessions?

- '… his ability to connect and empathise with the audience was excellent'.
- '… every opinion given to him [was] warmly received'.
- 'Enhancing the self-esteem of delegates who volunteered an answer'.
- 'I like your style in that you don't promote yourself as an exemplary practitioner who's got all the answers. Can relate more to that'.
- 'Barry has shown me it's not just the children who need confidence, it's the adults as well. [As a teaching assistant] it has made me feel that

I can make a difference just by believing in myself and my abilities to teach'.

- 'Loved the way everybody was listened to and how there was a chance for everybody to speak'.

or in the memories of values experienced in their negation and in their presence?

- 'I do draw subconsciously on my own experiences. When I was six my teacher shouted at me for asking how to spell "he." The whole class went quiet. I never forgot again but it was a horrible experience and I try never to do this to a child'.
- 'I had a fear of maths, but had a very understanding teacher who had patience and perseverance. Helped me to realise maths is not as hard if you look at it in a different light. I try to remember his patience'.

and in the recognition that the relational 'we' is a non-hierarchical 'we'?

- 'We are all still learning ourselves, so we can learn with the children as well'.
- 'That education is a two-lane road and that BOTH the teachers and the pupils are travelling along it'.
- 'It's in the connection with students, through listening, encouraging them to ask questions'.
- 'Valuing the child's experience and contribution to the learning process'.
- 'I would like to expand and use emotional maturity as a tool for learning and promoting a kinder atmosphere in class which would allow the space for constructive failure. This could also help in staff meetings!'

ACTIVITY-ORIENTED (A)

In his descriptions of applications of the activity-oriented 'jigsaw' technique in classrooms, Watkins (2005) offers this account from Alyson, a secondary school science teacher:

> Anyone who is used to a traditional classroom, whereby students are always sat still, in rows of desks listening attentively to the teacher, may have viewed my classroom during those learning sessions as unruly, noisy, disorganised etc. . . . [T]o the more discerning eye . . . I hope they would have noticed the agency that students were taking for their learning, the way in which they were helping and encouraging each other, the choices they were making for themselves, and the pleasure they took from constructing their knowledge together in order to make sense of what they needed to learn. (Watkins, 2005, p. 129)

Alyson is describing well the external and internal characteristics of activity-based, co-constructivist classrooms, where students, not teachers, are responsible for the co-generation of meaning and its subsequent interrogation for veracity. Further examples are to be found in classrooms practising such approaches as, for instance, P4C (Lipman, 1993, 2003), Thinking Actively in a Social Context (TASC) (Wallace & Bentley, 2002), Logo-Visual Thinking (Best, Blake & Varney, 2005) and Dilemma-Based Learning (Wood, Hymer & Michel, 2007). In all these cases, learning is a function of the intellectual activity generated between the focus or stimulus for thinking (content as conduit, not objective) and the various meanings being created from it in the minds of the community, alongside, perhaps even more importantly, the ensuing dialogical activity between all the agents of the learning episode.

Bruner (1966, p. 117) speaks of '. . . the energising lure of uncertainty made personal by one's effort to control it', and argues that 'To Channel curiosity into more powerful intellectual pursuits requires precisely that there be [a] transition from the passive, receptive, episodic form of curiosity to the sustained and active form' (ibidem). It is the 'sustained and active form' that our model holds precious as one of the core themes of gift creation, since gifts arise not through any lonely impulse of delight but through the sustained assault of persistent enquiry, with teachers acting as the facilitators or enablers of children's learning – not as repositories of data. This is a Vygotskyan method which '. . . is activity-based rather than knowledge/ epistemology-based . . . Knowledge is not separate from the activity of practising method; it is not "out there" waiting to be discovered through the use of an already-made tool' (Holzman 1997, p. 52).

Can you see the activity-based route to knowledge construction in the words of these educators, again reflecting on their practice – and their experience of others' practice – at the end of one- or two-day in-service training sessions?

- 'Confirms the importance of spending time floating and becoming involved with children as they need you and see you as an opportunity for learning'.
- 'I have always seen myself as an educator and not just a teacher – if all I am trying to do is give them knowledge I can get them to read a book'.
- 'To encourage children to be active thinkers – to ask questions about their learning'.
- 'To make links, discuss, question, evaluate, challenge and enjoy all that education has to offer – no more thinking in boxes or units of work'.
- 'I hope that learning and enjoying it are important all through my life – that there is always something to do and something else to find out about'.

- 'They [pupils] must set their own problems/challenges so they will produce personal responses to the stimuli'.

and the explicit valuing of process over product, and learning over performance?

- 'To question, ask, probe the entire process of learning. Doing not just listening – the experiential approach'.
- 'We don't teach – we help children to learn'.
- 'As a languages teacher it is so important that the learner knows the processes of learning the target language and is able to transfer learned skills into new contexts. Rote learning has little long-term value'.
- 'Children need to value their efforts and move on, rather than respond to stickers and purely external motivation'.
- 'I am privileged to work alongside a great headteacher who values all strengths in both staff and pupils. She actively encourages us all to be creative and challenging. I hope to take her gift with me when I'm a head one day!'

and a recognition that activity need not, and should not, be frenetic?

- 'Giving children time to think, contribute, listen and reflect'.
- 'To make connections to every child and not tell them what they need to know'.
- 'He was trying to open our minds to ways of introducing incremental learning and he did it incrementally'.

TEMPORAL/SOCIAL (TE)

This final theme, just like the preceding four, is underpinned by a foundational co-constructivist and research-buttressed belief that humans, being social animals, learn best in social settings. Moreover, the social contexts of learning will change over time. 'In a learning community the goal is to advance the collective knowledge and, in that way, support the growth of individual knowledge' (Scardamalia and Bereiter, 1994, p. 268).

We have modelled the temporal-social element in the co-writing of this book. It could not have been written by one of us alone, or even by all three of us together, but at another stage in our respective learning journeys. We recognise that each of us brings something unique to its creation, but that it benefits from the serendipitous convergence of 'distinct but complementary' skills, knowledge, motivations, histories – three narratives of lived experience. The words that you are now reading will have been filtered and recreated through three lenses, to the extent that original 'authorship' becomes immaterial. Even as they were first crafted, by just one of us, the echoes of others' internal voices were heard and attended to. This outworking of the 'exo-brain' is true, we believe, also of single-authored texts. It is a belief made explicit by Chris Watkins in the acknowledgements to his book, *Classrooms as Learning Communities* (2005, p. xi):

> The idea that this is my first "single-authored" book in fifteen years is a peculiar fiction. Our achievements are never exclusively our own. Many people have contributed, sometimes in ways that they do not know. Their voices will be found within these pages.

In the negation of the temporal-social theme of the G-T CReATe model are to be found many of the greatest absurdities in traditional conceptualisations of giftedness. The belief, for instance, that gifted development follows a neat, chronologically linear trajectory from 'gifted zygote' and prodigy (Simonton, 2008) through to fully realised gifted actualisation in any domain. The reality is, of course, far more fractured. Fully two-thirds of the group of over 300 eminent 20th century individuals studied by Goertzel, for instance, '. . . were not even described as precocious, much less as prodigies' (Winner, 1996, p. 289). Prodigious achievement in childhood requires a transformation from technical expertise and age-related eminence to creative and conceptual manifestations in adulthood, where 'age at the time of creation' carries only incidental weight. Where patterns of predicted achievement do exist, these often follow temporal-social felicities – such as the 'renaissance effect' (there is no corresponding flowering of Florentine genius in 2008) or the case of the outstandingly successful Moscow School No.2, which in 1958 attracted the world famous mathematicians Israel Gelfand and Eugene Dynkin as teachers. The quality of the school was clear from the beginning; teachers treated pupils with respect and created a special atmosphere of learning (Yurkevitch & Davidoff, 2008).

We will go further than suggesting that the temporal/social theme makes allowances for divergences from linear-sequential expectations in gifted performance. We suggest that it leads us to *expect* such divergences as are described in David Jesson's research at York University, which found that only 28% of pupils identified as gifted or talented in primary school went on to achieve their expected three A grades at A level, whilst many teenagers not previously highlighted as very able did achieve top grades. Traditional models, by contrast, are puzzled by such divergences, or seek to 'fix' these through additional layers of identification, tracking and monitoring systems, or by blaming teachers for their 'neglect of excellence'. Such blame is rarely accompanied, it would seem, by praise for 'finding' or 'redeeming' the initially unidentified!

As with the four themes described above, we conclude our brief description of the core themes underpinning the G-T CReATe model with educators' reflections on the fifth. Can you see the powerful interplay of activity-oriented and temporal-social factors in the observations of Meg Gleave, a retired head teacher, giving meaning to her existence and values in her life as a Voluntary Service Overseas (VSO) volunteer in Rwanda:

> As for writing something myself, where would I begin on such a topic? The gifts I see here and think about, tenacious optimism, courage in the face of the unimaginable horror and deprivation endured during and in the aftermath of the genocide, human resilience? I hardly think it would be appropriate. I am exercised by practical things to help and build relationships, you know me! But I wonder whether in the fullness of time I could write about the utter joy and sense of wonder I have gained and continue to gain by being here. (email from Meg Gleave to Barry, December 2006)

Can you also see the temporal-social theme in existence, often in harmony with accompanying themes, in the following stories?

- 'I had learning problems with literacy and maths, but with a small group learned more within a term than I'd done in years. This is what I do now with a small group of children'.
- '[I value] The opportunity to come together and face the dilemma of education'.
- '[I value] Having respect for/valuing each other's point of view/ideas/opinions'.
- '[I like] To agree or disagree in an atmosphere of safety and acknowledgement'.
- 'I am fortunate to work in an institution where the Head's vision links closely with the values (particularly that of social capital) of Barry'.
- 'Enabling us to become better learners by giving a safe environment in which to take risks, ask questions and explore ideas with each other'.
- 'Develop environment of positive thinking so that children value each other and are prepared to make mistakes'.
- '[In future I will . . .] allow children to work as a group in a cooperative way without teacher leading'.
- '[I will be] Incorporating self and peer evaluation of work so that it becomes part of classroom philosophy'.
- 'I feel strongly that G&T and SEN students should be given the same opportunities to fly and to fail – that we should be facilitating learning not trying to put our own knowledge "into" kids'.

In none of the comments reproduced in our descriptions of the five themes of the G-T CReATe model, nor in the more extensive population of evaluation returns (unreproduced but retained) from which these have been drawn as a representative sample, are we able to trace any meaningful linear, cause-and-effect, *tool-for-result* route between the course facilitator's action and the reflection evidenced by the participants. None, therefore, is claimed. Within the Vygotskyan conceptualisation of *tool-and-result*, perhaps this would be neither feasible nor desirable. The whole is greater than the sum, and the whole reflects an infinitely complex, catalytic, generative series of interactions and transactions between a course facilitator, course participants (with all the various personal, political, educational and cultural histories we bring to this engagement), environment and ethos, etc.

What we describe as generative-transformational giftedness (and the conditions under which we suggest it arises – the five themes outlined above), is of course not offered as a literal picture of 'the real world' but as a theoretical scientific model – a partial and provisional way of imagining the unobservable. The model is very closely related to and influenced by the Deweyan (and proto-Vygotskyan) emphasis on the significance of the future in the present, which in turn anticipates the malleable or incremental self-theory of intelligence described by Dweck:

> Everything we see in children is transitional, promises and signs of the future ... not to be treated as achievements, cut off and fixed; they are prophetic, signs of an accumulating power and interest. (Dewey, 1902, p. 14)

> For [people holding an incremental view of intelligence] intelligence is not a fixed trait that they simply possess, but something they can cultivate through learning. (Dweck, 1999, p. 3)

There is also a clear connection to the Marxian–Vygotskyan concept of development as continuously emergent, relational human activity – with the search for method as being necessarily *tool-and-result* (Vygotsky, 1978) rather than *tool-for-result*. Neither the tool nor the result can be independently meaningful – they exist in a unity, '. . . influencing each other in complex and changing ways as the totality tool-and-result develops' (Holzman, 1997, p. 58). We create our own meaning. In the words of one participant at a whole-school training event (23 September 2005): 'I have learned a lot in this session – but I don't think he "taught" me anything. How has this happened?'

We build now on the tables provided in Chapter 1, which drew ontological and epistemological comparisons between approaches to research and giftedness which were based variously on the self as perceived 'insider' and the self as perceived 'outsider'. In the table below, we offer a description of how traditional models of giftedness might be distinguished from those (such as G-T CReATe) which are framed from the perspective of the self as perceived 'insider' (Table 2.1):

Table 2.1 Two models of giftedness, reflecting contrasting ontological and epistemological stances

Domain	Traditional conceptualisation	G-T CReATe conceptualisation
Gift identification?	Yes, test and classify, the earlier the better	No; focus instead on gift creation; this happens at moments of coincidence between opportunity and need
Educators' emphasis	'Objective' data from past performances	Creating opportunities for present and future learning
G&T cohorts and labels?	Yes, distinct teaching and learning provision (often acceleration) on the grounds of ability and identification	No; inclusive initial provision, but extension opportunities on the grounds of interest and application
Nature or nurture?	Emphasis on individual intelligence and the provenance of nature, genetics, background influences	Emphasis on the impact of social factors in learning, on motivation and distributed intelligence
Teacher's role?	Teacher as neutral, impartial arbiter, separate from and independent of individual students	Teacher as involved co-participant in the construction of gifts and talents
Coordinator's role?	Coordinator role: administrator of systems for identification, tracking and monitoring	Coordinator role: peer-coach and co-learner, alert to new learning and teaching methodologies for dissemination and championing
Expectations for performance over time?	Assumptions of linear progression in performance based on fixed ability	Assumptions of variable performance based on, e.g. temporal-social, relational factors
Integration of affective factors?	Cognitive-emotional duality	Cognitive-emotional dialectical unity
Self theory? (Dweck 1999)	Feeds fixed, entity approach to intelligence and performance-led orientation	Feeds growth focused, incremental approach to intelligence and learning- or mastery-led orientation
Evidence of accountability?	Accountability through evidence of student performances and tracking and monitoring systems	Accountability through evidence of student learning, including 'soft data' (e.g. commitment, interest)

The right-hand column summarises some of the many things that remain vital and growthful in an inclusional and dynamic conceptualisation of gift-edness. These were summarised in the conclusions to a published plea for a rethink around the concept of *giftedness* (Hymer, 2005, p. 7):

> Gifted and talented education, for all the problems inherent in the terminology, has provided the world of education with many rich signposts over the 20th century. It continues to do so. This article is not intended as an assault on its existence, even though I'd welcome changes to its nomenclature. Early signs of a possible shift in emphasis in DfES thinking from "gifted and talented" to "challenge and engagement" are to be welcomed and encouraged. We should certainly continue to invest heavily in the pursuit of excellence and achieve-ment, confront anti-intellectual bigotry, and seek ways of raising aspirations within and without areas of deprivation.

We are aware from our contacts with hundreds of outstanding educators that whilst many generative educational practices (e.g. P4C, TASC, Dilemma-Based Learning) are not reliant on an affiliation to orthodox conceptualisa-tions of giftedness, they do, as described above and earlier in Chapter 1, embody many of the elements which are germane to non-deterministic, inclusive conceptualisations in the field – concepts such as *challenge, personal enquiry, extension* and *enrichment*, for instance. Whilst we have documented earlier the aetiology and the nature of our concerns with orthodox concep-tualisations of *giftedness*, and suggested ways in which crystallised, objectiv-ist, instrumentalist, dualistic, individualistic, pragmatic interpretations of the field might be supplanted by fluid, constructivist, social, relational, activity-oriented, dialectical interpretations – in particular the emergent concept of *generative-transformational giftedness*, we contend further that our experiences of the value and the emergence of *generative-transformational giftedness* when working in the *gaps* of dialogue and critical reflection with co-participants in classrooms, workshops and conference presentations can act as a model for the emergence of gift creation generally, and that this provides a possibility for repudiating fixed, crystallised, norm-referenced understandings of giftedness, in favour of the fluid, constructivist interpreta-tions described above.

From this socio-constructivist perspective, and drawing on Vygotskyan notions in particular, we argue that just as individuals build their knowledge through language and social interaction, so can gifts be *built, created or made* – rather than *identified, discovered or found*. This will, in large measure, be dependent on the social and relational element at the heart (in more than one sense) of *generative-transformational giftedness* – as socio-cognitive pro-cesses emerge through the activating and development of higher-order thinking skills, which in turn arise from the relationships a person sustains with his or her social environments (Mead, 1972).

In our work as teachers and researchers of our own practice, we have come to realise that the *relational* is seminal to arguments for a socio-constructivist understanding of *giftedness*, as described in Chapter 1 ff. In our work with children and with adults, we strive to live this relational, inclusional 'we' in our practice – as evidenced by the comments reproduced earlier from participants in these experiences. The 'we' helps to corrupt established and potentially oppressive *power-over* hierarchies. Within the field of giftedness, the *power-over* stance illuminated in narrative therapeutic understandings is as much an issue for the child 'having' *giftedness*, as it is for the child 'lacking' it. There is merit to be found, we believe, not in leaving the field to *power-over*, but in drawing it in to the *power-with*. It's all in the 'we'.

We recognise the power relationships in our culture and history that are sustaining 'power-over'. We do not underestimate the task of the cultural transformations in moving towards *power-with* in the expression and development of talents in the production of gifts. Rather than offering an imagined possibility for such a transformation that is grounded in our abstract rationalities, we prefer to focus on the living practices of those who are already engaged in such transformatory activities, in order to amplify their influences. We now turn to this amplification of the living practices that we see as moving towards such cultural transformations with gifts and talents in education.

CHAPTER 3

GIFTEDNESS AS A LIVING CONCEPT: WHAT IS A LIVING THEORY APPROACH TO ACTION RESEARCH AND HOW CAN IT CONTRIBUTE TO GIFT CREATION THROUGH STUDENT-LED ENQUIRY?

'Tread Softly, because You Tread on My Dreams' (Yeats, 1974) Principles of Reflective and Therapeutic Writing by Gillie Bolton

Once upon a time a young seeker after the truth set off to find the wisest person in the world. Travelling over mountains and valleys, oceans and deep forests, deserts and swamps, our adventurer eventually arrived at a high, lonely place. Here the wise one dwelt, but the dream of receiving wisdom seemed as distant as ever, as there was no suggestion of a tutorial. The only set activity was daily meditation, which lasted an unspecified time: three minutes, three hours, on one memorable occasion three days, the end being signalled by a bell. One day in furious frustration our student got up, grasped the beater, and rang the bell – hard – and then stood in fear and trembling at such audacity. The wise one got up slowly and creakily bowed, speaking for the first time: "Thank you. You have learned the first lesson: to take responsibility. We must all ring our own bells, and never give others the authority to ring them for us. Now your education can begin."

As a child I never grew out of asking *why?*, and just as often, *why not?* At boarding school from the age of nine, my days were fully organised,

Gifts, Talents and Education By Barry Hymer, Jack Whitehead and Marie Huxtable
© 2008 Wiley-Blackwell

apart from two hours on Saturday afternoons. I had no freedom of thought or enquiry, and no responsibility for my own actions or thinking. Little wonder I was the only girl in the entire school who never became a prefect of any sort. So when I left that stifling environment and entered the big world, I discovered I knew few life or study skills. But I still knew how to ask *why, when, where, with whom, what,* and *how?*

It was the time of the Vietnam war, and I discovered CND before I left school, later joining a group of questioning Quakers (Society of Friends) in Cambridge – what joy to find I was not a solitary freak after all in my pursuit of freedom and responsibility. At first I thought I could help change the world through primary school education. Later I found that a way of helping people to find their own bells, and ring them, was through expressive and explorative writing. For the last twenty years my practice and research has all involved writing.

In order to gain the most from writing (or any other art), I learned that we knowingly and willingly suspend our disbelief for the moment in whatever the writing presents us with, as Coleridge suggested. In this way art can bring us into different consciousness about ourselves and our place in the world. The sculptor Juan Munoz said, "You have to make [the viewer] trust for a second that what he wishes to believe is true. And maybe you can spin that into another reality and make him wonder."

This reality spinning often involves imaginatively entering the consciousness of others, to wonder what their experience might be like. Terry Eagleton has commented on its empathetic and ethical role in our lives: "There would seem to be a need for some special intuitive faculty which allows me to range beyond my own sense-data, transport myself into your emotional innards and empathise with what you are feeling. This is known as the imagination. It makes up for our natural state of isolation from one another. The moral and the aesthetic lie close together, since to be moral is to be able to feel what others are feeling." (2008, p. 19)

The activities of the culturally refined Nazis have, of course, forever disabused us of any notion that the aesthetic necessarily makes us act morally.

The imaginative faculty, which enables writers to enquire both into their own experience more deeply and into the possible experience of others, is both wise and fundamentally trustworthy. Insight and support are gained by writing if the self is respected, the processes of writing trusted, and reliable confidential readers carefully chosen.

Writing works when enquirers take full responsibility for all their actions, including writing and the sharing of it. It is essentially playful and straightforward: the greatest wisdom or inspiration is the simplest.

Writing can enable people to find out more about themselves and the way they relate to their home and work lives, significant others, and their wider society and culture. It offers relatively safe and confidential ways to express areas of experience otherwise difficult to communicate. Writing can offer this because in its initial expressive and explorative stages it is private, and is both physical and creative, as is art, music, and dance. This power is harnessed in professionally developmental reflective practice writing, and personally developing therapeutic writing.

This kind of writing can enable people to: a) explore narratives of experience from different perspectives, b) reflexively tease out and understand their own values, principles, ethics, feelings and professional identity, c) critically examine the metaphors they and their cultures use, d) harness the power of metaphor to express the otherwise inexpressible, e) observe acutely and imaginatively using all their senses.

The values underlying these explorations are: trust in the processes of writing, self-respect, responsibility, generosity, and positive regard. They are built upon my own experience of journal and poetry writing (I only recommend writing exercises I have done myself), my life-principles as a Quaker, and my reading (e.g. Sartre, Jung, Lao Tsu, Adrienne Rich, Sophocles, Plato (Socrates), Marion Milner, Winnicott, Paul Klee, Lewis Carroll, A.A. Milne, Coleridge and Wordsworth). These foundations can seem paradoxical; their power lies therein.

1. Trust in the processes of writing. Explorative and expressive writing can be trusted to lead to personal insight because its processes tap into the strong wise creative side of ourselves. We will always write the right thing. Although possibly initially unclear or lacking in understanding, we are the world's best authorities on our own experience and so cannot write wrongly about it. This writing takes free-rein: it is in letting go that we find our direction.
2. Self respect. Writing can give us confidence we have something vital to communicate, and can say it well. This is enhanced by knowing it is only for us to read, at least initially: there is no teacher-reader with a red pen. We therefore communicate respectfully with ourselves, tackling inevitable fears, hesitations, and the voice of destructive inner critics, in the process. With the certainty gained

from learning to respect ourselves, we can be creatively uncertain where we are going.

3. Responsibility. We are fully responsible for everything we write and our response to it, even when guided by a facilitator. We have full authority over our writing at every stage, including rereading to ourselves and possibly sharing with a confidential trusted reader. Writing fiction can offer significant insight (e.g. Munno 2006); in this, the writer is fully aware she is exploring how the situation might have been, or might have been perceived: in consciously writing fiction authors can gain clarity into what might actually have happened. It is in taking full responsibility for our actions that we gain freedom to explore and experiment playfully, and therefore with inspirational creativity.

4. Generosity. We willingly give ourselves time to write with energy and commitment, in a focused spirit of enquiry. This giving enables us to take inspiration from our own enhanced self-understanding.

5. Positive regard. We write about family and friends as well as colleagues and students, clients, patients, or members of the public. Any feeling can be explored within the privacy of writing, both for cathartic release, and in order to understand and discover appropriate ways to act in the future. Expressing and exploring negative memories can facilitate positive experience; celebrating positive ones can be life-enhancing.

"I, being poor, have only my dreams; / I have spread my dreams under your feet." (Yeats, 1974) Our sleeping dreams, and waking ones expressed in writing, are our riches. To find them spread openly under our feet, we only need basic literacy, pen, and paper. The above five principles enable reflective and therapeutic writing to work for us, and can help us ring our own life bells. Personal values are considered and reassessed in the process. Trust, self-respect, responsibility, generosity, and positive regard are sound foundations for individuals in society and for professional identity and practice.

We have explored in previous chapters the tensions we experience with the dominant approaches to gifted and talented education in the West, and have begun to explore different ways of understanding 'gifts and talents' educationally. The school curriculum embodies our society's beliefs about educational knowledge, the received wisdoms of our generation and cultural expectations. But an educator's role involves more than the transmission of the school curriculum. As educators, we want to enable our students to develop skills, understandings and an appreciative recognition of themselves and others which will enable them to contribute to their own well-being and that of our community. We want to help them learn to know themselves as the persons they want to be, confident and competent to develop their talents and offer them as valued, valuable gifts which will contribute to their living satisfying and productive lives.

A living educational theory is a story we create for ourselves and share with other people to account for our contribution to the creation of a more peaceful, just and productive world. We can each create our own descriptions and explanations for our own educational development as we answer questions of the kind, 'How do I live my values more fully in my practice?' By sharing such explanations, we can improve our own learning, contribute to that of other people, school and communities, and a world which supports the values of freedom, truth, beauty, goodness, integrity, justice and democracy. The sophistication with which it is approached may differ with age and experience; the particular frame and language used may be particular to the context, but underneath, there is a universality to it which makes it of particular relevance to educators.

We think of a living educational theory as a life story and as Winslade (2007) says, 'Stories should not be dismissed as either neutral mirrors or biased perspectives. Narratives play a part in producing a reality. Stories affect people's lives. They are not just reports of life' (p. 53).

In creating a living theory account, we are not just writing a history of what we have done; the phase in the research of creating a narrative which communicates is part of the research process: '... as we conduct our research and generate our own living educational theories. These theories are living in the sense that they are our theories of practice, generated from within our living practices, our present best thinking that incorporates yesterday into today, and which holds tomorrow already within itself' (Whitehead & McNiff, 2006, p. 3).

You may ask 'Why as an educator in a busy classroom should I bother with research and educational theory – mine or anyone else's?' We believe that the job of an educator is a professional one, and one of the distinguishing features of a profession is a body of theory which can help to justify and improve its practices. Educational theory and research has profound implications for the future of humanity because it is based on values which are communicated, through our practice, to our students. An individual's living educational theory is not simply an abstract and conceptual form of theory; it is a living theory embodied in practice. To research and to understand the embodied educational theories of the teaching profession is particularly important because they contain the values and understandings which constitute educative relationships with children and young people who are our future society.

We do not want you to feel that we are imposing our ideas on you, but rather we wish to invite you to share further in our thinking and to consider what relevance it may have for you as you see yourself, the world you want to be part of and how you wish to contribute to its improvement through your practice. We are asking you to engage with us in a trusting, creative relationship in which you will allow us to offer stories of our development as an invitation to you to open a space for enquiry about your ways of interpreting the world and of interpreting your actions and our own. In telling our stories, we want to appeal to your curiosity, originality and concern for integrity and vocational commitment. So, we will begin by introducing Living Theory through the story of its creation by Jack. A more detailed explanation can be found in *The Growth of Educational Knowledge: Creating Your Own Living Educational Theories* (Whitehead, 1993) and *Action Research Living Theory* (Whitehead & McNiff, 2006) and on visiting http://www.actionresearch.net/.

The story begins:

The time was the end of the 1960s in a period of educational, economic and artistic ferment. The place was inner-city London in a neighbourhood dominated by the activities of notorious gangsters such as the Kray and Richardson gangs. Jack had taken up his first teaching post in a comprehensive school in Tower Hamlets, fresh from an initial teacher education programme in the Department of Education of the University of Newcastle.

During this year, Jack had been inspired by his readings of the work of Erich Fromm on *Man for Himself* (1947) and *The Fear of Freedom* (1960). Fromm's writings helped Jack to articulate his own belief in the value of personal responsibility, in the recognition that if a person can face the truth without panic, then there is no purpose to life other than that individuals create for themselves through their own loving relationships and productive work. Jack still recalls the pleasure of being moved by Fromm's ontological insight that individuals are faced with a choice of uniting with the world in the spontaneity of love and productive work or of seeking a kind of security which destroys integrity and freedom.

His imagination and emotions had been captivated by Richard Peters' *Ethics and Education* (1966) with the idea that what was implied for a person seriously asking 'What ought I to do?' implied a commitment to live as fully as possible values of fairness, respect, worthwhile activities, freedom and consideration of interest with a commitment to procedural principles of democracy.

The ideas of John Dewey on *Democracy and Education* (1916) and on *Logic, the Theory of Inquiry* (1938) were particularly influential in developing the idea of a scientific form of living. In a scientific form of living, individuals learnt from their experience as they imagined possibilities for improving what they were doing; they acted and eliminated errors from their actions through their reflections and evaluations; they shared their learning with others.

The passion for learning and knowledge creation did not leave Jack as he took his first steps into the world of employment as a teacher. The desire to contribute to the creation of a new living form of educational theory first came to Jack as the resolution of a conflict he experienced in holding together his thinking about his teaching in an inner London comprehensive school during the day and his thinking about educational theory in the evening as a student at the Institute of Education of the University of London on the Academic Diploma and then the MA programme between 1968 and 1972.

The educational relationships during the day with the pupils were certainly distinguished by the expression of much life-affirming energy from both Jack and his pupils as he sought to communicate his passion to support them to develop their scientific understandings. He expended much effort in establishing forms of order conducive for developing scientific understandings in a large, lively, inner-city classroom filled with teenagers with other things than science on their minds.

Jack recognised that some of the difficulties in establishing this order were due to the differences in background between himself and his pupils. His own life had been largely influenced by the traditions of post-war, white, middle-class privilege in his progression through grammar school, university and into teaching, while some of his 14-year-old pupils were involved in prostitution or coping with racial violence and incidents of grievous bodily harm. The difference in the realities of his life and that of his pupils was graphically illustrated in an incident when he found himself pinned against a wall of the school by a gang leader called Big Kamara, together with his gang, after returning from the gentle, rational world of a philosophy seminar in the university one evening. This recognition fuelled his passion to help to develop scientific forms of living informed by values of love, care, fairness and respect.

In his evening studies at the Institute of Education, Jack would focus with the help of his tutors on developing his understanding of educational theory. In the late 1960s and 1970s, the dominant view of educational theory was that it was constituted by a 'disciplines' approach – the philosophy, psychology, sociology and history of education. The disconnection between the theories he was being taught and the reality of his experience of learning to improve his practice in school became increasingly obvious. It took Jack some 4 years to recognise the limitations in the traditional approach as he increasingly began to understand that his own interests in educational theory were focused on explanations of his educational influences in his own learning and in the learning of his students that could help to enhance these educational influences. Understandably, his tutors in the University were fascinated by developing and testing the theories in their discipline of education. Jack, however, was interested in the development of educational theories that could explain educational influences in learning from the ground of a discipline of educational enquiry in such questions as 'How do I improve what I am doing in my educational relationships with my pupils?'

It was during his time teaching in school that Jack understood what it was to experience himself as a living contradiction, and he recognised the power of video to help in self-studies of one's own practice.

In his studies of research methods in education during his time at the Institute of Education between 1968 and 1972, Jack began to see that no research methodology from any of the existing disciplines of education was appropriate for enquiring into the implications of asking, researching and answering the practical question 'How do I improve what I am doing?' in the context of educational relationships with pupils. This frustration with existing forms of educational theory and research methodologies in education led him in 1973 to become a lecturer in education at the University of Bath. His sense of vocation changed from being a science teacher to being an educational researcher with a focus on contributing to the generation of educational theories that could explain the educational influences of educators in their own learning and in the learning of their pupils. In 1980, he was arguing that a form of in-service education based on a teacher's practice should be the knowledge base of educational theory.

During 1975–1976, while coordinating and evaluating the Schools Council Local Curriculum Development Project on improving learning for 11- to 14-year-olds in mixed-ability groups, Jack began to understand the significance of action research cycles in enquiries of the kind 'How do I improve my practice?' This understanding developed with a group of six teachers he worked with for over 12 months. The responses of the teachers to his accounts of the project helped him to understand that the way they worked together to improve their learning and the learning of the pupils could be understood as action reflection cycles which involved

(a) Expressing concerns when our values were not lived as fully as we believed it possible to live them.
(b) Imagining possible ways forward and choosing one idea as an action plan to act on.
(c) Acting and gathering data on which to make a judgement about our effectiveness in living our values more fully and in developing our understandings.
(d) Evaluating our effectiveness.

(e) Modifying our concerns, ideas and actions in the light of our evaluations.

(f) Producing an explanation of our learning whose validity had been submitted to democratic evaluation by our peers.

As he videotaped himself working on the development of enquiry learning with a group of pupils in a secondary school in Bath, Jack came to appreciate the significance of including 'I' as a living contradiction in explanations of educational influence in learning. It was the desire to overcome the tension of feeling that he wasn't living his values as fully as he could do with his pupils that moved him to seek to improve his practice.

So, in a living theory approach to action research, individual practitioners produce validated explanations of their educational influences in their own learning and in the learning of others as they ask, research and answer questions of the kind 'How do I improve what I am doing?' Here is the action planning process that Jack uses with his masters students.

ACTION PLANNING IN CREATING YOUR LIVING EDUCATIONAL THEORY: EXPLORING THE IMPLICATIONS OF ASKING, RESEARCHING AND ANSWERING 'HOW DO I IMPROVE WHAT I AM DOING?'

Your living educational theory is your explanation for your educational influences in your own learning, in the learning of others and in the learning of the social formations in which you are living and working. You can see a more detailed description in the 1989a paper on living educational theories in the *Cambridge Journal of Education* at http://www.actionresearch.net/writings/livtheory.html.

In the creation of living educational theories in enquiries of the kind 'How do I improve what I am doing?' many researchers have found it useful to start their enquiries with the help of action reflection cycles in an action planner that contains written responses to such questions as

(1) What do I want to improve?
(2) Why do I feel that something could be improved in what I am doing? (This is concerned with what really matters to me in terms of the values that give meaning and purpose in my life. These are the explanatory principles that explain why I do what I do.)
(3) What could I do that might improve what I am doing? (Imagining possibilities and choosing one of them to act on in an action plan.)

(4) As I am acting, what data will I collect to enable me to judge my educational influence in my professional context as I answer my question?

(5) As I evaluate the educational influences of my actions in my own learning and the learning of others, who might be willing to help me to strengthen the validity of my explanation of my learning about my influence? Who might provide me with responses to questions such as

   (i) Is my explanation as comprehensible as it could be?

   (ii) Could I improve the evidential basis of my claims to know what I am doing?

   (iii) Does my explanation include an awareness of historical and cultural influences in what I am doing and draw on the most advanced social theories of the day?

   (iv) Am I showing that I am committed to the values that I claim to be living by?

(6) In the light of the evaluation, it is often the case that the concerns, action plans and actions are modified and the process of improvement and educational knowledge creation continues.

In his tutoring, Jack usually begins with conversations between pairs of practitioner-researchers in which they take some 4 minutes each to outline their context, what really matters to them and what they would like to improve. He encourages individuals to hold themselves and others to account for sustaining enquiries into living their values and developing their understandings as fully as they can in improving their practice.

There are many different approaches to the creation of living educational theories using action reflection cycles. One that Jack particularly likes because of its attractive visual presentation includes the Thinking Actively in a Social Context (TASC) wheel generated by Belle Wallace. It has been used by Joy Mounter in her research with her 6-year-old pupils in exploring the question 'Can children carry out action research about learning, creating their own learning theory?' You can access this account at http://www.jackwhitehead. com/tuesdayma/joymounterull.htm. We think you will be particularly inspired by the three video clips in Appendix 2 that show three pupils explaining to Joy how they think the TASC wheel should be modified to give a more appropriate representation of their learning (Figure 3.1).

You can access the WebQuest Library at http://www.webquestuk.org.uk/ webquestuk_library.htm and see how the TASC approach has been used in the teaching of thinking skills across the curriculum (Wallace, 2001).

Having introduced a living theory approach to action research, we now want to show how it can contribute to gift creation through student-led enquiry. Jack's sense of giftedness as a living concept had its genesis in a meeting with Barry. Barry's focus on gift creation influenced Jack's recognition that

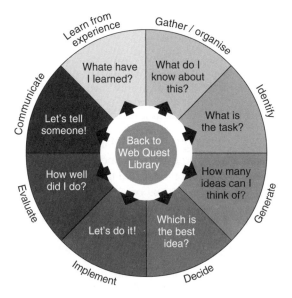

Figure 3.1   TASC wheel (Wallace 2000).

what he had been doing in making public the living theories of practitioner-researchers through his web site http://www.actionresearch.net was to freely offer these living theories as gifts for others that might influence their lives for good.

We want to be clear about our shared meaning of gifts in gifted and talented education. By a gift, we are meaning something that is produced with one's developing talents and that is freely given. This meaning differs markedly from the following, where the 'we' in the DCSF statement below refers to statements on the UK government's standards site. We experience the definitions provided below as an attempt to colonise the meaning of 'gifted' and impose it on those of us who live in England and are working with a different understanding of gifts and talents:

DCSF – What do we mean by gifted and talented?

Gifted and talented children are those who have one or more abilities developed to a level significantly ahead of their year group (or with the potential to develop these abilities).

IN England the term "gifted" refers to those pupils who are capable of excelling in academic subjects such as English or History. "Talented" refers to those pupils who may excel in areas requiring visuo-spatial skills or practical abilities, such as in games and PE, drama, or art.

Some gifted and talented pupils may be intellectually able but also appear on the Special Educational Needs (SEN) register for behavioural, literacy or physical difficulties.

Provision for gifted and talented pupils can act to counteract disadvantage. Direct intervention is particularly critical for pupils from disadvantaged backgrounds to enable them to make full use of their abilities and to raise their aspirations accordingly. (DfES, 2007, Standards Site http://www.standards. dfes.gov.uk/giftedandtalented/identification/gandt/)

A living theory approach to gifted and talented education unmasks such colonising tendencies by asking questions about whose interests the concept serves and includes the value of individual intellectual respect as a contributor to the creation of generative-transformational giftedness:

I articulate in narrative form the meanings of my embodied ontological values through their emergence in my practice – specifically in my practice of philosophy with children, in creating webs of meaning through dilemma-based learning, and in seeking to unmask (Foucault, in Rabinow, 1984) the concept of giftedness – by asking whose interests the concept serves. In the process of living, clarifying and communicating the meanings of these practices are formed, I argue, living epistemological standards of judgement for a new, relationally dynamic epistemology of educational enquiry. I record also how through my professional activity, my reflections on and revisions of this activity, and the process of creating this account, I have moved in the direction of creating and living my core personal and educational values and realising the critical standards of judgment which are both consisting in and attendant on these values. These include the value of individual intellectual respect as a contributor to the creation of generative-transformational giftedness – i.e. giftedness which is co-constructed (not identified) in a social, relationally respectful, activity-oriented, dialectical, tool-and-result (Vygotsky, 1978) manner and context. (Hymer, 2007a, D.Ed.Psy. Abstract)

Barry has produced his doctoral thesis using his talents for original enquiry and critical judgement while engaging with the ideas of others. His talents include the expression of the values that give meaning and purpose to his life – that is, his ontological values. Within the narrative form of his thesis, he has clarified the meanings of these values and formed them into the standards of judgement to which he holds himself accountable and which are offered as standards of judgement to evaluate the validity of his contributions to educational knowledge.

As a research student, Barry produced his thesis from his student-led enquiry. It is student-led in the sense that the enquiry has made public the unique constellation of values and understanding that constituted his embodied professional knowledge. That is the knowledge that he expresses in his practice as an educator.

Drawing evidence from other student-led enquiries from lifelong learning, we want to show how a living theory approach to action research, in relation to gift creation, could transform the knowledge base of education and enhance the flow of values and understandings that carry hope for the future of humanity. What we have in mind are the gifts created through the talents of action researchers in developing and expressing their living educational theories and offered freely to others.

It might be helpful at this point if we say that in our understandings of what counts as educational, we need to develop a values-based language of education and educational influence in learning that is related to but distinct from 'learning and teaching'. We agree with Biesta's (2006) understandings of the need to go beyond a language of learning into a language of education. The idea of learning does not appear to us to carry the values that distinguish learning as educational. For example, many people learn to express themselves in ways that damage others. Human beings have a history of killing each other on grounds of ethnic difference. They learn to do such things through socio-cultural influences. We do not believe that such learning is educational. We distinguish this learning from that which carries a sense of educational responsibility for enhancing the flows of energy, values and understandings that in turn carry hope for the future of humanity.

We agree with Biesta that we come into the world as unique individuals through the ways in which we respond responsibly to what and who is 'other'. He argues persuasively '. . . that the responsibility of the educator extends to asking questions that summon us to respond responsively and responsibly to otherness and difference in our own, unique ways' (Biesta, 2006, p. ix).

Instead of seeing learning as an attempt to acquire, to master, to control, to internalise or any other possessive metaphors we can think of, Biesta (2006) says that we might instead see learning as a reaction to a disturbance, as an attempt to recognise and reintegrate as a result of disintegration. He says that we might look at learning as a response to what is other and different, to what challenges, irritates or even disturbs us, rather than as the acquisition of something we want to possess. We agree with him that both ways of looking at learning – learning as acquisition and learning as responding – might be equally valid, depending, that is, on the situation in which we raise questions about the definition of learning. However, we also agree that the '. . . second conception of learning is educationally the more significant, if it is conceded that education is not just about the transmission of knowledge, skills and values, but is concerned with the individuality, subjectivity, or personhood of the student, with their "coming into the world" as unique, singular beings' (p. 27).

Student-led educational enquiries are distinguished by their coming into the world as unique singular beings, and they include transforming engagements with a 'given curriculum' into the students' living curricula.

These distinguishing qualities of an educational enquiry can be seen in Joy Mounter's (2007a) work with her pupils as she asks and enquires with her 6-year-old pupils 'Can children carry out action research about learning, creating their own learning theory?' When we say that 'These distinguishing qualities of an educational enquiry can be seen in Joy Mounter's work with her pupils', we mean this literally in the sense that we think you will need to see Joy at work with her pupils in their educational relationships. If you access the video clips in Appendix 2 of Joy's account with her pupils from http://www.jackwhitehead.com/tuesdayma/joymounterull.htm, we think it will repay your effort because of the non-verbal meanings of a flow of life-affirming energy being communicated through the visual medium of the video in the space of creative conversation generated by Joy and her pupils. There is a given curriculum in schools that carries the government's disciplinary power of national assessment. In the creation of their living educational theories, individuals can develop their living curricula in their creative and engaged responses to the given curriculum in generating their own living theories.

We think that you will see the embodied expression of a similar flow of life-affirming energy with the value of educational responsibility in Claire Formby's (2007) educational enquiry 'How do I sustain a loving, receptively responsive educational relationship with my pupils which will motivate them in their learning and encourage me in my teaching?' You can access this visual narrative with the video clips at http://www.jackwhitehead.com/tuesdayma/formbyEE300907.htm.

In their flow through web space, these accounts are freely given as gifts by Joy and Claire for sharing by other practitioner-researchers who are seeking to enhance their educational influences with their pupils and students. These gifts embody what we are meaning by a living concept of giftedness. What we particularly value about the accounts is that Joy and Claire are willing freely to share the values and understandings that give meaning and purpose to their lives and to show that they hold themselves to account in relation to their educational influences with their pupils. Perhaps more importantly, they show how they are influenced by the gifts of their pupils as their pupils share their own accounts of their learning. Writing about a new era in educative relations, Jack emphasises the importance of hearing student values and voices in the responses of educators to their students:

> What I am suggesting is that asking, answering and researching such questions can lead to living forms of curriculum theorising through which learners can create their own curriculum vitae in dialogue with others. In creating their own curriculum vitae, they can answer for themselves questions of the kind, "How do I live a good and productive life?" Such curriculum studies involve the self-creation of the learner in asking, answering and researching good questions in their own disciplined, educational enquiries. Researching such

questions does require the courage of an educator and educational researcher in being accountable to those they teach, as well as to the wider community, for the values they choose to live by and the educational knowledge they produce. It will be of no small interest to this educator to see if amongst the contributions to Curriculum Studies, the voices and values of professional educators and their students can be heard. (Whitehead, 1999, p. 87)

Drawing again on Biesta to emphasise the importance of offering the gifts of our living theories to others, we want to highlight the importance of our educational responsibility for coming into the world with other unique and singular beings. Claire Formby (2007) and Joy Mounter (2007b) have shown their expression of this educational responsibility in their educational relationships with their pupils. We are suggesting that we reinforce Biesta's advocacy of the need to develop a language of education that embraces this educational responsibility:

> . . . I have presented a different way to understand and approach education, one that isn't based on a truth about the human being, one that doesn't claim to know what the humanity of the human being consists of, and one that doesn't think of education as the production of particular identities or subjectivities or the insertion of newcomers into an existing social order. Instead I have argued for an approach that focuses on the multifarious ways in which human beings as unique, singular individuals come into the world. I have argued that we come into the world as unique, singular beings through the ways in which we take up our responsibility for the otherness of the others, because it is in those situations that we speak with our own "voice" and not with the representative voice of the rational community. I have shown that the world in which we come into presence is a world of plurality and difference, because we can only come into the world if others, who are not like us, take up our beginnings in such a way that they can bring their beginnings into the world as well. I have therefore argued that the educational responsibility is not only a responsibility for the coming into the world of unique and singular beings; it is also a responsibility for the world as a world of plurality and difference. The creation of such a world, the creation of a worldly space, is not something that can be done in a straightforward manner. It rather entails a "double duty" for the creation of worldly spaces and for their undoing. Along these lines I have tried to articulate a way to understand education that itself responds to the challenges we are faced with today, including the disappearance of a language of education in the age of learning. (Biesta, 2006, pp. 117, 118)

One of Jack's desires is to look back on a productive life in which he has contributed to the educational knowledge of a language of education that carries hope for the future of humanity. At the age of 63, Jack is now looking back, as well as forward, from some 40 years of professional and vocational commitment to education. He derives great satisfaction from seeing the research programmes of doctoral researchers he has worked with, offered freely as gifts in the living theory doctorates flowing through web space from http://www.actionresearch.net and other web sites. In developing the theme of giftedness as a living concept, we are asking you to think about differences between concepts as abstractions of the kind that constitute traditional propositional theories and concepts as embodied living meanings through which you constitute who you are, together with your understandings of the world and your contributions to it. In the history of dialectics, there is a transformation in thinking of ascending from the abstract to the concrete. Marx emphasised the importance of this in his critique of Hegel's dialectic while stressing the idea that philosophers interpret the world while the point is to change it. In our text, we are stressing the importance of ascending from the abstract to the concrete in expressing living concepts of giftedness in improving the world.

In answering the questions 'What is a living theory approach to action research?' and 'How can it contribute to gift creation through student-led enquiry?' we are now going to focus on enquiries that have taken over 5 years of sustained commitment that have evolved into successfully completed doctoral theses.

In developing their talents in the course of their doctoral research programmes, the following practitioner-researchers have offered their living theories as gifts that they hope you will find helpful in enhancing your loving and productive life. The theses legitimated at the Universities of Limerick and Bath were completed with the supervision of Jean McNiff or Jack Whitehead, and the theses legitimated by the Universities of Worcester, Coventry, Plymouth, Newcastle, West of England and Kingston had other supervisors.

The extracts from the narratives below are all taken from the abstracts used by the narrators to tell their own story in their doctoral research programmes. One of the reasons the abstracts are so important is that they distil the essence of the evolution of the individual's talents as they offer their theses as gifts to others in their flow through web space. They show the living meanings of the giftedness of the givers.

The following five living theories represent a remarkable accomplishment in the University of Limerick. Margaret Cahill, Mairin Glenn, Mary Roche and Bernie Sullivan have shown courage and persistence of a high order in first completing their masters degrees and then completing their doctorates with enquiries into living their values as fully as they can in their professional practices with the support of Professor Jean McNiff. If you access the supporting web page for this book at http://www.actionresearch.net, you will be able to access any of the contents for any of the doctorates with the URLs included below. One of the ways of acknowledging the accomplishment would be to recognise the scholarly and intellectual capital these theses bring into the University. They certainly establish the University's reputation as a creative space for generating and legitimating the new epistemology for the new scholarship of teaching. Another way of recognising the accomplishment would be to go beyond a language of economic rationality, valuable though that might be, in seeing the theses in their flow through web space as showing the living meanings of the giftedness of the givers.

We attach great significance to the titles, the questions and the abstracts below. The titles and questions are often the last meaning to emerge from the writings as the writer becomes increasingly aware of what they have accomplished and the question(s) they have answered. In the evolution of one doctoral narrative, the abstract went through 16 iterations before the final version at the front of the thesis. By the time the abstract is produced, practitioner-researchers are clear about the meanings of the ontological values that give meaning and purpose to their lives and that are formed into the standards of judgement to which they hold themselves accountable. We do hope that you will give yourself the time to appreciate the significance of the following stories and that the values communicate a life-affirming energy with values and understanding that resonate with your own.

Margaret Cahill (2007) My Living Educational Theory of Inclusional Practice. http://www.jeanmcniff.com/margaretcahill/index.html

This thesis is the articulation of my living educational theory of inclusional practice, which evolved through undertaking research in the area of educational provision for marginalised children. It is a narrative account in which I offer descriptions of and explanations for my practice, as I transform my educational contexts into a celebration of democratically-constituted inclusional practices.

The thesis demonstrates how my embodied values of justice, inclusion and equality compelled me to develop social and educational practices that included potentially marginalised children. My living educational theory of inclusional practice therefore contains within itself a living theory of social justice premised on the idea that all are equal participants in democratic public discourses. I explain how I have transformed these values into the living critical standards of judgement by which I wish my work to be evaluated.

My original contributions to knowledge are to do with how I demonstrate the development of inclusional practices that are grounded in the realisation of my values that honour the individual and enable them to become agents in the creation of an inclusive society. From the grounds of my evidence base, I claim to have developed an inclusional practice that has profound implications of the education of the teaching profession and other social formations.

Mairin M. Glenn (2006) Working with Collaborative Projects: My Living Theory of a Holistic Educational Practice. http://www. jeanmcniff.com/glennabstract.html

This thesis is the narrative account of my research programme that has enabled me to make my original claim to have developed a living epistemology of practice that is grounded in dialogical, holistic and creative ways of knowing. From my belief that each individual is capable of developing their potential for learning and knowledge creation, I have come to see the interconnectedness of people and their environments as a locus of learning which may be embraced through technology.

Through my research I have developed my capacity for critical engagement, especially in relation to critiquing many normative practices in dominant forms of education; specifically in terms of their underpinning technical rational ontologies and epistemologies of fragmentation. My original contributions to knowledge are to do with how I show that I can account for how I have transformed my own erstwhile fragmented epistemologies into holistic and inclusional forms of knowing and practice. From the grounds of my research-based practice, I am able to make my original claim that I have developed my living theory of a holistic educational practice, through collaborative multimedia projects, and I ground my evidence in the multimedia narrative of my research account.

A distinctive feature of my research account is my articulation of how my ontological values of love and care have transformed into my living critical epistemological standards of judgement, as I produce my multimedia evidence-based living theory of a holistic educational practice. Through working with collaborative multimedia projects, I explain how I have developed an epistemology of practice that enables me to account for my educational influence in learning.

Mary Roche (2007) Towards a Living Theory of Caring Pedagogy: Interrogating My Practice to Nurture a Critical, Emancipatory and Just Community of Enquiry. http://www.jeanmcniff.com/ MaryRoche/index.html

In this narrative of my self-study action research into my practice I describe and explain my living theory of caring pedagogical practice as I claim to know my own educational development (Whitehead, 1989a) in relation to teaching children to realise their capacity to think critically, within a context of a new scholarship of educational practice (Boyer, 1990). I claim that as I researched dialogical pedagogies that would support my aims of encouraging children to be critical thinkers, I also reconceptualised my own identity as a critical thinker and began to challenge dominant orthodoxies that have traditionally determined who is seen as a knower in a primary classroom and who is seen as an educational researcher.

I articulate how my ontological values of care, freedom and justice in relation to others were transformed through their emergence into the living standards of judgment by which I evaluated the educational influence in learning of my developing dialogical practice.

I claim that I have generated a personal living educational theory about teaching children to be critical thinkers that is grounded in the idea of "being" rather than "having" (Fromm, 1979), and this stands as my original contribution to knowledge in my field. I explain how I experienced a dissonance between my values and my practice that led me to critique dominant didactic norms as located in an abstract concept of a generalised "Other", whereas my dialogical practice was located in the idea of relationships with real, concrete others (Benhabib, 1986). I explain the significance of my research, grounded in my multimedia evidence base, for my own educational development, for my institution, and for the wider educational research community, as I clarify the developmental processes of my capacity to theorise my practice.

Bernie Sullivan (2006) A Living Theory of a Practice of Social Justice: Realising the Right of Traveller Children to Educational Equality. http://www.jeanmcniff.com/bernieabstract.html

This thesis is an articulation of my living theory of social justice that evolved through undertaking research in the area of educational provision for Traveller children. It demonstrates how my embodied values of social justice and equality compelled me to engage in social and educational practices that refused to privilege some children at the expense of minority or marginalised groups. I explain how I transformed these values into the living critical standards of judgement by which I wish my work to be evaluated. Through using a self-study approach, within an action research methodology, I was able to reflect on my practice, with a view to learning how to improve it. This process contributed to an enhancement of my personal and professional development, and enabled me to theorise my practice as a form of emancipatory education. My emergent living theory of practice, therefore, incorporates a theory of social justice that reflects an ethos of equality of respect for all. It goes beyond traditional propositional theories of justice in that it has evolved from the lived reality of social practices in an educational institution. I explain how I arrived at an understanding that a practice of inclusion is more appropriate for a living theory of justice than one of assimilation, which often seeks to deny difference, or integration, which frequently attempts to eliminate difference. A practice of inclusion that is grounded in an intercultural ethos may take account of individual differences and transcend normative institutional hegemonic structures and discourses that are grounded in a logic of domination. Through developing my living theory of social justice as equality of respect for all, and as the recognition and acceptance of diversity, I became aware of the possibility that a process of inclusion could have a greater probability of success in achieving sustainable social evolution if it originated from the marginalised space. In this context, my research could have significance for other marginalised groups, as well as for the Traveller children in whose interests the research was undertaken.

Margaret Follows (2006) Looking for a Fairer Assessment of Children's Learning, Development and Attainment in the Infant Years: an Educational Action Research Case Study. http://www. jackwhitehead.com/followsphd/followsphd7livth.pdf

This thesis tells the story of an infant head teacher researcher's journey into the heart of a living educational assessment landscape. She embarks on this journey to search for a fairer assessment of young children's learning, development and attainment. It is a journey that forces her to question everything about the professional world in which she works and lives.

The story is intended to use and evoke the human senses within the context of a real infant school (for children aged 3–7 years) – seeing, touching, hearing, and listening. It provides the vehicle to experience and gain an insight into an evolutionary and exploratory journey of people working and learning together as they reflect on the creative, emotional, social, moral and sensual feelings of practice. In particular, it offers insights into the professional identity of the writer as she critically examines the impact of educational assessment on a school community and the people working in it. The research methodology is adapted from critical action research in which the researcher's educational values are the yardstick against which the tacit knowledge of action (practice) is evaluated. Professional stories of past practice are used to represent implicit theories that are collaboratively reflected upon as they are deconstructed and explored. The creative research process is uniquely represented by the visual metaphor of a multi-layered jigsaw puzzle that enables the researcher to uncover successive, significant layers of professional knowledge in the infant school that relate to the concept of a fairer assessment of children's learning, development and attainment. The educational assessment landscape or "sensescape" is traversed in order to make sense of the conceptual model of a fairer assessment of children's learning, development and attainment as a living educational theory. The research offers an original contribution to educational knowledge in that it clarifies meanings of the researcher's ontological value of a fairer assessment of children's learning, development and attainment and transforms that value into a living epistemological standard of critical judgement.

Swaroop Rawal (2006) The Role of Drama in Enhancing Life Skills in Children with Specific Learning Difficulties in a Mumbai School: My Reflective Account. Graduated from Coventry University in Collaboration with the University of Worcester. http://www.actionresearch.net/rawal.shtml

This thesis is a reflective account of an action research project set in a drama classroom. It is a multi-voiced patchwork text which is created and built imaginatively to re-present my students and my experience in the drama classroom. On one level it deals with the question "How can drama be used to enhance life skills in children with specific learning disabilities studying in a school in Mumbai?" On the second level it is related to the question "How can I improve my practice?" This research is concerned with a teacher's capacity to recognise and realise the opportunity of an alternate reality in teaching. The reality of loving and caring for the students. The reality of an empathetic, compassionate, just and democratic classroom. The foundation of this study was laid when I saw the children in need suffer due to insensitive teaching practices and uncooperative peers and family. I was concerned with the trauma faced by students in the prevalent educational setting in India. I believe that what I do in education should help make changes for the better in our society. Life skills enhancement, in my under-standing, was a way to alleviate the stress the children experienced seeing that life skill education promotes mental well-being in young people and behavioural preparedness. As a drama teacher I see drama as a tool for education. It is a natural vehicle for explorative and experiential learning. The aim of my thesis is to describe and reflect on the learning process and the context in which it occurs. I present the critical points with close analysis of the choices made by me as I taught my pupils using drama as a learning medium. Additionally, this study investigates the influences of action research on my practice and the impact of engaging in the stages of action research which provided me with a methodical structure for implementing and analyzing the teaching and the learning process. This defined structure guided me through systematic and conscious data collection, data analysis, and reflection. The data is composed of classroom observations and tran-scripts, a collection of the students and my work and interviews with their schoolteachers and parents. The main objective of this research was to enable a gain in positive behavioural intentions and improved psychosocial com-petence in children. This was accomplished through augmentation of cre-ativity, emotional understanding and development, improved self-esteem and a notion of the joy of autonomy to enable the students to deal effectively with the demands and challenges of everyday life.

Mike Bosher through the University of Bath and John Loftus through Kingston University demonstrated courage, persistence and resilience in completing their doctoral enquiries. While the idea of being a master educator and a doctor educator has yet to receive widespread recognition in the UK context, we believe that the profession of education would benefit from such formal recognition. Mike embraces the idea of being an educator within his doctoral enquiry in a secondary school and John brings his embodied knowledge as a professional educator and head teacher into the academy.

Mike Bosher (2001) How Can I as an Educator and Professional Development Manager Working with Teachers, Support and Enhance the Learning and Achievement of Pupils in a Whole School Improvement Process? http://www.actionresearch.net/bosher.shtml

This thesis is a personal journey through an educational world of continuing professional development. It is located at school level, and the fields of School Effectiveness and School Improvement act as a context within which this learning process is framed. I claim three aspects of originality in this thesis.

The first claim is the manner in which the thesis has engaged in a personal learning process using insights from the paradigm of Action Research, and the fields of School Effectiveness and School Improvement. These are combined and grounded in my day-to-day professional life as an educator and provide a means of showing how my learning is integrated into a school improvement process. It also shows how my living educational theory develops.

My second claim is that I develop my critical judgement and living theory as I evaluate a school's development. This is in terms of improving the teaching and learning experiences with its staff and pupils and as I engage with, and use the ideas from others.

I express my originality of mind and critical judgement in creating my own living educational theory as I show how the scholarships of discovery, integration, application and teaching, are included within my scholarship of educational enquiry.

John Loftus (1999) An Action Research Enquiry into the Marketing of an Established First School in Its Transition to Full Primary Status. http://www.actionresearch.net/loftus.shtml

This thesis is based on a five year research study, in which I have looked at my own practice as a headteacher in the marketing of a newly formed primary school, using action research methodology. The study was undertaken as I was aware that because of LMS formula funding, open enrolment, opting out, SATs, league tables, OFSTED inspections, schools had been forced into competition with each other and consequently had to market themselves. I, as headteacher, was aware that although I would have to both operate under and implement the above reforms in our school, I was of the opinion that the above reforms could indeed damage education. Therefore, I looked for a mechanism whereby I could reduce the damage which the reforms may cause. This thesis describes how I worked within these reforms, utilising them so as to give enhanced learning opportunities for the pupils in our school. The research required long-term observation and reflection and also extensive literature reviews of marketing strategies (both industrial and educational) and primary headship. A distinctive feature of the research is the account of the author's exploration of his educational values within the context of external pressure to initiate the process of marketing the case study school. As a result of my enquiry, I am able to make the following claims about my practice:

Claim Number One. This thesis contributes to the professional knowledge-base of education in a description and explanation of how a headteacher in a newly formed primary school has asked, researched and answered questions of the form "How can I improve my own leadership and management?"

Claim Number Two. This thesis makes an original contribution to knowledge in an analysis of the extent to which industrial marketing strategies were effective in the educational context of marketing a primary school.

Claim Number Three. This thesis is an original study of a headteacher in a primary school striving to live his values in his practice so as to maintain his integrity in the light of incessant changing education reforms.

The gifts of the following four living theories of Eleanor Lohr, Madeline Church, Marian Naidoo from the University of Bath and of Robyn Pound from the University of the West of England make original contributions to educational knowledge from outside the teacher profession itself.

Eleanor breaks new ground through bringing love at work from being a director of social housing, as a living standard of judgement into the academy.

Madeline works as a network coordinator, action researcher, activist and evaluator in national and international contexts. Addressing the experience of being bullied, Madeline shows how her approach to her work is rooted in the values of compassion, love and fairness, and is inspired by art.

Marian researches her work in improving relationships and communications in a multi-professional and multi-agency healthcare setting in order to improve both the quality of care provided and the well-being of the system. Marian brings a passion for compassion as a living standard of judgement into the academy.

Robyn researches her work as a health visitor and shows how her embodied value of alongsideness is expressed in her relationships and formed into a living standard of judgement for explaining her professional influence.

Eleanor Lohr (2004) Love at Work: What Is My Lived Experience of Love, and How May I Become an Instrument of Love's Purpose? http://www.actionresearch.net/lohr.shtml

This is a first person action research account in which I immerse myself in my embodied experience of love. My aim is to learn through love how my practice, as a Director in social housing, and as a teacher of yoga, might be improved by giving primacy to a value laden theorising of my lived experience.

I combine journalling and spiritual practice to bring an intimate and non-verbal experience of love into professional practice. I bring this inner felt experience into language taking a phenomenological and hermeneutical approach. I immerse myself in the relation between physical, emotional and spiritual knowledge. I analyse the movement of knowledge between the personal and the social in the language of inclusionality (Rayner, 2004), and show how social relations mediate my inner non-verbal experience.

I situate my method within the action research paradigm and my philosophy within a holistic and subjectivist frame. As I write I realise my knowledge in the relation between thinking and the act of writing. My knowledge and its production are deliberately value-laden. I cultivate reasoned emotion in order to influence my thought process. My claim to originality of mind emerges from this subjective experience as I show how I bring my ontological values of love into practice through a "pedagogy of presence" that is integral to my action.

I judge the worth of my action and its loving dimension in silent reflective spiritual practice. I also judge the worth of my action and its loving dimension in the feedback I get from others. I set criteria that focus on seeking harmony and wholeness, and which do not ignore challenge and difference. I argue that the creative dynamism arising from difference is an important component of love at work.

I provide evidence for my claim in an account of current practice, through pictures, drawings and a video clip, and it is further evidenced by the coherence of my writing and the rigorous application of my own criteria against which I judge the worth of my actions. My claim to truth can also be substantiated by my application of method, and by situating my inquiry firmly within a post-modern narrative.

Madeline Church (2004) Creating an Uncompromised Place to Belong: Why Do I Find Myself in Networks? http://www.actionresearch.net/church.shtml

My inquiry sits within the reflective paradigm. I start from an understanding that knowing myself better will enhance my capacity for good action in the world. Through questioning myself and writing myself on to the page, I trace how I resist community formations, while simultaneously wanting to be in community with others. This paradox has its roots in my multiple experiences of being bullied, and finds transformation in my stubborn refusal to retreat into disconnection.

I notice the way bullying is part of my fabric. I trace my resistance to these experiences in my embodied experience of connecting to others, through a form of shape-changing. I see how question-forming is both an expression of my own bullying tendencies, and an intention to overcome them. Through my connection to others and my curiosity, I form a networked community in which I can work in the world as a network coordinator, action-researcher, activist and evaluator.

I show how my approach to this work is rooted in the values of compassion, love, and fairness, and inspired by art. I hold myself to account in relation to these values, as living standards by which I judge myself and my action in the world. This finds expression in research that helps us to design more appropriate criteria for the evaluation of international social change networks. Through this process I inquire with others into the nature of networks, and their potential for supporting us in lightly-held communities which liberate us to be dynamic, diverse and creative individuals working together for common purpose. I tentatively conclude that networks have the potential to increase my and our capacity for love.

Through this research I am developing new ways of knowing about what we are doing as reflective practitioners, and by what standards we can invite others to judge our work. I am, through my practice, making space for us to flourish, as individuals and communities. In this way I use the energy released by my response to bullying in the service of transformation.

Marian Naidoo (2005) I Am Because We Are (a Never Ending Story). The Emergence of a Living Theory of Inclusional and Responsive Practice. http://www.actionresearch.net/naidoo.shtml

I believe that this original account of my emerging practice demonstrates how I have been able to turn my ontological commitment to a passion for compassion into a living epistemological standard of judgement by which my inclusional and responsive practice may be held accountable.

I am a story teller and the focus of this narrative is on my learning and the development of my living educational theory as I have engaged with others in a creative and critical practice over a sustained period of time. This narrative self-study demonstrates how I have encouraged people to work creatively and critically in order to improve the way we relate and communicate in a multi-professional and multi-agency healthcare setting in order to improve both the quality of care provided and the well being of the system.

In telling the story of the unique development of my inclusional and responsive practice I will show how I have been influenced by the work of theatre practitioners such as Augusto Boal, educational theorists such as Paulo Freire and drawn on, incorporated and developed ideas from complexity theory and living theory action research. I will also describe how my engagement with the thinking of others has enabled my own practice to develop and from that to develop a living, inclusional and responsive theory of my practice. Through this research and the writing of this thesis, I now also understand that my ontological commitment to a passion for compassion has its roots in significant events in my past.

Robyn Pound How Can I Improve My Health Visiting Support of Parenting? The Creation of an Alongside Epistemology through Action Enquiry. http://www.actionresearch.net/pound.shtml

Motivated initially by rights for children, particularly freedom from violence, this thesis explores the enhancement of children's well-being in family life. It shows the creation of a living theory of health visiting as I seek to understand, improve, evaluate and explain my support of developing family relationships. From increasingly collaborative relationships with parents, colleagues, educational researchers and others, alongsideness emerges as an explanation I found appropriate to my parenting, health visiting and researching. Alongsideness, meaning creating and sustaining connections that enhance collaborative enquiry, intends to support the generation of personal theory for application in practice.

The thesis shows how I found theory of human emotional need useful for understanding and raising awareness about the needs of people in relationships and for problem-solving. It illuminates the health-enhancing and educational possibilities of alongsideness for myself, children, their families and the communities they form. It shows how I question personal beliefs arising from my history, as I reflect on my values and attempt to embody them for living as I practise. Self-study enabled me to grapple with the dynamic, multi-dimensions of alongsideness in diverse situations, the dilemmas arising for understanding myself and for clarifying my practice values.

The thesis contributes to a new scholarship of enquiry for health visiting. It shows how values generated and embodied in the process of enquiring can be transformed into living standards of judgement both for evaluating practice and for judging my claims to knowledge. It explains how the generation of living theory through reflective action enquiry has potential for the improvement and explanation of practice.

Moving back into accounts from educational organisations, we have the living theories of Margaret Farren and Jacqueline Delong legitimated by the University of Bath.

Margaret's living theory emerged from her work and research as a lecturer in e-learning from Dublin City University with students on the MSc in Computer Applications for Education and the MSc in Education and Training Management (ICT). In developing a pedagogy of the unique, Margaret shows how her Celtic spirituality in a 'web of betweenness' enhances her capacity to respond to and creatively respond to the risks, courage and challenges in her enquiry.

Jacqueline's living theory emerged from her research and work as Superintendent of Schools in the Grand Erie District School Board in Ontario. Jacqueline's gift includes an understanding of the educational significance of developing a culture of enquiry to support practitioner-researchers as they explore the implications of asking, researching and answering questions of the kind 'How do I improve what I am doing?' In developing our idea of giftedness as a living concept, we appreciate the significance of educating social formations of working and researching to enhance our cultural influences because of the importance of these in the development of social movements.

Margaret Farren (2005) How Can I Create a Pedagogy of the Unique through a Web of Betweenness? http://www. actionresearch.net/farren.shtml

This thesis examines the growth of my educational knowledge and development of my practice, as higher education educator, over six years of self-study. The thesis sets out to report on this research and to explain the evolution of my educational influence in my own learning, the learning of others and in the education of social formations. By education of social formations I refer to Whitehead's (2005a) meaning of living values that carry hope for the future of humanity more fully in the rules and processes that govern its social organization.

The context of my research was the collaborative process that developed between myself and participants on the M.Sc. in Computer Applications for Education and the M.Sc. Education and Training Management (ICT) at Dublin City University. Within that context, I worked with a sense of research-based professionalism, seeking to improve my practice through using a "living educational theory" approach that has sustained me in asking, researching and answering the question; "How do I improve my practice?" This has enabled me to critically examine my own assumptions and values.

I clarify the meaning of my embodied values in the course of their emergence in my practice-based research. My values have been transformed into living standards of judgement that include a "web of betweenness" and a "pedagogy of the unique." The "web of betweenness" refers to how we learn in relation to one another and also how ICT can enable us to get closer to communicating the meanings of our embodied values. I see it as a way of expressing my understanding of education as "power with," rather than "power over," others. It is this "power with" that I have tried to embrace as I attempt to create a learning environment in which I, and practitioner-researchers, can grow personally and professionally. A "pedagogy of the unique" respects the unique constellation of values and standards of judgement that each practitioner-researcher contributes to a knowledge base of practice.

As a researcher, I have supported practitioners in bringing their embodied knowledge and values into the public domain as they design, develop and evaluate multimedia and web based artefacts for use in their own practice contexts. This has involved the supervision of Master degree "living educational theory" enquiries. My PhD enquiry has been a professional journey that has involved risks, courage and challenges, but I have learned that in creating my "pedagogy of the unique," I learn and grow, recognising the contribution I myself make as an individual, and also recognising the contribution dialogue, participation and collaboration with others achievers.

Jacqueline Delong (2002) How Can I Improve My Practice as a Superintendent of Schools and Create My Own Living Educational Theory? http://www.actionresearch.net/delong.shtml

One of the basic tenets of my philosophy is that the development of a culture for improving learning rests upon supporting the knowledge-creating capacity in each individual in the system. Thus, I start with my own. This thesis sets out a claim to know my own learning in my educational inquiry, "How can I improve my practice as a superintendent of schools?"

Out of this philosophy emerges my belief that the professional development of each teacher rests in their own knowledge-creating capacities as they examine their own practice in helping their students to improve their learning. In creating my own educational theory and supporting teachers in creating theirs, we engage with and use insights from the theories of others in the process of improving student learning.

The originality of the contribution of this thesis to the academic and professional knowledge-base of education is in the systematic way I transform my embodied educational values into educational standards of practice and judgement in the creation of my living educational theory. In the thesis I demonstrate how these values and standards can be used critically both to test the validity of my knowledge-claims and to be a powerful motivator in my living educational inquiry.

The values and standards are defined in terms of valuing the other in my professional practice, building a culture of inquiry, reflection and scholarship and creating knowledge.

CHAPTER 4

BEYOND IDENTIFICATION – THE TEACHER'S ROLE IN CREATING GIFTS: TEACHERS AND STUDENTS AS COMMITTED CO-ENQUIRERS, RESEARCHING THEIR OWN LIVES

Burning to Learn by Andrew Leggett

Like many teachers, I have been inspired by learning to the point where I burn to inspire. Yet that was by no means a certain process given my own education. As a child, my early learning was best characterised by embarrassment. I was (and remain) highly inquisitive: I asked far too many questions compared to my peers and the responses frequently mortified me.

Born in rural Norfolk, I was one of the last to take the "Eleven Plus" – a test that was used until 1976 to sort the wheat from the chaff. Taking the "verbal reasoning" element was one significant example of how learning became a source of embarrassment to me. I remember being puzzled by the cultural bias inherent in the test questions. One particular question hinged on an understanding of the word "champagne". As a child of working class parents with very limited reading materials I had not encountered this word before. I asked my teacher for assistance. Determined not to cheat on the test, I asked only how to pronounce the word hoping that it might jog some memory from my reading of fiction.

"Oh, do you mean sham-pag-ny?" he replied.

Gifts, Talents and Education By Barry Hymer, Jack Whitehead and Marie Huxtable
© 2008 Wiley-Blackwell

The sniggers from some of my classmates alerted me to the fact that I had, once again, asked a really stupid question.

Like three others in my class, I passed. However, my rural primary school was only allocated two "places" for the local grammar school. The four names were placed in a hat, in assembly, and two were drawn as the winners in our educational lottery. Thus I began my secondary schooling with a clear sense of the arbitrary processes which judged me a loser and judged my questioning an embarrassment, not an asset. Well, I wasn't going to make that mistake again: I would keep the questions in my head.

Teachers at secondary modern schools in the 1970s expected little from students who had already been designated as unworthy of the grammar school. Not that I was unhappy with this state of affairs. Learning was something that I could do on my own, a submergent thinker, largely outside the classroom. My school had more books than I had ever seen; I realised that I could attend night-school classes with no cost; and my natural introspection and inquisitive mind meant that my learning ranged broadly.

It was with a genuine sense of surprise that, towards the end of my compulsory schooling, I noticed teachers' interest in my answers, compositions and test scores. They realised that something had gone wrong with the sorting process at eleven and tried to make amends.

Blinking in the light of this scrutiny, I awoke to find some truly inspirational teachers, including many who went well beyond their remit in order to make sure that I achieved what is recognised as educational success. More importantly, I grew and discovered that enquiry was laudable not laughable. Here was something larger than my own endeavours: creating the world anew through discussion, guidance, direction and support. Thankfully the experiences that defined my early learning persisted as a set of values that developed into a desire to share.

As a teacher I am motivated to enable others to experience that growth. Underpinning my work are those values of fairness and equality, integrity and compassion, mutual growth and development through learning. Alongside them is experience of the potential in each student to encounter learning through a rich range of stimuli. Intrinsic in all, is that this complex process of development exists beyond external measures of success and is concerned with enriching lives in ways that are often too subtle to measure.

Think of a student performing in their school play. Is the experience as educationally convincing as say, learning how to plot the graphs of simple linear functions? Well, most would agree that the student gains "something" from the "experience" but seldom is the idea explored beyond that. On reflection they might concede that the student has learned turn-taking, timing, representation, poetics, characterisation and to have a greater sense of confidence and self-worth. These elements of learning change a person and yet are seldom appreciated in the same way as say, a facility with number.

Clearly these values underpin my practice and inform a pedagogy that has at its heart the idea of creating a learning space. At a simple level this informs my selection of approach and activity; on a more complex one it underpins each encounter with a student. A high degree of empathy, acute listening skills and the ability to value each student's contributions are central to this. Perhaps most importantly, the ability to focus the moment as an opportunity for sharing and mutual growth is how I define my work. In practice this means using empathy to recognise and value the person at the point where we encounter each other; to be aware of the frequently incongruous schema imposed upon those encounters by national learning "specifications," and simultaneously to hold those at bay and move towards the larger goals expressed in them.

In professional relationships the process is similar. Teachers, like learners, become distracted by the mundane. We can lose sight of the unmeasured growth that results from learning – however small the steps. Worse still, mundanities make islands of us, weakening our ability to cooperate. Paradoxically, in stillness we often make the greatest strides and much of my work with colleagues concerns listening, finding the centre of their concerns and helping them to meet their goals cooperatively.

A Student's Prayer by Umberto Maturana

Don't impose on me what you know,
I want to explore the unknown
And be the source of my own discoveries.
Let the known be my liberation, not my slavery.

The world of your truth can be my limitation;
Your wisdom my negation.
Don't instruct me; let's walk together.
Let my riches begin where yours ends.

Show me so that I can stand
On your shoulders.
Reveal yourself so that I can be
Something different.

You believe that every human being
Can love and create.
I understand, then, your fear
When I ask you to live according to your wisdom.

You will not know who I am
By listening to yourself.
Don't instruct me; let me be.
Your failure is that I be identical to you.

We like the way Buckingham & Coffman (1999) write about the way great managers think about talents. We share their meanings. They say that great managers describe a talent as a recurring pattern of thought, feeling or behaviour that can be productively applied. The emphasis here is on the word 'recurring'. Your talents, they say, are the behaviours you find yourself doing often. You have a mental filter that sifts through your world, forcing you to pay attention to some stimuli, while others slip past you, unnoticed. Your instinctive ability to remember names, rather than just faces, is a talent. Your need to alphabetise your spice rack and colour code your wardrobe is a talent. So is your love of crossword puzzles, or your fascination with risk or your impatience. Any recurring patterns of behaviour that can be productively applied are talents. The key to excellent performance, of course, is finding the match between your talents and your role. (Buckingham & Coffman, 1999).

As previously described, we are working with the idea of a gift being something we freely give. We are working with the idea that we express and use our talents to produce something we value and that our gifts are what we offer freely to others. What fascinates us about other people is listening to stories of their lives which allow us to understand the meanings and purpose they find in, and give to, their existence. From these stories, such as Andrew's, introducing this chapter, we find ourselves selecting the values that seem to us to carry hope for the future of humanity and seeking to understand how to avoid those behaviours that can suck individuals and their social formations into vortices of destruction and disability. We particularly like to understand the values that individuals use to explain why they are doing what they are doing. As we have said, we call the explanations that individuals produce for their educational influences in their own learning, in the learning of others and in the learning of the social formations in which we live and work, living educational theories. We like to hear the histories of individuals in which they have encountered and responded to challenges to their values and understandings. We like to hear what they think of events in their global context and about what they believe we should be doing about contemporary issues of human rights, poverty, corruption, the environment and of education. We view these stories as the gifts produced from their talents.

These stories do not simply happen. They are created. So too, with the story of giftedness. By this point in the book, we have thought about gifted and talented education as traditionally understood and suggested that we find it counterproductive. We have begun to clarify how we identify where and when we feel concerns that we are not living our values as fully as we desire, and what we mean when we say we experience ourselves as living contradictions. We have gone on to explain what a living theory approach is and what it has to offer to student-led enquiry. We have imagined a way forward through a living theory approach to the development of talents and the creation of gifts. Now what do I do as an educator in a world of constraints and demands? How do I act? What is my role? What am I trying to achieve? What data can I gather to show I am more effective in supporting my students to develop their talents to offer as gifts? Am I the educator that I believe my students deserve?

In advocating a living theory approach to the expression and development of talents and the creation of gifts, we recognise the importance of accounting for our practice to ourselves and each other in terms of our values and understandings. The title of this chapter, 'I act in the direction of the imagined solution', contains 'I' and to be authentic, we each need to show ourselves acting in the direction of our imagined solution.

In a living theory approach, we recognise that 'how we are' and 'what we do', as much as 'what we say', communicates our embodied values, theories, knowledge, talents and gifts which we have developed and created during the course of our lives and which contribute to the educational influence we have in our students' learning. Ghandi said 'Be the changes you want to see in the world!' We would suggest you *are* the educational changes you want to see in the way you live through your practices.

In the role of educator, we imagine you, like us, are wanting to support your students to develop as thought-full, thoughtful learners, knowing themselves, with informing aspirations and the confidence and competences to pursue them; able to contribute to, and benefit from, their own learning and that of others.

The role of the educator in respect to living theory and inclusional pedagogy could be thought of as having various foci which are held together in a creative tension. We have used the metaphor of a challah before (Hymer, 2007a), which might serve us here. A challah is a type of plaited bread; each strand is recognisable as distinct but not discrete, and the baking brings the strands together into a new dynamic relationship with each other and within the whole. For this metaphor to be useful, we need to have some shared experiences of a challah. So it is with trying to describe and explain our understanding of the role of the educator; we need to begin by establishing some shared experiences with you of teachers in the role of meaning makers, as an inclusional pedagogist, as an educator working with a living theory approach to gifted and talented education.

We will first shift our gaze to the teacher and learner as creators of knowledge. We will explore the role we have as educator: facilitating the acquisition and increasing sophistication in use and development of the tools for enquiring, illuminating such contexts and constraints as the given curriculum, the dominant wisdoms, making accessible what is known in the field, pointing and moving to fertile ground, relaxing boundaries and opening spaces for creativity. As we act, we may be asking questions such as

– How do we enable students to recognise and value the contribution they make to their own learning and that of others?
– How can we contribute as creators and co-creators of knowledge in the student's enquiry?
– In what ways can we create and hold the educational space open, invitational and safe?
– When do we make opportunities to notice what the student is seeking to do: the learning, the skills, the understanding and talents they are trying to develop, and the gifts they are trying to create – and support them in their endeavour?
– How do we connect the 'given' (the curriculum, the prevailing wisdoms, the knowledge that exists in the discipline) to the 'living' (the focus of the student's enquiry) without imposing?
– How can we attract the attention of the student educationally (Mai Li, 2005) to the unexplored and unimagined?
– How do we sustain the commitment of ourselves and our students to learning and to contributing to the learning of others?

Then we want to focus on bringing into presence the uniqueness of the individual (Biesta, 2006). We can't talk about the role of ourselves as educators without talking about our educational qualities, values, embodied knowledge and the theories that we communicate through our practice, often unknowingly. As the ancient Greeks would have said: 'Educator – know yourself!' And in knowing our unique and professional selves, we can come to recognise and know our students, perhaps even better than they might know themselves at times, and contribute to their knowing who they are and who they want to be, and the lives they want to live as worthwhile.

The sorts of questions we ask ourselves here might be, for instance,

– How do we enable the student to recognise and value his or her self?
– In what ways do we recognise the student and reflect back what we see?

– When do we enable the student to see the 'other', to value this 'other', and to feel recognised and valued by the 'other'?

– When do we provide opportunities for the student to reflect on their emerging living values, the standards by which they judge their lives, and the stories they are developing which inform their careers? (Maree, 2007)

We will focus on the educator's role with regard to the educational relationship, and responsibilities expressed, between themselves and the learner with questions such as

– How can we be sensitive to the qualities of the inclusive and inclusional educational relationship with the student?

– What are the qualities of the educational relationship between teacher and student we want to improve?

– How do we enable students to express their educational responsibility towards themselves and others?

Towards the end of this chapter, we will describe in some detail an approach to using video as a means of data collection and analysis that helps us to recognise our values emerging through our practice.

We will finish the chapter with an outline of the role educators might want to take in introducing their students to constructing their own living theory research: learning to recognise their aptitudes, dispositions, enthusiasms, motivation; values which are at the heart of their living standards by which they judge their lives as satisfying and worthwhile.

As individuals construct their living educational theories, we draw the distinction between explaining learning and explaining one's educational influence in learning that is borrowed from Biesta (2006) and which is described in Chapter 3. The distinction between what is educational and what is learning can be understood with the idea of educational responsibility. Individuals can learn many things that we do not see as educational. They can learn to relate to others with a sense of superiority or inferiority based on differences in skin colour, social class, gender or other differences that should not be used in recognising the other as another human being of value. In our understandings, learning is always involved in what counts as educational, but not all learning is educational. In distinguishing what is educational in learning, we need to recognise the exercise of the learner's responsibility for including values in the learning that carry energy and hope for the humanity of others and their own.

RECOGNISING LEARNERS AS CREATORS OF KNOWLEDGE

Let us take you on an imaginary journey. Think back to the last lesson that you emerged from with a sense of pleasure, a glow that comes when you know that you have done something you really believe in and you did it well. Maybe you were teaching 5-year-old children in a nursery, or maybe you were lecturing adults in a university or conference venue. Just think of yourself as the educator in a space where you wanted to have an educational influence. What was it like? Remember what you did? How did you judge your success? Did you share your learning? Did you explain your learning? Our experiences may be different from yours, but we think there is only a small chance that you will have shared your experiences beyond an intimate circle; in English culture, the expectation is for people to be self-effacing and diffident. If you had a crashing failure, the chances are you kept even quieter; it is not usually prudent to share stories of ruin (McLure, 1996) even though it is often in moments of failure that we have the opportunity to learn the most – an idea taken up in the contradictory-dialectical element of our G-T (Generative-Transformational) CReATe model – cf. Chapter 2. Either way, it is even less likely that you gave an explanation to account for your learning or clarified the standards by which you judged your practice.

We have suggested that one reason for not sharing or researching our learning is English reserve, but another might be that we have learnt, through our own experiences as children and adults at school and beyond, that our own embodied knowledge, our own theorising and ability to create knowledge, is not valued or perceived as valuable. Despite the rhetoric of supporting educators to lead in their own learning development, the predominant form of professional development is still by and large that of delivered in-service training which infantilises the teaching force with learning represented as a product, and knowledge something others more worthy than ourselves have created for us to be helped to acquire and reproduce. Biesta (2006) communicates something of this:

> What is learning? Learning theorists of both an individualistic and a socio-cultural bent have developed a range of accounts of how learning – or more precisely, how the process of learning – takes place. Although they differ in their description and explanation of the process, for example, by focusing on processes in the brain or legitimate peripheral participation, many of such accounts assume that learning has to do with the acquisition of something "external," something that existed before the act of learning and that, as a result of learning, becomes the possession of the learner. This is what many people have in mind when they say that someone has learned something. (p. 26)

In a living theory approach, we are working with the assumption that we are all capable of creating valued and valuable knowledge; learning is a process we all engage in and we can become more skilful and sophisticated in our learning if we work at it. 'Working at it' doesn't just mean devoting time and energy (though it means that too): it means being prepared to challenge, critique, transform and transcend what we have been doing and thinking and to engage creatively to progress. We recognise that this is all part of the process of learning which is reflected in the generation of new knowledge.

It is our belief that it is only the learner who can do the learning; no one can impose learning or do the learning for another. The role the educator plays can contribute to or diminish the student's recognising and fulfilling their aspirations but cannot extinguish what seems to be a very human quality – the creative desire to learn. MacBeath (2006) is often quoted in national strategies (such as personalisation of learning and the study support framework) expressing similar sentiments:

> Personalised learning is not something that can be "done" by teachers to pupils. Rather it arises when pupils themselves take charge of their own goals and progress, together with a heightened awareness of their own learning styles and preferences. When young people enjoy a range of opportunities to test themselves, to explore their talents and cultivate new interests, they come to a deeper appreciation of how learning works, what can inhibit it and in what ways it can nourish self belief. When there are rich extended sites for learning, young people grasp that the purpose of school is not to provide an education but to stimulate a thirst for learning, and to give it life beyond the school gate. (p. 12)

We know from experience that learning is not just a cognitive activity – it can also be experienced very personally and emotionally. We can have an emotional investment in some learning and theories that is not necessarily obvious to ourselves or others; sometimes there is a commitment to new understandings, sometimes to knowledge that has been superseded, that is not rooted in the rational. Galileo learnt that when he was pressurised to change his mind about the knowledge he was seeking to share about the form of the world. On being shown the instruments of his promised torture, he recognised not only the emotional investment of others in maintaining their knowledge base, irrespective of the rightness of the new knowledge he had created, but also the power relationships that can be challenged unwittingly. He recanted – at least outwardly. Educators seeking to develop their role as inclusional pedagogists might feel a sense of discomfort as the power relationships expressed between themselves and their students are exposed. We will return to this point later where we explore the responsibility of the educator and student towards each other and their learning.

To accept that we are all capable of creating valued and valuable knowledge places responsibilities on individuals for their own learning. Some may resist that responsibility for a variety of reasons including self-preservation, financial security and emotional well-being; they may lack confidence in themselves or wish for a raft of reasons to be helpless. The role of the teacher then is not just to enable skills and understandings to be acquired but to hold the learner in an educational space he or she may find uncomfortable. At one time, the behaviouristically derived instructional notion of errorless learning and short, easily acquired, steps was popular. This proved successful for reintroducing students to opportunities to learn they had previously found aversive. However, there was the unintended consequence of the student becoming dependent on the instructor and ultimately learning to be helpless as learners. Edison recognised the problem decades ago when he observed that many of life's 'failures' are people who did not realise how close they were to success when they gave up. Claxton's (2002) work on *Building Learning Power* emphasises the importance of providing opportunities for risk taking and becoming more resilient. Curiously and disappointingly, this work has been introduced in many schools as a 'package' to be implemented rather than as engaging in a thinking, acting and reflecting journey, to contribute to the knowledge the learning community is creating.

Biesta (2006) draws this distinction between making knowledge and implementing someone else's knowledge when he points out that learning is not easy and the teacher's role is not to make it so; rather, their role is to enable the learner to gain confidence in their ability to learn and to value the influence they can have in their own learning and that of others. Dweck (1999, 2006) picks up on this in her books on self-theories and mindset, and shows how inadvertently educators, with the best of intentions, can convey disempowering messages. She talks of a 'fixed' theory of intelligence; put simply, you believe you are or are not intelligent, contrasted with a 'growth' theory of intelligence in which learners believe that they can learn to behave more intelligently, more proficiently, more creatively. With a 'fixed mindset', the learner is more likely to construe challenging and difficult experiences as a challenge to their self-image as a 'bright' student, whereas someone with a 'growth mindset' is more likely to see such experiences as opportunities to learn rather than to repeat what another has already produced. When a person does something correctly, she's had a chance to practise something. When she makes a mistake, she's had a chance to learn something.

That all are capable of creating extraordinary knowledge is not a revolutionary concept in all parts of the world, as Freeman (2002) points out:

> The major cultural dichotomy affecting educational provision for the gifted and talented is between the largely Eastern perception – "all children have gifted potential" – and the largely Western one – "only some children have gifted potential". (p. 9)

The role of educators developing a living theory approach to gifted and talented *education* is concerned with *all* learners developing their talents and creating gifts. The educator's perspective moves from that of definer and categoriser of children, offered by Galton's theories of intelligence – which as White (2006) points out dominates the school systems in Britain and

America – to that of opening a child's eyes to the possibilities that life offers, given the courage and tenacity to pursue their dreams.

Robert Burns described what gift the teacher can give in their role as educator:

> O' wad some power, the giftie gi us
> To see ourselves as ithers see us! . . . !
> *It wad frae monie a blunder free us,*
> *An' foolish notion*

The 'blunder' and 'foolish notion' is often to see ourselves as incapable and having nothing of worth to offer. In recognising the individual student's abilities to create knowledge of value and in enabling them to offer and share the gifts they create, the teacher can give their student the opportunity to see with another's eyes what they really are capable of creating, which can confer the courage to strive.

Denise Shekerjian (1991) in her book *Uncommon Genius* declares, 'Everyone has an aptitude for something. The trick is to recognise it, to honour it, to work with it'. Perhaps the trick is for the educator not simply to recognise and honour the student's aptitudes, and try to entice or enforce the student to work with them, but rather to enable their students to do the recognising and honouring and knowing how to work with their aptitudes in a direction that is satisfying and productive.

When we say that the role of the teacher is not only to recognise their students as learners able to create valued and valuable knowledge but to enable them to recognise themselves as such, we are not thinking this is restricted to a particular age. In reading the accounts of Joy Mounter (2007a, 2007b), we hope you can also appreciate the educational influence they are having in their teacher's learning. As Joy demonstrates in her work with her pupils, one way of empowering pupils is to engage them in their own research, creating their own living theory accounts to offer to others. We will come back to this later.

Creating something of worth is not quick and it is not easy, and the learner needs the attributes as well as the skills of a productive learner, such as Claxton's (2002) 'four Rs of learning' – resilience, resourcefulness, reciprocity and reflection. It concerns the deep and profound learning that West-Burnham (2003) describes. The difference between deep and profound learning he describes in an article on leadership:

> Deep learning in this context is manifested in the ability to develop a personal model of the change process which is a synthesis of a range of sources and the ability to translate that model into action. Experience is mediated through reflection, which allows for personal interpretation and a sense of autonomy.

Profound learning, however, results in the creation of personal meaning – integrating principle, values and practice so that behaviour is intuitive and the response to change is creative, challenging, ethically driven and integrative. (p. 4)

BRINGING INTO PRESENCE THE UNIQUENESS OF THE INDIVIDUAL

Everything seems so much simpler in orthodox understandings of learning: the teacher is instructor, imparter/transmitter of knowledge or trainer of the uninformed trainee. Learning is seen as a quantity best delivered in bite-sized, easily digested, well-sweetened doses, and the ingestion can in turn be quantified. The role of the teacher then is to ensure 'successful learning' principally through focusing on improving their technical efficiency. Out come the stopwatches, the time sampling, the learning behaviours to be observed, the learning outcomes carefully defined and 'pace and challenge' quantified and qualified. However attractive, such approaches bring with them problems which you must be more than aware of – or you wouldn't be reading this book! We ask you to step outside this space for a moment and bring to mind an educator who influenced you. Was it what they did that influenced you or what they were like? In our experience, there is a tendency to remember their passionate enthusiasm for what they were doing and/or their capacity to communicate an interest and confidence in you as a person. Or, if you were really lucky, both!

Barry's research illustrates this point well when working with adults:

> [I had thought it necessary to focus] . . . my energies on the quality and rigour of my arguments and evidence-base (an empirical foundation), and the technical "efficiency" and persuasiveness of my presentations (the dark arts and tools of sophistry). However, the evaluative feedback I have received in the course of recent research (Hymer, 2007) has suggested, on the contrary, that beyond certain baseline presentational skills (e.g. of timekeeping, voice-projection, pace, use of audio-visual aids, content-audience match, etc.) only a relatively small part of the significant meanings (deep learning) gained by participants can be attributable to the course content ("knowledge") and presentational technique. (Hymer, 2007)

Think back; who has influenced your life in ways that you valued? Who has helped you see something in yourself that you hadn't seen before? That time someone saw something in you that you were not aware of and helped you see yourself with their eyes. It may not have been a 'road to Damascus moment', or resulted in launching you on your vocation or career path, or in enabling you to know in what way you wanted to dedicate your life or lead you to make a world-leading contribution. But that vision of something of value in yourself enhanced the quality of your life. Many theorists have written about the importance of that quality of recognition. For instance, Fukuyama (1992) wrote:

> Human beings seek recognition of their own worth, or of the people, things, or principles that they invest with worth. The desire for recognition, and the accompanying emotions of anger, shame and pride, are parts of the human personality critical to political life. According to Hegel, they are what drive the whole historical process. (p. xvii)

And most recently, Feldman (2007):

> Although it is possible to conceptualize a way of being in terms of emotions ... or spirituality . . . , I see it as an existential concept. It is not a teacher characteristic, such as the teacher's knowledge or reasoning skills; rather, it is the way a person is in the situation that is defined and informed by what was and is for the teacher, and his or her intentions for what could be. The teacher's way of being a teacher is essentially the way in which that person is a teacher – where "teacher" is one of the many ways that that person is and can be. ... In the present paper I argue that an awareness of their existential freedom allows teachers to act responsibly to construct educational situations that help pupils to become aware of the way that they exist in the world. For this to happen, teachers and their pupils must recognize that each is an individual human being who is situated, whose self emerges through experience and who has freedom to choose. Because this appears to be rare in American schools I have examined the ways that teachers' participation in collaborative action research can help them to become more aware of their existential freedom. (pp. 240, 241)

The recognition of the student, for it to be authentic, offers a mutual recognition; they are allowed to see something of you and your values being lived. We are not talking about an egotistical view but something that comes from a selfless confidence and love of self as Fromm (1957) describes. You can test the veracity of this contention yourself. Think again of those educators that have been influential in your story – what did you recognise in them? Bullough & Pinnegar (2004) emphasise the importance of focusing on one's being in and towards the world: 'The consideration of ontology, of one's being in and toward the world, should be a central feature of any discussion of the value of self-study research' (p. 319).

In an easily missed moment in a video seen by ourselves, a pupil brushes some dust from her teacher's jacket; the teacher turns on being touched, and in a brief moment there is the mutual recognition in the gaze between teacher and student that captures this bringing of the other into presence. It is the human moment of sharing a look that is important; that could only happen in a context where there was trust and an invitational space.

Biesta (2006) talks of that uniqueness, what it is that only 'I' can say, what is it that would not exist if 'I' were not in the world and the role of the educator in bringing the individual into presence.

It is the recognition and valuing by ourselves and others of the uniqueness that we each bring to the world that not only contributes to our mental well-being but enables us to contribute without 'fear or veneer'. This is perhaps a bold statement, for which we are asking you to test the validity through your experience. There is a difference between fulsome praise and authentic recognition. Dweck (1999) highlights this difference, and the result of meaningless praise. The token of a 'gold star' at times can be an overt symbolic recognition of something valued in the other or an appreciation of the quality of a gift they have created and shared. It can also be nothing more than tokenistic, and the inadvertent result can then be demeaning or disempowering.

What does it mean for you to see students, for example, reaching out beyond their own expectations so that they see themselves as capable people? Isn't that a marvellous achievement for both of you? It goes beyond recognising aptitudes and dispositions – it is a connection with the ontological values of the other – what it is that gives meaning and purpose to their lives. We do not suddenly recognise ourselves. There is a growing awareness of our sense of self, the person we are and how we want to be in the world. To develop our talents to create and offer our gifts to others requires a sense of self that gives a root to the courage and energy required.

What influences the evolution of our ontology? There is a growing aware-ness of the role of the teacher in enhancing self-esteem, self-image, self-confidence and the development of morals and ethics. Many approaches have been mechanistic and treat children as objects to be moulded rather than as creators of themselves with living standards by which they judge their lives as worthwhile. A living theory approach to gift creation is based on a belief that everyone has embodied values and knowledge not just about the world but about themselves which the educator respects and seeks to enhance. You can see the influence of that recognition or the lack of it in the personal stories told in these chapters.

How do we as educators open opportunities to recognise and enhance students' evolving ontologies? How do we enable those in our learning community to feel the quality of recognition?

You are possibly thinking that this is all well and good, but I have too many pupils to be able to recognise them all as themselves. Sometimes there can be recognition even when it can't be 'up close and personal'. This is one example of an educator in a Chinese University who had classes in the region of 100 students, but who wanted to enable her students to feel recognised. To give you the context, Moira wrote:

> There were 103 students in that class. It was one of the two "teaching method-ology" classes I had. The other had 98 students. I didn't know them all by

name, I'll be honest. I had each class once a week for two hours and in that time I had to put across to them that teaching is about relationships and making contact at personal levels and yet I didn't know all their names. What I did do, though, every single lesson was say hello and goodbye to every student, sometimes shaking hands, even sometimes embracing each other. I had three students in my penultimate year, two girls and a boy (about 22 years old) who would regularly give me hugs. Once, when I was passing one of these students I praised his homework and he was so pleased he jumped out of his seat (we were in a lecture theatre, another real difficulty in making contact with individuals) and hugged me, asked first, I said yes (of course) and he gave me this huge bearhug. He said when he was at kindergarten, his teacher hugged him. She was the only person who ever had – a lot of children are never hugged in China; it's not cruel, it's cultural. Anyway, he realised I was a teacher who hugged too and he wanted some. It started a bit of a trend, actually, but that's another story.

Jack had turned the video off at what was 'the end' of the session and turned it back on when he noticed the educational significance of what was happening at the door. Jack wrote:

This one-minute clip shows the flow form of mainly non-verbal communications at the end of a lesson in Guyuan Teachers College (now Ningxia Teachers University in China). The last student in the clip is being congratulated by Moira for showing courage in questioning something Moira asked her to do. [Moira's account of her 5 years on VSO in China posted in December 2006]

Buber (1961) also expressed the importance of the educator recognising the student as a unique person poetically when he wrote:

If this educator should ever believe that for the sake of education he has to practise selection and arrangement, then he will be guided by another criterion than that of inclination, however legitimate this may be in its own sphere; he will be guided by the recognition of values which is in his glance as an educator. But even then his selection remains suspended, under constant correction by the special humility of the educator for whom the life and particular being of all his pupils is the decisive factor to which his "hierarchical" recognition is subordinated. For in the manifold variety of the children the variety of creation is placed before him. (p. 122)

Mai Li Juan (2005), an educator in China, in asking and researching her question 'How can I attract my students' attention educationally?' describes some of those educational qualities of recognition which we believe are expressed through the role of educator. For instance,

There is an anonymously-authored poem in English, which ends: "Before I teach you, I must first reach you." This expresses brilliantly, in my opinion, the role of a teacher. The NC (Chinese New Curriculum) guidelines are very precise about this as well. The NC documentation, in the spring of 2005, states that teachers need to get to know their students as individuals, in order to promote independence in learning, and pay attention to the students' individual emotions and feelings as a springboard to development. It is necessary to observe students when giving a class, and ask questions in your heart.

If you find the prospect of recognising your 'I' embarrassing, just remember that others do not recoil in horror from you. As we start to try to communicate the role of the teacher, it feels a bit like an impossible list of saintly qualities or the basis for a 'performance review' where we are required to identify 'aspirational targets for improvement'. If you can suspend such inquisitorial feelings and look with gentle eyes on yourself as educator, we think you will recognise the qualities not only of what you want to achieve as educator but are already unconsciously embodying. A living theory methodology recognises your embodied knowledge as an educator and provides a process for enhancing that knowledge that is communicated through your practice.

In recognising and valuing your own qualities, your own unique living 'I', we suggest you invite others to recognise, value and share theirs. It is that growing appreciation of our own values that informs the living standards by which we live and judge our lives as worthwhile. It is that which fuels our dreams and aspirations and provides the energy necessary for the creation of gifts of extraordinary value. The role for the educator is to open the eyes of the student to possibilities rather than to be a purloiner of their dreams.

EDUCATIONAL RELATIONSHIPS AND RESPONSIBILITIES

We said at the start of this chapter that our focus would shift, and no priority is seen in the different interconnecting strands. We have explored the role of the teacher with enquiry, learning and knowledge creation in focus. We then shifted our gaze to ontological awareness and recognition. Now, what of the relationship between educator and student? What are their respective responsibilities?

We need first to acknowledge the power of the educator to determine the nature of the relationships. A move from relationships rooted in traditional pedagogies towards those which are consistent with inclusive and inclusional ones has implications. These are illuminated by Costa (2001) in his introduction (titled 'The Vision') to *Developing Minds: A Resource Book for Teaching Thinking*:

> Our perceptions of learning need to shift from educational outcomes that are primarily an individual's collections of sub-skills to include successful participation in socially organised activities and the development of students'

identities as conscious, flexible, efficacious and interdependent meaning-makers. We must let go of having learners acquire OUR meanings and have faith in the processes of individuals' construction of their own and shared meanings through individual activity and social interaction. That's scary, because the individual and the group may NOT construct the meaning we want them to: a real challenge to the basic educational framework with which most schools are comfortable.

Educational relationships are understood in their expression, not in defini-tions. We believe that we are each unique and express our educational responsibilities in our unique ways. We don't accept a responsibility for the other, but we do accept a responsibility towards the other. The difference is important as we find oppressive the idea that anyone should feel a respon-sibility for us as distinct from towards us. We want people to feel, accept and respect that we are each responsible for ourselves, while recognising the significance of internal and external influences. Covey (2004) puts it rather well when he says, 'Between stimulus and response there is a space. In that space lies our freedom and power to choose our response. In those choices lies our growth and our happiness' (p. 43).

We appreciate the adult has particular duties of care towards children and young people in enabling them to express that responsibility for their learn-ing and their choices. This is reflected by the national focus on how to enhance the voice of children and young people in their own learning, that of others and the communities in which they live. One example of a national strategy is Social and Emotional Aspects of Learning (SEAL); another is the growth in schools' councils and young people's parliaments, and the 'inclu-sion agenda'.

As we research the expression of our educational responsibility, we are seeking to help pupils or students to experience themselves with a flow of life-affirming energy and of being of value to us and to themselves. We include the value of individual respect as a contributor to the creation of an individual's gifts and talents (Hymer, 2007, Abstract). That respect has to be extended to ourselves, and the question that reasonably follows is 'How do I recognise, generate, develop and share my own gifts and talents? What is the connection between our expression of our egoless love for ourselves and our educational relationships with our students?' Buber (1961) puts it as follows:

> The relation in education is one of pure dialogue ... Trust, trust in the world, because this human being exists – that is the most inward achievement of the relation in education. Because this human being exists, meaninglessness, however hard pressed you are by it, cannot be the real truth. Because this human being exists, in the darkness the light lies hidden, in fear salvation, and in the callousness of one's fellow-men the great Love. (pp. 125, 126)

We are now going to focus on the meanings of values as these are explicated and communicated in educational relationships in the course of the enquiry. In understanding 'who I am' and 'what I do', we think our focus on values is vital. We believe that the world will become a better place to be if we could find a way of enhancing the flow of values and understandings into the world in which we live and work. We see making public your embodied knowledge and placing this in the flow of educational knowledge and living educational theories through web space as a contribution to making the world a better place to be.

In our understanding of 'who I am' and 'what I do', it is important to recognise each other's talents and to create gifts that can be used by others if they wish. We understand the need to engage in paid labour, so that we can pay for the material necessities we need to live. In our own productive lives, we have worked out ways of sustaining a creative and productive space in which we can do what we believe in and get paid for it. In understanding our desire to exercise and develop our talents as part of our productive life, we smile with the pleasure of recognising the motivational power of the early writings of Marx (Bernstein, 1971, p. 48) in which he answers the question of what it means to produce something as a human being:

> Suppose we had produced things as human beings: in his production each of us would have twice affirmed himself and the other.
>
> In my production I would have objectified my individuality and its particularity, and in the course of the activity I would have enjoyed an individual life, in viewing the object I would have experienced the individual joy of knowing my personality as an objective, sensuously perceptible, and indubitable power.
>
> In your satisfaction and your use of my product I would have had the direct and conscious satisfaction that my work satisfied a human need, that it objectified human nature, and that it created an object appropriate to the need of another human being.
>
> I would have been the mediator between you and the species and you would have experienced me as a reintegration of your own nature and a necessary part of yourself; I would have been affirmed in your thought as well as your love.
>
> In my individual life I would have directly created your life, in my individual activity I would have immediately confirmed and realized my true human nature.

So, in seeing the originality of our students expressed in their unique narratives of their educational influences in their own learning and the learning of others, we feel that they are affirming themselves in producing something that embodies what really matters to them. As we see their accounts communicating to others, we feel affirmed in our own productive lives: we see their values and understandings being offered as gifts to others for their use in living their own loving and productive lives in making the world a better place to be.

We will return to the educational relationships and responsibilities in the next section on the use of video in living theory research.

COLLECTING DATA OF THE INFLUENCE WE WANT TO BE USING VIDEO

Drawing on the work of Eisner (1988, 1993), especially on his idea of re-imagining schools, we recognise the limitations of purely textual forms of representation on printed pages for communicating the meanings of our values in explanations for what we do. 'I hope we will even learn how to see what we are not able to describe in words, much less measure. And, through the consciousness borne of such an attitude, I hope we will be creative enough to invent methods and languages that do justice to what we have seen' (Eisner, 1988, p. 20).

Our use of multimedia representations of what we are doing and learning enables us to communicate our understandings of our educational influences to and with ourselves and others. If you had a video running and trained on you, you could rerun it and have the opportunity to reflect when not engaged in the action. But too rarely do we turn it on ourselves and use it as a tool to help us improve our educational influence in our own learning.

Video also offers us a unique opportunity to see ourselves as others see us, so that we can include these visual data into our explanations of our educational influences in learning. We believe that the visual data help us to communicate the values that really matter to us in education as we express these embodied values in our educational relationships. We also believe that the visual data help us to gain confidence in ways of explaining our educational influences that recognise our uniqueness, our singularity and the expression of our educational values, including responsibility, in our educational relationships.

An opportunity to experience yourself as a living contradiction brings the energising possibility of understanding a little more about your embodied values and imagining ways by which you might live them more fully. How can you obtain video data? You can set a video camera up in the corner of the room and leave it running. Make sure you have sought the permissions of whoever might be caught on camera with you. Better still, ask someone to video you – not video your students, but video you. When you look at it, you can remember that you are looking through their eyes and they might be able to help by sharing with you their analysis to put alongside your own. You might find a student more than willing do the videoing for you if you explain to her that you want her to help you understand what you are doing so you can improve your practice. You might like to ask her to help you recognise where you are acting in harmony with your educational values. You may be surprised at what the student focuses on and find it difficult initially to recognise the educational significance of what you see.

There is a more than an even chance that you, our reader, have feelings not dissimilar to at least one of the authors – who still finds looking at herself on video a far from pleasant experience. However, we are wanting you to 'feel the fear (or embarrassment) and do it anyway', with the optimism that something useful will emerge given the chance. On video, educators and learners are willing to share something of themselves. They make public their embodied knowledge – not as an ego booster but as a generous gift freely given to contribute to their own learning and ours.

In the flow of relationships, you may recognise as significant something you have previously dismissed in understanding your talents and the gifts you are bringing into the educational space. When reviewing videoed footage of yourself as an educator, as you run the cursor backwards and forward, feel the meanings of your communications being responded to by others. Feel the meanings in your receptive responsiveness with others.

In particular, look with gentle eyes on yourself and see if you can find places where you appreciate your movements through the space and then in relation to the people and then in relation to the values and understandings that give meaning and purpose to your life. You might be surprised to find that you are not doing what you thought you were doing, which was Jack's experience when he was given one of the first video cameras to experiment with as a science teacher. Here are Jack's reflections on viewing himself teaching:

> In the academic year 1971/2 the inspectorate in Barking asked me to explore the potential of video for improving education in the Science Department of Erkenwald Comprehensive School. As Head of the Science Department I emphasised the importance of enquiry learning in science and believed that I had created the conditions to enable my pupils to generate some of their own questions in developing their scientific understanding. Having video-taped a lesson I watched myself with a feeling of embarrassment as I saw that I was providing my pupils with the questions which could be answered with the scientific equipment previously organised for the lesson. I had not established the conditions for enquiry learning. This feeling of being a living contradiction was accompanied by imagined possibilities as to how I might improve my practice to establish the conditions for enquiry learning. I acted on a chosen possibility and with the help of video gathered data that could help me evalu-

ate the effectiveness of my practice in creating the conditions for enquiry learning. With the help of the video I evaluated my practice and could see that some of my pupils were involved in genuine explorations of their own enquiries. Some years later I integrated this use of video in a local curriculum development to develop enquiry learning with science teachers and their pupils. The recognition of existing as living contradictions in relation to their values provided a stimulus to imagined possibilities for improving practice and powerful motivation to sustain the commitment to help to enhance the quality of pupils' learning. (Whitehead, 1976)

THE EDUCATOR'S ROLE IN SUPPORTING CHILDREN AND YOUNG PEOPLE RESEARCHING THEIR OWN LIVES, RECOGNISING THEIR OWN VALUES AND LIVING STANDARDS OF JUDGEMENT

On the world stage, UNICEF promotes children as community researchers (http://www.unicef.org/teachers/researchers/) and gives the pedagogical rationale, affirming the activity-oriented element of our G-T CReATe model: 'It has long been recognized that learning is most effective when children are actively engaged in the creation of knowledge'. But for the most part, the opportunities for children to enquire as researchers appear to have focused on their part as social researchers rather than as opportunities to transform educational practice and engage children as collaborative enquirers, creating valued knowledge. A few examples can be seen with the establishment of the Children's Research Centre within the Open University (http://www.childrens-research-centre.open.ac.uk):

> The CRC is all about children by children. Our primary objective is to empower children and young people as active researchers. The CRC recognises that children are experts on their own lives. We value the child's perspective and believe in promoting child voice by supporting children to carry out research on topics that are important to them.

With the first few sentences to the introduction of her book *How to Develop Children as Researchers*, Kellett (2005) expresses the sentiment 'In the adult world research process is greatly valued as an advanced learning tool and whetstone for critical thinking. The importance of research in professional and personal development is increasingly being acknowledged. So why should children not benefit in a similar way?' but she does not develop the idea of research beyond a traditional scientific methodology where children focus on others as objects of investigation and the educational intent seems to melt away. What we are proposing here is that with your support, students can go beyond simply acting as social science researchers to be able to research themselves, construct their own theories of their learning and create their own living standards of judgement based on their own values.

If you have reached this point and are thinking that a living theory approach to talent development and gift creation is restricted to older students, we want to draw your attention again to the work of Joy Mounter (2007a, 2007b), now a head teacher but whose research began as a teacher of 6- and 7-year-olds. Louise Cripps (2007) as a head teacher wrote:

> As educators we have the responsibility and privilege on a daily basis to communicate and affirm a child's intrinsic value to them. It's no good just believing it ourselves, or in telling children that they are special regardless of what they can or can't do which is going to make any difference to them. It needs to be in the way we live and learn alongside them. A crucial aspect of this is in the time we have for others, and our willingness to spend time in listening to them, and in really hearing what they say.
>
> As significant adults the verbal and non-verbal responses we make in our discussions with children both individually and in various size groups, are incredibly important and rewarding.
>
> Although as educators, we often control the classroom agenda, it is as we are willing to share the learning agenda with others that true engagement in learning is more likely to flourish. The more we are able to show the areas we need support in, the balance of power changes. It is our need that leaves space for others to lead the learning. It is not absolving us of our responsibility. If as leaders of learning we are always self sufficient, we leave no room for others to lead the learning. We deny others the opportunity to learn what they are capable of.

This is not bound by nationality. We have already drawn your attention to the work of Moira Laidlaw (http://www.actionresearch.net/moira.shtml) and Mai Li Juan (2005, http://www.jackwhitehead.com/china/malijuanar3.html) in China. Branko Bognar has provided video evidence from Croatia of 10-year-old children as action researchers, presenting their research to their peers for validation (http://www.e-lar.net/videos/Validation.wmv).

In asking the question 'How do I support my students to research their own lives . . .?' we are suggesting your answers will be unique to you and will emerge through recognising and valuing yourself and your students as knowledge creators, as unique individuals developing understandings of self, with a delightful diversity of talents to develop and gifts to create and offer. You will be researching educational relationships and responsibilities together and experimenting with video to enhance your understandings of the dynamic interrelational nature of your role as educator. There are no formulas; you can turn to action research cycles or Thinking Actively in a Social Context (TASC) for inspiration and threads to get you going, but it is through your researching your own practice and engaging your imagination to create your own methods that answers will emerge that make a difference. As Eisner (1993) said, 'We do research to understand. We try to understand in order to make our schools better places for both the children and the adults who share their lives there' (p. 5).

We began this chapter asking what do I do as a teacher? How do I act? What is my role? What am I trying to achieve? What data can I gather to show I am more effective in supporting my students to develop their talents for gift creation? Moving on to explore the next point in the action reflection cycle, we will refocus on your role in your own learning. We look at how you might evaluate the outcome of your imagined solutions and actions through enhancing your understanding of your living standards of judgement by which you determine whether your practice is improving. This is essentially a process of understanding of self in using talents to produce gifts through living theory.

We now move on to consider views of talented and gifted education that are different from our own and some of which feel antithetically to our own perspectives shared below as we develop our generative-transformational approach to gift creation. In the growth of our educational knowledge, we do appreciate the importance of understanding and communicating what we are seeing as limitations and errors in other approaches to gift creation, as well as our own. As we engage with the ideas of others, we acknowledge that they contain valuable insights as well as limitations and errors. We hope that our own learning from our critical engagements with the ideas of others will be of some use in the growth of your own educational knowledge.

CHAPTER 5

'I CONSIDER IMPLICATIONS FOR FUTURE PRACTICE': HOW CAN I CONTINUE TO INFLUENCE MY OWN LEARNING, THE LEARNING OF OTHERS, AND THE SCHOOLS AND LEARNING COMMUNITIES OF WHICH I AM PART?

Molly by Moira Laidlaw

I remember a particular time when my philosophy, methodology and practice were unified: Molly was an elective mute. When she came to the school she had not been speaking for several months. She engaged in all the activities, except speaking of course. I felt sorry for her. She seemed a sad little soul to me. Some teachers suggested we should force her to speak. That rather reminded me of first-world war soldiers who were muted by their traumatic experiences in the trenches, and subsequently, in order to make them fit for service again, were given electric shock treatment and other savageries to force them to speak. This little girl seemed to me to have been engaged in her own kind of trench warfare. Anyway, I was always gentle and kind to her. She occasionally smiled at me but not a word she spoke. I put her in situations, which showed I "colluded" with her choice not to speak, telling her she wasn't allowed to speak in this role and so on. In my classroom was a cupboard that housed all my teaching materials, books, folders and so on. It also housed about fifty stuffed frogs. Children were

---

Gifts, Talents and Education By Barry Hymer, Jack Whitehead and Marie Huxtable
© 2008 Wiley-Blackwell

encouraged to come into the classroom as early as they could to choose the frog they wanted for the lesson. Molly arrived early one day and took the biggest frog, Reginald, from the cupboard and sat down with him, almost entirely hidden from the class with Reginald sitting plump on her desk. She got out her books for the lesson and sat and waited. I chatted with her and the other girls as they came in and chose their frogs and got settled. About ten minutes into the lesson, I asked a question and several hands went up, including Reginald's. Molly sat behind him, manoeuvring his bright red hand and waving it in the air to attract attention.

"Reginald!" I said. All the girls were silent and waited. "Reginald" gave the answer, which was correct. Everyone clapped and cheered. Molly beamed with pleasure behind the frog. I felt like crying with joy. I was happy because I always believed that love will cure harm and pain, and that we cannot force a child to do anything, neither should we try. Molly spoke, I believe, because she was allowed *not* to. She was respected within her choice. She was respected. Her space wasn't violated. She had the right to choose. Equally gratifying were the other children's responses. They were wholly supportive of Molly and her quietness, and were truly delighted when she chose to speak. I wanted a learning community in my classroom, where the values of trust, love, truth, honour, respect, responsible freedoms and fairness were the order of the day.

'Only Connect': Constructing Learning by Chris Reck

I have a quotation in my classroom – apparently attributable to Leonardo da Vinci – which states that "Everything in some way connects to everything else." I find this an invaluable insight, as it has helped me to conceptualise that learning is a process of "fire lighting" and that when we first learn something new, it is slow going, a necessary struggle, perhaps similar to cutting a path for the first time in a large, dense forest.

My search for a "living theory" of teaching came after my own struggle with what I call the "reptilian regulations" inherent not just in our education system but also our culture: a culture that does not seem to value the notion of time to think. I therefore decided that my teaching practice would focus on and celebrate the connectivity of the thinking process, the time needed to develop this learning disposition as well as role-modelling the necessary struggle that underpins all worthwhile learning. In other words, I would try and engage in the learning process with the students, let things emerge and, if possible, let there be some very long pauses! Or, as Claxton and Lucas (2004, p. 63) state, "It is worth emphasising the importance of patience. Experience does not give up its most intricate secrets quickly, and the acquired inability to let things emerge, to let situations speak for themselves is a very definite form of stupidity."

My own approach to practising this form of teaching is very much influenced by what I read about Ezra Pound's view of poetry. For Pound, poetry is "language charged with meaning." Therefore it makes sense to me that learning is activated by the same restless and creative source of energy – that is, "meaning".

There is currently a great deal of reference to learning being "relevant" to students' lives. This is, on the surface, a laudable aim but in my opinion misdirected. "Relevance" is time-bound and therefore restric-tive, whereas "meaning" is part of the human journey: where we are from, where we are now and where we are likely to go. We need to connect students learning dispositions to this continuum. We need to connect students learning dispositions with a sense of where they fit into this journey. An appreciation of this "human journey" requires us to cast our nets further for our students so that we can connect their learning with personal sources of inspiration. For example, when studying Shakespeare we can connect his creativity to the necessary disposition of empathy by using Jorge Luis Borges' short narrative, "Everything and Nothing" where Borges' narrator suggests that Shakespeare's creativity came from "that controlled hallucination," or by reflecting upon Mihaly Csikzsentmihalyi's observation that we all are capable of reaching that state of effortless concentration and enjoy-ment called "flow." The challenge for the teacher comes from finding ways of personalising these sources of inspiration; or how to motivate a desire to construct a personal sense of learning.

Through this book, we have offered a new educational concept of gifts and talents which is inclusive, relational and dynamic. We have introduced you to a living theory approach to the development of talents for gift creation which can be used by adults and children. The living theory approach values individuals' embodied knowledge, their ability to create valued knowledge about and for themselves and their world, and to make decisions based on their own living values as standards of judgement. We recognise that the new brings challenges but also excitement. We also recognise how difficult it is to break established habits, so here we intend to focus on some of the issues that arise to take you beyond the initial steps. The questions that will guide us in writing this chapter are

- How amongst the impositions and demands can we recognise, create and maintain an educational space?
- How can we know we are making a difference and how do we communicate this to those imbued with the traditional social science perspectives?
- How can we improve our educational influence in the learning of our colleagues and the learning of our school?
- How might we contribute to shaping educational policy and practice?

As you read this final chapter, we would like you to think about why it is important that you give thought to the influence you have in 'social formations', the communities you affect through your practice. Perhaps the point is best made by this true story:

> A little girl, seven years of age, enjoyed a happy time in her school. She was learning well, progressing through the curriculum with confident strides. Her school was successful, well placed in the league tables, and had good OFSTED reports. The school had a gifted and talented register as expected by the DCSF and she was on it. This gave her access to other opportunities beyond the curriculum and beyond school, as the school used the register to decide who they offered these to. She thoroughly enjoyed the Saturday workshops she went to as a result, meeting other children from different schools who shared her enthusiasms. Then she moved to another school. This one also was successful, well placed in the league tables and had good OFSTED reports. Like the first school, it had an enthusiastic staff committed to developing a creative, positive experience for their pupils. However, as a consequence of changes in her personal life, the little girl was not thriving and she felt out of place. She no longer hurtled through the curriculum targets set her. Her progress faltered and stalled, and her self esteem went with it. The second school also, like the first, had a gifted and talented register and used it to decide who to offer the Saturday workshop opportunities to. The difference was the little girl was not on the register and was no longer offered the chance of going to any of the Saturday workshops she loved and felt a part of.

What response would you have offered? By this point, we hope we have made the argument sufficiently clearly that the issue is not who to put on or off the register. There is a problem with the theory which is the driver of such excluding and depersonalising practice.

This story is a graphic example of the unintended, but known collateral damage that is inherent in the prevailing theory and practice. Through this book, we are trying to say we have an educational responsibility towards that little girl and all children. Accepting those responsibilities means we have to look at the scope of our influence beyond the classroom door, the school reception hall or the boundaries drawn on the map of a local authority and realise our power to influence others as well as to be influenced by them.

Through the course of our book, we have introduced you to a notion of giftedness that arises from our educational values, and a belief that the world would be a better place if we could enhance the possibility of each person developing talents and offering the gifts they create within an appreciative community. We see these values reflecting ideals of egalitarianism, democracy, mutual respect and responsibilities. An inclusive concept of 'gifted and talented education' reflects our desire to create a humane world where the uniqueness of the individual is recognised and valued as an integral, valued and valuable member of our broader neighbourhood, with a contribution to make towards a world which is more hopeful and loving.

We have offered educational practice which is enquiry based, in which the 'given' curriculum, which communicates the knowledge and wisdom of previous generations, is made accessible to the student as they create their living curriculum. Through enquiry, the students build pictures of themselves, their emerging values, an understanding of their aptitudes, passions, motivations, how they want to contribute to the world, and what they want to devote time and energy to as adults.

As students and educators, we can build the skills, understandings and sophistication needed for a life of creating gifts and developing talents through living theory research. We recognise that we build pictures of ourselves irrespective of the pedagogy of the educator. When that image is built, it can be very difficult, but not impossible to change. The process we are advocating gives explicit attention to the picture a person is creating of herself. It is intended to enhance the sophistication individuals develop in doing that which is integral to the development of their talents and the creation of their gifts and the consequent contribution they make to the world.

We have shown how the educator's role moves from 'sage on the stage' or 'guide on the side' to one of co-enquirer with responsibilities towards students as unique individuals, gaining skills and understandings and creating, valuing and sharing knowledge about themselves and their worlds, and the enquiry which enfranchises both.

In previous chapters, we have illustrated how we might have an educational influence in our own learning and that of our students. Now our concern is with understanding the educational influence we may have in the learning of other educators and the social contexts we work in, and how we might contribute to shaping national policy and practice. In this chapter, we will explore the implications for educators in the classroom, the school and local community, and set it in the context of national policy and practice in which we want to thrive.

There are many inspiring examples of educational practice from those working at school and organisational levels which we will share. We also recognise that we work in a context where traditional thinking still predominates and traditional concepts rooted in the values of a bygone age are the prevailing power – therefore, caution is advised. We will share some experiences which might help you to get started, survive and thrive in an initially unsympathetic and sometimes hostile environment.

We wish you to keep in mind as you read towards the conclusion of this book that we believe the questions and the answers you create will be specific to you. There is no formula and responses are living, continually shaped by the intra- and interpersonal contexts, and the social structures and demands you face. Our intention has been to share our thinking, experiences and work that inspires us, in the hope that these might contribute to yours, stimulate your imagination and inspire you to create your own evolving narratives, not to dictate or impose ours on you.

We cannot overemphasise the importance of your creativity and responsiveness to your unique context in generating a school for gift creation. We have experienced at first hand the influence of educational leaders and managers who have helped to generate supportive conditions for gift creation. We have also experienced the struggles to express a generative transformational approach to giftedness when working within power relations that serve to stifle creativity. It is important to be resilient and courageous in sustaining one's integrity in the face of these power relations and to respond to the supportive conditions as quickly and energetically as possible. You may know the story of Socrates taking hemlock after being found guilty of corrupting the youth of Athens. In Plato's dialogues, he acknowledges the creative influence of his mentor Socrates in his educational conversations as well as his responses to the disciplinary power of the State in condemning his educational practices. These stories continue to inspire many. We make this point to emphasise that the passion to generate the educational relationships for the expression and development of gifts and talents has a history of over 2,500 years. In creating schools for giftedness, educational leadership that inspires and protects the creativity of teachers and pupils is necessary. The influences of individual teachers with their pupils are, for us, the most important mediating relationship between the culture of the school and support for gift creation of pupils.

Some of the most inspiring work in generating such creative spaces in the face of unsupportive government pressures and supportive educational leadership has been documented from the late 1980s to the early 1990s with teacher-researcher groups: e.g. Kevin Eames at Wootton Bassett School, and Erica Holley and Andy Larter at Greendown Schools in Wiltshire, Moira Laidlaw at Oldfield School between 1995 and 2001, Simon Riding, Mark Potts, Karen Riding and other teacher-researchers at Westwood St. Thomas School (now Salisbury High School) between 2000 and 2004, and with Simon Riding at Bitterne Park School between 2004 and 2005.

Kevin Eames has explained how the supportive conditions for the production of accounts of educational influences in learning were generated and sustained over a number of years in the aptly titled paper 'Growing Your Own' (Eames, 1990). Eames completed an MPhil research degree in 1987 and then continued to research his own practice in his doctoral enquiry (Eames, 1995a), 'How do I, as a teacher and educational action-researcher, describe and explain the nature of my professional knowledge?'

In his analysis of a language of education, Biesta (2006) focuses on the importance of responsibility in persuasive abstract conceptualisations. In his living educational theory, Eames (1995a) focuses on the lived meanings of moral responsibility within a dialogical community and embodied practice in the generation of educational knowledge:

> This thesis is an attempt to make an original contribution to educational knowledge through a study of my own professional and educational development in action-research enquiries of the kind, "How do I improve what I am doing?" The study includes analyses of my educative relationships in a classroom, educative conversations and correspondences with other teachers and academics. It also integrates the ideas of others from the wider field of knowledge and from dialectical communities of professional educators based at Bath University, Wootton Bassett School and elsewhere. The analyses I make of the resulting challenges to my thinking and practice show how educators in schools can work together, embodying a form of professional knowledge which draws on Thomism and other manifestations of dialectical rationality. Contributions to educational knowledge are made in relation to educational action research and professional knowledge. The first is concerned with the nature of professional knowledge in education, and how action research can constitute the form of professional knowledge which I see as lacking at present. The second contribution is concerned with how we represent an individual's claim to know their own educational development. These contributions contain an analysis in terms of a dialectical epistemology of professional knowledge, which includes contradiction, negation, transformation and moral responsibility within a dialogical community.

Also working at this time with pressure from the economic rationalist policies of the Thatcher government (that appeared to deny the educational values being celebrated in this book), Andy Larter and Erica Holley were researching their own practices with colleagues and pupils in the Greendown Action Research Group.

In his MPhil dissertation 'An Action Research Approach to Classroom Discussion in the Examination years', Andy submitted the first living theory account to be legitimated in a dialogical form. It highlights the importance of including educational conversations in explanations of the educational influences of educators with their pupils. Andy's thesis in which he shows his talent for generating and researching dialogical educational relationships is offered as a gift through its flow in web space: http://www.actionresearch.net/andy.shtml. This dissertation is an action research approach to understanding his attempts to improve the quality of education in his own classroom:

> Three reports provide the detailed explanations of what occurred when I attempted to put my planned interventions into operation. My concern was with a group of students in the last two years of their compulsory schooling and how they discussed and made sense of issues arising from the events in my own classroom. To this end, I have attempted to integrate the following: 1. transcripts of classroom events; 2. my reflections upon the transcripts and the events; and 3. literature from the field of oracy.
>
> The dissertation is presented in a dialogical form as part of an exploration of a logic of question and answer and generates the possibility of a different definition of generalisation. This is also an attempt to reflect the nature of the research itself – that is, discussions between students, colleagues and myself as well as internal dialogues. I have also been concerned with issues of validity which have been raised in this form of enquiry. Because of the dialogical nature of the research, the dissertation contains extracts from conversations between colleagues and myself who discussed video films, sound recordings, students' writing as well as my own writing about what I observed. Within this dialogue and reflection, I have attempted to integrate literature from the field of educational research. This integration takes the form of dialogues with the texts as well as with my own reflections. (Larter, 1987; http://www.actionresearch.net/andy.shtml)

Working in the Greendown Action Research Group with Andy Larter and other colleagues, Erica Holley explored the implications of asking, researching and answering: 'How Do I as a Teacher-Researcher Contribute to the Development of a Living Educational Theory through an Exploration of My Values in My Professional Practice?'

We urge you to access Erica Holley's dissertation. Not only because of the foci in the abstract,

> My thesis is a description and explanation of my life as a teacher and researcher in an 11 to 16 comprehensive school in Swindon from 1990 to 1996. I claim that it is a contribution to educational knowledge and educational research methodology through the understanding it shows of the form, meaning and values in my living educational theory as an individual practitioner as I researched my question,

How do I improve what I am doing in my professional practice?

With its focus on the development of the meanings of my educational values and educational knowledge in my professional practice I intend this thesis to show the integration of the educational processes of transforming myself by my own knowledge and the knowledge of others and of transforming my educational knowledge through action and reflection. I also intend the thesis to be a contribution to debates about the use of values as being living standards of judgment in educational research. (Holley, 1997; http://www.actionresearch.net/erica.shtml)

... but also because the titles and contents of the seven chapters show an individual educator's creative responses to issues and values that resonate with our own and that we believe will resonate with you:

Chapter 1. My values and where they come from.

Chapter 2. What is educational research? What is good quality educational research?

Chapter 3. How my research started and how I reformulated my initial question.

Chapter 4. I can speak for myself. My account of working with Poppy and how I struggled to come to terms with what I saw as academic accounts of teaching?

Chapter 5. "Accounting for myself" – a description of my work with a whole class and an attempt to explain what I mean by accountability.

Chapter 6. "Accounting for my work" – a description and explanation of what went on in the appraisal I did with a member of my department and how it conflicted with the monitoring role I was expected to have by the school management.

Chapter 7. "Accounting for the negative" – how the politics of oppression affected my work and how I found a creative response.

Chapter 8. How I understood that my educational knowledge was a living educational theory whose validity could be judged by living standards of judgement.

Working with Mark Potts, Karen Collins and other colleagues, with the generative support of the head teacher of Westwood St. Thomas School in Salisbury (now Salisbury High School), Simon Riding researched his own practice in supporting an in-house teacher-research group. His explanation of learning and influence is another gift freely flowing through web space:

This Action Research dissertation explores, through an autobiographical account, the influence of an in-house teacher-research group at Westwood St Thomas School in Salisbury, Wiltshire. It considers the potential impact of using a teacher-research group within a school and explores the potential benefits of the existence of such a group on a school. It considers how the writer has worked with the members of this group to explore the educational value of living through others. It accounts for the professional growth of the writer as he matures through his active interactions both dialogical and relational with other teacher-researchers. It also provides a brief account of how this group has developed and moved forward over the three years of its existence. (Riding, 2003; http://www.actionresearch.net/module/srmadis.pdf)

Mark Potts' master's dissertation 'How Can I Improve My Practice by Communicating More Effectively with Others in My Role as a Professional Educator?' like Mike Bosher's doctorate described in Chapter 2, explicitly embraces the identity of a professional educator. We are suggesting that the pioneering work of these educators, in bringing their embodied knowledge, as educators, into the public domain and in gaining accreditation for this knowledge from the academy is helping to establish the knowledge base of the profession as the knowledge of master and doctor educators – a most significant gift for the profession. Here is Mark's description of his dissertation:

> In this dissertation I seek to show my learning as an educator as I try to improve my practice and gain an understanding of how it is that I influence others. Using my own values as an educator and drawing on ideas such as presencing (Scharmer 2000) and mindfulness (Claxton 1997), I seek to understand better how I communicate with others and connect with them at a deeper level, influencing their actions. Words are not enough to express my meaning and therefore I have presented this dissertation with video clips to try to demonstrate my meaning more completely. It is written as a narrative with events recounted mostly chronologically. There is a limited amount of re-ordering. This is the narrative of my life as a teacher researcher with many different demands on my time. I have taken time, usually during school holidays, to reflect on the problem of how to be a more effective communicator allowing slow, unforced development extending over a year. This approach has allowed my deeper thoughts to surface and to guide my writing. I have so many interactions each day with my colleagues and my students that I seek here to understand how I can ensure good intuitive responses, making a lot out of a little. (Potts, 2004; http://www.jackwhitehead.com/monday/mpmadis.pdf)

Each of the educators above has contributed to the generation and sustaining of an educational space for the expression and development of talents and the generation of gifts.

HOW AMONGST THE IMPOSITIONS AND DEMANDS CAN WE RECOGNISE, CREATE AND MAINTAIN AN EDUCATIONAL SPACE?

We live in a world which is overflowing with targets, implementation strategies, performance indicators, demands for prescribing learning outcomes and defined plans of action – the list goes on. We are not saying that there is no place for goals and plans but that we recognise they are tools and servants of the educator – not the masters. How do we create the space and energy to do what we believe is right as educators without, to put it bluntly, losing our jobs or our will to live? Claire Formby (2007) described in her master's enquiry the inner turmoil that can result from recognising that her values were being denied – and a way forward that she found:

Where do I begin? "We need others physically, emotionally, intellectually: we need them if we are to know anything, even ourselves". (Lewis, 1960, p. 7) The question that stimulates this writing is as much about me as it is about the children I teach, because when I reflect on what the children will take with them when they leave my class, I will ask myself what I have done that will influence them for better after they have gone. I will not therefore be as concerned with what they have learned, rather with how they have learned and how I may have supported and encouraged that learning and that child.

Those words are easy for me to write; however the reality of living them is tough, as I consider the constraints that sometimes suppress and depress me, preventing me somehow from living my values in the classroom. At times I feel under such pressure to meet targets, deadlines and to cover the curriculum that I almost forget my relationship with the children. Yet when I am freed from or cope well with these constraints it is central once more.

What do I mean by being receptively responsive? For me, receptive responsiveness is about relationship, specifically the relationship I try to create and nurture with each child in my class but also in the relationships I have in other areas of my life. The fact that I am even able to write about receptively responsive relationships amazes me. Up until two years ago I did not spend long thinking about or reflecting on the importance of my relationships in or out of the classroom. Although I had a vague awareness of my values and how I wanted my class to "be," I did not talk about this with anyone. If I'm honest I have always doubted that people would want to listen to what I had to say. For as long as I can remember I have struggled with feelings of inadequacy and this has continued in the nine years of my teaching career. However since starting my MA course with its weekly discussion groups I have experienced receptive responsiveness first hand myself in educational conversations and have been . . ." energized by the educational processes of learning". (Whitehead, 2007a)

What I have experienced in the safe space of the Tuesday MA (university master's programme) group is a forum where it is possible for each of us to try out our developing ideas, listen to one another's responses and possibly adjust our own thinking. We support and encourage, challenge, look at the writings and work of others, sometimes disagree, often laugh and ultimately consider our educational influence in the learning of our pupils. During a recent meeting, one of the group, Louise, expressed her feeling ". . . that it was often through understanding someone else better that she came to a better understanding of herself" (Whitehead, 2007a). That thought has stayed with me, both in relation to me and also to the children in my class. As much as possible I try to recreate that safe space in my classroom where each person feels able to take part in those educational conversations because, "We feel an energizing flow of pleasure in living productive lives as we support others in enhancing their own learning as they develop their own values, skills and understandings and as we improve our own." (Whitehead, 2007a) I want each child to begin to understand themselves and one another better and develop their thinking and learning.

Claire's story, of how she creates space and energy as a class teacher in a busy classroom with SATs (Standzalised Assessment Tests) looming, is inspirational and worth reading in its entirety, but here we will just draw out a couple of points. Claire does not waste her time trying to fight what is obviously going to be a losing battle. SATs are currently a fact of life in English schools, and head teachers, parents, local authorities and government have expectations of 'results'. There has been a great deal written over the years about the penalties of high-stakes tests, but research studies, reason and rational argument have done nothing to move American or English politicians from their determination to extend the dominion of the testing industry.

Sometimes we have no choice but to do something which we find antithetical. In this case, like Claire, we try to do so by keeping in check our inclination to waste time on futile, energy-sapping moaning and argument. That is not to say that *reasoned* argument does not have a role to play in moving forward. Through making our research and narratives public, we hope to contribute to the weight of that reasoned argument by offering a living theory approach to developing inclusive concepts of gifts and talents. In doing so, we are also offering educational values as standards of judgement about the effectiveness of our practice and new forms of evidence that contribute to, rather than negate, the efforts of educators to improve the quality of the educational experience of children and young people.

Recognising and seeking to respond creatively to impositions of inappropriate theories and practice in education can open a possibility for learning something constructive. Since we recognise that we live in a world dominated by targets, gross use of improperly understood statistics and the like, how we deal with such issues can enable our students to learn something from the way we face these demands.

One example is recognising when a strategic response is needed and developing the skills and mindset which help us to survive within the system. This is more often recognised in university teaching than in school teaching, and Lublin (2003) gives a good summary on the University of Dublin web site:

> The strategic or achieving approach is that approach which students are said to take when they wish to achieve positive outcomes in terms of obtaining a pass or better in the subject. Students taking this approach:

- Intend to obtain high grades
- Organise their time and distribute their effort to greatest effect
- Ensure that the conditions and materials for studying are appropriate
- Use previous exam papers to predict questions
- Are alert to cues about marking schemes

This approach when allied to a deep approach to learning in the subject would seem likely to deliver both an intelligent engagement with the subject as well as success in the subject.

We mentioned in Chapter 3 the ideas of deep and profound learning which are gaining more prominence in work being referred to by the Department for Schools Children and Families (DCSF). We have found an idea familiar in the business world also to be useful – as described here by McBarnett (2006) in the abstract of her conference paper presented at the American Society of Criminology:

> "Creative compliance" is the practice, routinely employed by corporations, of using the letter of the law to construct devices which can be claimed as "perfectly legal" even though they totally undermine the purpose of the law. It is a means of seeking simultaneously to evade legal control and the risk of stigma and sanctions that would accompany out and out white collar crime. Attempts to control creative compliance through law can be shown empirically to have major limitations in practice.

Meier (2005), of international repute as an educator best known for founding Central Park East Elementary Schools and the Central Park East Secondary Schools in New York, describes the circumstances under which creative compliance has thrived in schools, with both positive and negative effects, and the difficulty in changing ourselves:

> The school change we need cannot be undertaken by a faculty that is not convinced and involved. Even when teachers are engaged, it's tough to change the habits of a lifetime, embedded as such habits are in the way we talk about schooling and the way our students and their families expect it to be delivered. Such a task must be the work of the participants themselves in a climate of self-governance.
>
> The kinds of change required by today's agenda can only be the work of thoughtful teachers. Either we acknowledge and create conditions based on this fact, conditions for teachers to work collectively and collaboratively and openly, or we create conditions that encourage resistance, secrecy, and sabotage. Teachers who believe in spelling tests every Friday or are "hooked on phonics" sneak them in, even when they're taboo. And so do those who want good books or fewer workbooks, regardless of school regulations. The braver and more conscientious cheat the most, but even the timid can't practice well what they don't believe in.

What she also points out is how much less effective we are when even the most timid of us are required to do what we don't believe in. But habits are tough to change and that is still the case – even when we recognise the habit as destructive. What Claire Formby offers is an example of how focusing on our educational values, searching for evidence of them being lived in our practice and finding colleagues to share our journey with, can open a space for us to create, value and offer educational gifts of our own. And in doing that, we open a space for our students. Ginott (1993), a child psychologist and educator, voices this recognition of how powerful an influence a teacher is in the way they live their values through their practice when he writes as a young teacher:

> I have come to a frightening conclusion. I am the decisive element in the class-room. It is my personal approach that creates the climate. It is my daily mood that makes the weather. As a teacher I possess tremendous power to make a child's life miserable or joyous. I can be a tool of torture or an instrument of inspiration. I can humiliate or humour, hurt or heal. In all situations, it is my response that decides whether a crisis will be escalated or de-escalated, and a child humanized or de-humanized. (p. 15)

It is not just in the direct deliberate interactions between student and educa-tor that the student learns. The student is not a passive recipient of just what the teacher intentionally communicates; everything that comprises the envi-ronment and context the student is in and part of offers opportunities to learn. As Ginott points out, the influence of educators is subtle and extends to the climate and culture they create around them in the classroom and beyond. One thing the student can learn from the educator is how to survive and thrive amongst the trials, tribulations and challenges of living in a complex world. As the educator takes responsibility for creating, recognising and opening the space for gift creation, they offer an opportunity for the student to learn from their example. As Covey (2004) points out, 'Between stimulus and response there is a space. In that space lies our freedom and power to choose our response. In those choices lies our growth and our hap-piness' (p. 43). No matter how small the space, it is there, and how we choose to respond can expand or contract the space, not just for ourselves but for our students and our colleagues. This narrative by Moira Laidlaw describes what we mean (the names have been changed):

> When I was a teacher in my first couple of years, I'm talking about 1979/80, I had a drama class, a year seven, although of course at that time, it was a first year; boys and girls, all willing and able and energetic. I wasn't drama-trained at all, but I was required to teach a single lesson a week from the English stable. This one time, I'd asked the class to rehearse a solo-slot, after working for a term on how to communicate character and so on, leading on from books we were reading in English. Anyway, a lad, John Wallace, was last up in the lesson. We were all sitting in a circle – in the round, I suppose you'd say – and he came on stage, his head bowed. He stood, no talking. The silence became a little weird. Kids didn't laugh, but looked at each other awkwardly. John rode

the silence, milked it, stretched it. He did things with time you wouldn't believe, and then, eventually, when I felt I couldn't bear it anymore, he looked up at us, turning slowly, making eye-contact with each child and with me. "I'm a clown!" he said, his mouth turned down, his voice muted and miserable. "But nobody wants a clown like me anymore. Am I funny? Am I?" He looked at us accusingly, as if we'd sacked him, or jeered at him ourselves. "You're not laughing. Why aren't you laughing? Go on, then, laugh, why don't you laugh?" Tears started pricking my eyes, This child was a sad clown. This wasn't a characterisation, this was reality. I bit my lip because I could have bloody sobbed. "Go on! Laugh!" he exhorted us. "Just laugh, why don't you? Not funny now, is it? Not bloody funny now!" And he drooped his head once more, turned once around to each one of us, eyes cast on the ground, and then made his way out of the circle. No one moved. No one clapped. No one did anything. We just stood there, mute and shamed into silence and then someone clapped, and someone cheered and then the whole room erupted in praise. John turned back to us, tears in his eyes. "All right, Miss?" he said, gulping, and I just cried and hugged him, and so did everyone else (cry, I mean). And that was the first time I got this huge emotional reaction to authenticity, this sense of awe of being in the presence of something or someone so authentic in talent and ability (and by the way, John was considered an "average" child, whatever the hell that means) that I just KNEW it was "good" in every sense of the word – goodness, ethical, meaningful, significant, healthy, potentially brilliant, worth pursuing and working for.

Moira created the space that allowed that student to be recognised and for gifts to be created and shared, not as product or performance but as a mutual process which, as humans, express the humanity which we delight in. Biesta (2006) is right; we need a language of education not simply of learning. Cho (2005) tries to extend our vocabulary when he distinguishes love in educational relationships. He says that love means the pursuit of real knowledge, knowledge that is no longer limited to particular content passed from one to the other, but rather knowledge that can only be attained by each partner seeking it in the world. To put this differently, Cho says that knowledge is by definition the enquiry we make into the world, which is a pursuit inaugurated by a loving encounter with a teacher:

> With love, education becomes an open space for thought from which emerges knowledge. If education is to be a space where teacher and student search for knowledge, then with love, both teacher and student become self-aware and recognize a space for both lovers to preserve the distinctiveness of their positions by turning away from one another and toward the world in order to produce knowledge through inquiry and thought. (pp. 94, 95).

These narratives describe for us how invitational educational spaces and relationships are created through focusing on what we believe to be educationally important and what we love about our work as educators. In describing these spaces and relationships, they also offer evidence of the difference the educator was making, judged against their living standards of judgement rooted in their educational values. The educational spaces and relationships we are talking of do not involve changing timetables but in changing ourselves. As Carl Jung said, 'Children are educated by what the grown-up is and not by his talk'.

There is a saying, 'If it is a problem it can be solved; if it can't be solved it is a fact of life and you have to learn to live with it'. However, at times, we rail against 'learning to live with it' and find a good moan cathartic, which has the advantage of also diverting attention from our own lack of agency by focusing on the constraints and frustrations offered by others. Perhaps Alfred Adler was right in his assertion that 'It is easier to fight for one's principles than to live up to them'.

At times, we also find it easier to say we can't live up to our principles because of the impositions and demands we have to live with; a lot of energy is expended on moaning, but nothing is changed. The trick is learning, where necessary, 'to live with it' in the least damaging way possible while focusing our energy on living our values as fully as possible. Claire Formby and Moira Laidlaw offer real inspiration of what can be achieved by keeping in focus what is important; in doing so, we find, and open, educational space for individuals to make a real contribution to their own lives and the lives of us all.

There is an important point we want to make about generative and transformational giftedness as a relational process. Sometimes it may be that such giftedness can appear to die in one context while thriving in another. It is important to recognise the importance of feeding life with death, rather than death with life in advocating generative and transformational giftedness. In advocating the spread of influence of generative and transformational giftedness, we are doing what we can to catch the fire of imaginations to try out ideas in their own contexts. We have seen ideas with their genesis in the work of teacher-researchers associated with the University of Bath sometimes appear to die as the contexts where they initially grew kill off the innovation. We have also seen a life-enhancing process of a relational dynamic in which ideas generated in one context are kept alive in creative transformations in other contexts. For example, ideas generated in Bath with Moira Laidlaw (1996) on action research, living theory and living standards of judgement have been creatively transformed into the generation of collaborative living educational theories in Ningxia Teachers University in China (http://www.actionresearch.net/moira.shtml; Tian & Laidlaw, 2006). Ideas generated at Wootton Bassett School have been used and transformed into the creation of a culture of enquiry in the Grand Erie District School Board in Ontario (Delong, 2002; Delong, Black, Wideman, 2005) with a passion for making a difference in professional practice (Delong, Black & Knill-Griesser, 2001–2007).

HOW DO WE KNOW WE ARE MAKING A DIFFERENCE AND COMMUNICATE THAT TO OTHERS IMBUED WITH THE TRADITIONAL SOCIAL SCIENCE PERSPECTIVES?

Although these may appear to be two separate questions, we find trying to communicate our meanings to those who are challenging them can improve the quality of our thinking. Medawar (1969), a world-leading scientist and winner of the Nobel Prize for Medicine in 1960, said, 'The critical task of science is not complete and never will be, for it is the merest truism that we do not abandon mythologies and superstitions but merely substitute new variants for old' (p. 6).

It is sometimes easier to see the mythologies and superstitions expressed in other people than in ourselves; in trying to communicate with people who are challenging our values and methods, we can sometimes see more clearly our own mistakes and improve our own internal dialogues. The value for us of seeking to improve our communication with those who do not share our perspectives is in the process of rigorously clarifying, testing and articulating our theory and practice, and in that way, we create new understandings and recognise those previously veiled.

How we go about answering the question 'How do we know we are making a difference?' rests on a number of assumptions which are often not articulated but have considerable bearing on our research and practice. Eisner (1993) believes '. . . we do research to understand. We try to understand in order to make our schools better places for both the children and the adults who share their lives there' (p. 10).

There is an interrelationship between how we understand and what we understand; an interrelationship between how we look and what we see; there are differences between how we look at our practice through the mediating lens of living theory methodology and traditional social science methodologies which will influence what we see, the sense we make of our observations, what we understand and the theories we create to account for our understandings.

Questions such as 'How do I help my students learn to live satisfying and productive lives?' are at the core of improving our practice as educators, yet are beyond the scope of most traditional research in education. You can't ask a question until you recognise there is a question to be asked and you know the nature of the answer you are seeking to create. There is a dynamic interrelationship between the question, answer and the 'terrain' that is not acknowledged in traditional research methods. Medawar (1969) describes this organic process:

> The purpose of scientific enquiry is not to compile an inventory of factual information, nor to build up a totalitarian world picture of natural Laws in which every event that is not compulsory is forbidden. We should think of it rather as a logically articulated structure of justifiable beliefs about nature. It begins as a story about a Possible World – a story which we invent and criticise and modify as we go along, so that it ends by being, as nearly as we can make it, a story about real life. (p. 59)

Living theory research approaches explicitly acknowledge that the question arises through the answer created; not in a static link but through a creative, dynamic, interactive process where the research methods, and the enquirer's values, embodied knowledge and personal theories of the world, contribute to the terrain in which the enquiry happens. Joy Mounter (2008) expresses this beautifully in her response to the poem *The Road Not Taken* by Robert Frost, which ends with

> Two roads diverged in a wood, and I—
> I took the one less travelled by,
> And that has made all the difference.

She reflects on how we each need to see our own journey from our own perspective and that we periodically need to stop and consider the journey we are on. Sometimes, she speculates, we choose a path with a desire for something new but instead find we can see clearer the truths that others have found before us. With ever-enduring curiosity, we speculate with hindsight what it might have been to have taken the other path which may have brought us different pain and pleasure, and in doing so, we enhance our perspectives of where we are and where we are going, which both challenge and change us.

We are not trying to say social science methodologies do not have their uses, for instance, when we have to decide between instructional approaches. The problem is that the strategies that are apparently most cost effective in terms of improving skilled performance can actually be at odds with what educationally we wish to achieve. For instance, children may acquire exam grades at the expense of a love of learning.

Many traditional research methods are not about asking questions; they are about determining whether an answer is right or not right. As Medawar (1969) says, 'It is a truism to say that a "good" experiment is precisely that which spares us the exertion of thinking: the better it is, the less we have to worry about its interpretation, about what it "really" means' (p. 15).

The form of question which can be explored in this sort of 'experimental design' has to be fairly simple such as 'Do children's test scores increase if they are taught in this way?' – otherwise, there is the challenge of 'too many variables'. The hypothesis is not a question but a pre-statement of an answer with the intention of showing it to be 'true' or not 'true'. The answer gives no connection with educational questions such as 'Which teaching strategies contribute to the development of a more educated person?' Yet whatever we do in our practice as educators, we should surely be connected with questions of that nature; otherwise, we run the real risk of creating practice which increases the number of people who are well schooled but poorly educated.

When asking 'How do we know if we are making an *educational* difference?' we need to recognise the limitations of methods of enquiry where the systematic and systemic relationship between questions and responses and the person, or people, asking them cannot be held together.

Let us go back a step. Questions about 'How do we know we are making a difference?' are often expressed in the form 'How do I measure the impact of "the package"?' – where 'the package' is any finite entity such as the National Primary Strategy, the national Social, Emotional Aspects of Learning (SEAL) programme, etc. – which are rooted in forms of logic that demand that you can claim to be able to 'measure' whatever it is you are looking at; that numbers can be assigned and they will not be treated just as nominal data (as labels or names), but they can be arranged and manipulated as ordinal and ratio data. Ordinal data can be put in an order of importance or size or ratio, so that the 'amount' or 'unit' between 1 and 2 is the same as between 2 and 3. 4 can therefore be said to be twice 2. This is easily understood as making no sense when you go back to the educational concepts that we are interested in exploring. It makes no sense to say this child reads twice as well today as he did yesterday; this person is three times more emotionally literate as that person; this child's talents are double another's; the mathematical gift that Einstein offered the world was five times more valuable than the gift of love that Nelson Mandela created and offered from his years of imprisonment – such statements are manifestly silly.

We are not saying that numbers are not useful and we accept that sometimes we want to be able to use statistics. But we are saying that the dominating methods in education value number in a way that is often destructive of the educational concept that is being explored. We find the word 'evidence' rather than 'measure' more often opens us to possibilities of making meaning of what we experience in our explorations of educational theory and practice.

'Measure the impact of the package' – the next assumption comes through the use of the word 'impact'. The notion of 'impact' often seems to lead to a simplistic (not simple) search for cause and effect relationships which are singular and discretely definable and identifiable. It leads to research methods with baselines, matched groups, control of variables and statistical analysis, and takes for granted that such attempts are possible and desirable. Our desire to feel we are being productive leads us to want to make such claims about how we affect others. It is ironic that such benevolent aspirations should have the unintended potential for such malevolent consequences. We may talk about the impact that a person, an idea or an experience has had on us, but we need to recognise we are misguided if we try to ascribe a unique value to a singular event.

There is also within the traditional search for 'impact' an implied power relationship; there is one right way to do something and this is it and you will do it. We believe the responsibility for anyone's life rests with the person himself/herself and he/she may not pass that responsibility over, any more than another should try to take it from him/her.

One of Ginott's (1993) main points was that he believed dependence breeds hostility, and educators should not do for a child what that child is capable of doing for him or herself. Dweck (1999) shows the possibilities that open for children to learn when they are empowered by being encouraged and allowed to take responsibility for themselves as learners. The strategies that work with Vygotsky's (1978) ideas of scaffolding a young person's learning is not a contradiction of this but an elaboration. Independent learning should not be confused with learning as a solitary activity.

'Power with' is a respectful acknowledgement of the person, irrespective of age, as being a responsible and valued part of the community. In shifting our language and practice from constructing measures of impact to looking for evidence of our educational influence in our own learning, the learning of others and communities in which we live, we explicitly acknowledge the complexity of relationships, contextualised responsibility and rights of the individual, and a mutuality of power.

The demand to 'measure impact of the package' is rooted in a form of pedagogy that considers learning as a product, something to be delivered or received, not as a process and even less as a dynamic relationship. Through this book, we have been thinking of gifts not as an entity but as a dynamic that might be expressed within a phrase such as 'gifts might be understood in their creation, offering and valuing'. In creating our living theory accounts. we write communicable stories (theories) of how we account for ourselves and the influence that we are having in our world, which enable us to improve and share our understandings and contribute to the world we want to live in. There is an explicit acknowledgement that I cannot delete myself from an account. It is curious that as educators, we desperately want to know if we are being influential, but in so much research in education, the teacher is viewed as a contaminant to be eliminated – as an undesirable 'variable' where possible.

There is no noun 'learn'; it is a verb – and people do it. A research method that purports to contribute explanations of learning must surely hold the possibilities of embracing a dynamic concept. To explore educational questions, the methods selected for research must be grounded in logic and epistemologies that allow educational answers to emerge, and judgements made about the efficacy of our practice should reflect our educational values. The purpose of evaluation is to enhance and contribute to our learning, not to justify what we have done.

To improve educational practice requires not just an intellectual shift but an emotional and personal one. In asking 'How do we know we are making a difference?' evaluative approaches have to embrace and reflect our educational values. The tools available are crude and distorting as Donmoyer (1996) points out, drawing on Lather:

> First the practical problem: Today there is as much variation among qualitative researchers as there is between qualitative and quantitatively orientated scholars. Anyone doubting this claim need only compare Miles and Huberman's (1994) relatively traditional conception of validity "The meanings emerging from the data have to be tested for their plausibility, their sturdiness, their "confirmability" – that is, their validity" (p. 11) with Lather's discussion of ironic validity:

> Contrary to dominant validity practices where the rhetorical nature of scientific claims is masked with methodological assurances, a strategy of ironic validity proliferates forms, recognizing that they are rhetorical and without foundation, postepistemic, lacking in epistemological support. The text is resituated as a representation of its "failure to represent what it points toward but can never reach. . . ." (Lather, 1994, p. 40-41) (p. 21)

How do you communicate an open mind, a creative thought, an educational relationship? How do you provide evidence that your students are behaving more intelligently, are wiser, have developed their aesthetic appreciation of the world, let alone demonstrate your influence in their learning?

To communicate to and with others requires negotiation of the meanings of language employed – and this requires more than a dictionary of words. It requires a genuine desire, intention and confidence to hold open the possibility for something new to emerge. For us to understand if we are making a difference, we need both to create a language of education and to explore different forms of communication which can get closer to the subtle, dynamic and interrelational qualities of the standards of judgement that we are using. We believe the extracts from the narratives of Claire Formby and Moira Laidlaw you have read enable us to understand what values these educators were living through their practice, the difference they wanted to make, and provide evidence of the difference they were making. Master's accounts accepted by the University of Bath demonstrate that this form of evidence communicates effectively – and is gaining acceptance amongst the bastions of the social science orthodoxies.

HOW CAN WE IMPROVE OUR EDUCATIONAL INFLUENCE IN THE LEARNING OF OUR COLLEAGUES AND THE LEARNING OF OUR SCHOOL AND OTHER COMMUNITIES?

Before we offer a response to our question concerning how we might improve our educational influence in the learning of others, we want to return to why we want to do this.

We recognise that how we are in the world has an influence on other people – whether we realise it or not. We hope you are persuaded by the argument we offered in the previous Section that how we are and how we deal with life's challenges, not just how we behave as instructors, has an educational influence in the learning of our students. Our educational influence is not bounded by the category we might ascribe people to. We cannot help but continually learn, regardless of age, position or inclination. We may not do so explicitly or with a particular focus as we do as students, and we may often feel as though we are going round in circles, but nonetheless, we learn. Our learning is influenced by our own internal dialogues and by the world and communities we inhabit and are part of.

A common mistake is to assume if you do not communicate 'content', or you do not intentionally share your learning, that you are not having an influence on anyone except yourself or your students. Think about teachers you know who tell you nothing of their practice, never stroll beyond their classroom door, don't go to development and training events; how does that apparent 'non-action' communicate and influence the culture within which we live and learn?

We see the offering by educators of the accounts they create through researching to improve their practice and their appreciative openness to the gifts of others as acts of generosity; we believe that we have a responsibility without obligation to be as generous. One of the key features implicit in traditional thinking concerning 'gifted and talented education' is the valuing recognition of the uniqueness of the contribution a person can make to a community which identifies them as individuals worthy of recognition. But only a few people are singled out for appreciation. As Fukuyama (1992) so eloquently said, 'Human beings seek recognition of their own worth, or of the people, things, or principles that they invest with worth. The desire for recognition, and the accompanying emotions of anger, shame and pride, are parts of the human personality critical to political life' (p. xvii).

In developing a living theory approach to developing inclusive gifted and talented educational theories and practice, we want to emphasise the importance of 'recognition' of the uniqueness of each person as capable of creating valued and valuable gifts. Some gifts noticeably influence those in our local communities; some extend to national or international communities, and some transcend time. Irrespective of the extent of their communication or visibility, all contribute to the world in which we live. If you think you have nothing to offer your colleagues, school or the wider learning community, perhaps this very well-known piece, based on a passage by Marianne Williamson, and sometimes wrongly attributed to Nelson Mandela (who used it in his presidential inaugural address), might help you think again:

> Our deepest fear is not that we are inadequate. Our deepest fear is that we are powerful beyond measure. It is our light, not our darkness, that most frightens us. We ask ourselves, – who am I to be brilliant, gorgeous, talented, fabulous? Actually, who are you not to be? Your playing small doesn't serve the world. There's nothing enlightened about shrinking so that other people won't feel insecure around you. We are all meant to shine, as children do … It's not just in some of us; it's in everyone. And as we let our own light shine, we subconsciously give other people permission to do the same. As we're liberated from our own fear, our presence automatically liberates others. (a non-theistic interpretation of Marianne Williamson, *A Return To Love*, 1992)

Our living theories are in effect the stories we develop to account for our lives and the way we believe the world works. Their creation and sharing not only improves the influence we have in our own learning, but also has an influence in the learning of those with whom we share them. Winslade (2007) articulates this position well when describing the construction of a career narrative.

> Just what kind of project a career is depends on how we think about it. If we entertain a narrative conception of this project, then we might develop not just an actual career, but an account of a career, a sustaining and guiding narrative to which we can refer in moments of confusion and contradiction. The assumption here is that the representation of an event or object, the story of it, plays a role in creation. Stories should not be dismissed as either neutral mirrors or biased perspectives. Narratives play a part in producing a reality. Stories affect people's lives. They are not just reports of life. Hence, in counselling we can work directly with the narrative in order to have an effect on the way a story is lived out. The task of career counselling then becomes one of eliciting a person's narrative of meaningful action in the world. (p. 53)

Like Winslade, we view our research accounts as narratives of our meaningful action in the world and in the construction of an account that communicates to others we extend our research; our accounts can be seen as transition structures in the process of transformation. Tolstoy is reputed to have said:

> I know that most men, including those at ease with problems of the greatest complexity, can seldom accept the simplest and most obvious truth if it be such as would oblige them to admit the falsity of conclusions which they have proudly taught to others, and which they have woven, thread by thread, into the fabrics of their life.

We know we will never convince some people of the rightness of approaches or concepts rooted in a very different logic and epistemology to the traditional, and we have no interest in their approbation or abuse. So, while we value well-intentioned criticism and are interested in responding constructively to critiques which help us find ways to do things better, we see no need to continue responding beyond this point to those who wish merely to be destructive.

We realise, like many, that not everyone (ourselves included) is open at any predetermined moment in time to new learning; we don't expect this to be the case, or to judge ourselves or them accordingly. We have found that trying to understand the various reasons for this reluctance, and even at times aggressive resistance, is helpful both in understanding ourselves and enabling us to respond more appropriately to those who seem to be determined to eliminate new ways of knowing and thinking.

Some of these reasons may be a function of an education system obsessed with norm-referenced comparisons and external judgements of worth, as a consequence of which many people stopped learning a long time ago, and content themselves instead with endlessly cataloguing their achievements and 'perfect practice', and criticising the 'inadequacies' of others. 'Evaluation' becomes a repeated search for justification of practice and confirmation of a universal rightness which confers acceptance on adherents. White (2006) offers some interesting thoughts about the still influential origins of concepts of intelligence, and the school curriculum, as expressed in England and America. He proposes these have been linked at the level of policy for centuries and contests: 'However influential the two core notions have been, if you look for sound supporting arguments behind them, you will be disappointed. There are no solid grounds for innate differences in IQ; and there are none for the traditional subject-based curriculum' (p. 1).

White provides evidence to support his assertion that the two ideas have common origins which can be traced back to the radical forms of Protestantism in the 16th century and more recently to the men with the same cultural roots and affiliations who are responsible for the current notions of intelligence and our present school system. How far have those same religious notions of unquestionable 'perfection' influenced academic thinking in the disciplines?

In our society, it is not usual to openly admit, as Sternberg (2007) does, to error or uncertainty or that growth can occur when we are at our most open and vulnerable: 'Everything I have ever done in my professional life has been the result of a failure, usually my own. I've spent my life trying to turn lemons into lemonade, starting from my early years. . . . In sum, I have found my own failures and those of others to be some of the most useful sources of ideas. I can only hope that I find a few more failures in my life, so that I can try to turn those lemons, too, into lemonade' (pp. 210–212).

To maintain a mindset that is open to seizing times of apparent failure or struggle as opportunities to learn, as Dweck (2000) describes, determination is needed. Opposition can come when individuals with a 'fixed mindset' feel that they are faced with recognising their own mistakes, and the perceived challenges to their theory of self may be resisted with increasing vehemence.

What responses do you make when you ask yourself why examples of 'outstanding practice' translated into frames of reference which are not based on values – e.g. GCSE (school exams) data – are continually being compiled? Is approval or compliments for aspects of your own work that you do not value of worth to you? We doubt it. In the end, your own evaluative responses, recognition and valuing of your contribution and continuing journeying are what contributes to your feelings of fulfilment and of being at peace with yourself. It is that which is affirmed when another expresses the pleasure of sharing in a gift of worth that you value and have crafted and offered. The other road, Dweck and others have found, is one of increasing disappointment, bitterness, resentment, anger and depression, and a need to pull others down in order to feel worthy oneself. Growth occurs in working with those who have the courage and mindset required to make themselves open to attacks, and through future-oriented self-criticism and remaining open to others' well-meant critiques.

We have offered some theories of why it may at times be difficult to change our own behaviour and to communicate with those imbued with the traditional perspectives; you will have your own theories.

Why have we spent time on thinking about blocks to thinking and learning? As we have pointed out, to ask whether we are making a difference has the possible answer 'not a lot'. As educators, with a burning desire to make a difference to the lives of others, to recognise when we are actually contradicting and negating the very values that are at the foundation of our being presents emotional challenges. If we are not prepared to face an answer we do not like, then we cannot learn; forewarned is forearmed.

HOW MIGHT WE CONTRIBUTE TO SHAPING EDUCATIONAL POLICY AND PRACTICE?

In stressing the importance of developing ourselves as creators and co-creators of knowledge, we want to integrate insights from the most significant policy initiatives of the day. Through supporting teacher-researchers in improving the educational opportunities and experiences of their pupils, we believe that we will be contributing to enabling schools to respond productively to the expectations of the DCSF and OFSTED while improving the quality of their gifted and talented educational provision. Ros Hurford (2007) offers us an inspiring example of this in her accredited master's enquiry as she offers as a gift her journey in creating answers to her question, 'How Does the Writing of a New Gifted and Talented Policy Enable Me to Reflect upon and Evaluate My Personal Values about Gifts and Talents? In What Ways Am I Living My Values in This Area?'

> Those of us there at the beginning of the changes (1997) will remember the enthusiasm of the then head teacher who insisted the whole staff attended an after school meeting on Bloom's Taxonomy. We came away with a higher awareness of learning, instead of the gardening expertise we had anticipated!
>
> But maybe that isn't such a bad description of what takes place as your knowledge increases. Just like plants, our change in attitude has been gradual and constantly growing, nurtured by new courses on Thinking Skills and generating "giftedness." It is one of those situations where one day you suddenly wonder why you ever thought anything else – and yet the changes have come through small steps of staff development and their implementation in the classroom to enhance the learning of each child. Whether we are "old" staff or "new" staff, in our professional conversations we all seem to share the same values that each child has the potential to become gifted and talented.

Ros illustrates well how making a contribution to shaping policy and practice requires commitment, determination, a willingness to learn and a courage to share knowledge created. This particular reflection by Ros also illustrates the difficulty we each have in recognising the extent of our influence. The head teacher that Ros mentions, Kate St John, died a number of years ago. It is only now, through Ros's recognition, that you can see evidence of the enduring influence of Kate St John's enthusiasm, courage and faith in her staff as educators who shared her values and ability to learn.

Through the generation of our living theories, we can show and explain how we are providing opportunities to develop our collective wisdom in terms of approaches to improving the quality of gifted and talented education for all. As we engage in policy formation, implementation and evaluation, we can develop our responses to shaping educational policy collaboratively in the belief that this is the most powerful and effective way of engagement in real learning taking place.

To defy or attempt to beat 'power', you run the real risk of being removed from the field; for instance, you can be sacked. This is one approach but not one that is often successful in bringing about change. Another is to appreciate some of the forces which can be mobilised to suppress dissenting voices or those trying to tell an *alternative story* (White & Epston, 1990) to that which currently remains in the ascendant.

In July 2006, following the appearance of an article Barry had written for an educational journal questioning national policy in gifted education (Hymer, 2005), he received a private email from a highly respected academic with considerable expertise in the field of gifted education: '. . . I am so pleased that you have raised this debate . . . It has been a field with such little real debate and I am really grateful that you have begun something that will hopefully rattle all our cages'. He replied thanking her for her kind words and intellectually open attitude, but doubting that he'd succeed in raising a debate. We know personally of one internationally renowned academic who was disinvited from giving a keynote presentation at a National Academy for Gifted and Talented Yorth (NAGTY) conference, on the strength it seems of a too-discomforting paper published in a journal for school 'G&T coordinators'. Should we really prefer easy answers to awkward questions – especially in a field like giftedness? The awkward question is directed at the underpinning of the edifice, not the edifice per se, but even so, some care needs to be paid as to time and place if the questioner is to survive to ask another day.

Another approach to responding to the impositions of power is to connect with the energy of the values behind the policies and strategies and find those which resonate for you and with those wielding 'power', and to use some of the practices they advocate to advantage. For example, we can sometimes work with the educational visions expressed by leaders of the day, such as Gordon Brown (the current British Prime Minister) who expressed a belief that world-class performance comes from consistent brilliance from teachers in every classroom, professionals who seek continuous improvement, who teach better lessons tomorrow than they did yesterday because they are learning all the time.

We can explore the implications of the belief expressed in the personalising learning strategy and the study support framework, that schools should be helping children become more aspirational: educators should be shaping education around the unique needs and aspirations of the child, and we engage pupils in their own learning, giving them a thirst for education and knowledge that will stay with them long after they have left school.

> Personalised learning is not something that can be "done" by teachers to pupils. Rather it arises when pupils themselves take charge of their own goals and progress, together with a heightened awareness of their own learning styles and preferences. When young people enjoy a range of opportunities to test themselves, to explore their talents and cultivate new interests, they come to a deeper appreciation of how learning works, what can inhibit it and in what ways it can nourish self belief. When there are rich extended sites for learning, young people grasp that the purpose of school is not to provide an education

but to stimulate a thirst for learning, and to give it life beyond the school gate. (MacBeath, 2006, p. 12)

This applies to adults as well as to children and young people; learning is something that cannot be done to another, and it is when people are empowered to take charge of their own goals, to test themselves, to explore their talents and the educational gifts they can offer, and feel valued that they can recognise the difference they can make to shaping policy.

In relation to the Department for Children, Schools and Families, we can make central to the role of the teacher leading in improving their school's gifted and talented education the notions of networking, collaborative learning and supported professional development, together with that of progressive improvement linked to self-evaluation.

We see the value of visual narratives in communicating our meanings, especially in terms of the value-laden expression of talents and gifts. We also recognise the limitations of words on pages of text to communicate some of these meanings. This is why we are supporting this text with video resources. Technology is becoming increasingly accepted and video narratives particularly offer an opportunity to communicate qualities of the educational experience which are lost in the traditional academic prose of research accounts as this extract from the doctoral thesis of Eden Charles (2007) illustrates:

> The video clip above marks a defining moment for me in the life of the Sankofa Learning Centre. As I questioned the value of what I had been engaged in over the years I watched this video again. I was struck by a sense of achievement. Here, in living form, embodied by others was evidence of the positive influence that the centre had been. The young man speaking is embraced in the gaze of the adults and I see an appreciative and affirmative quality in that gaze. He has come to show his support at this meeting not because he feels obligated but because he desires to be part of a meeting that could determine the future of the centre. I see people of all different ages and genders, and celebrate this intergenerational connection, quality and warmth of interaction evidenced here. I see a welcoming enjoyment in his presence and feel that this evidences a living Ubuntu together. We are each because of the other. Through watching video clips like this I discover evidence of the educative influence I have been in my role of helping create, maintain and determine the educational direction of the centre. (Section 5, p. 1)

AND IN CONCLUSION

The purpose of offering a living theory approach to developing the talents of all of our students for creating, valuing and sharing their gifts is an expression of the values we wish to see lived more fully in education. Our theories and practice reflect our ideals of egalitarianism, democracy, emancipation, mutual respect and the hope of contributing to a more harmonious world. What we do in our lives, how we live, how we talk to others and treat others, every action, every decision, every pronouncement of reality – all these are descriptions of our values and describe our humanity. If your last thought is – 'well that sounds very worthy but I am faced with 32 demanding children and . . .' we hope this book has stimulated your imagination as to a few possibilities you might wish to experiment with to recognise, value and share more of the gifts created amongst the pressures you face daily. This letter, in the epilogue of Haim Ginott's *Teacher and Child* (1993), is from a school principal sent to teachers at the beginning of each new school year. It communicates graphically the significant influence and responsibility of educators and the importance of explicating the value base of educational theory and practice:

> Dear Teacher,
>
> I am a survivor of a concentration camp. My eyes saw what no man should witness:
>
> Gas chambers built by *learned* engineers.
>
> Children poisoned by *educated* physicians.
>
> Infants killed by *trained* nurses.
>
> Women and babies shot and burned by *high school* and *college* graduates.
>
> So, I am suspicious of education.
>
> My request is: Help your students become human. Your efforts must never produce learned monsters, skilled psychopaths, educated Eichmanns.
>
> Reading, writing and arithmetic are important only if they serve to make our children more humane. (p. 317)

As educators, we are privileged to have such a possibility for influencing for the good, and we would like to conclude this book with the joy and optimism of an inspirational educator, Belle Wallace. We hope that her story of the educational gift, Thinking Actively in a Social Context (TASC), which she has dedicated a large part of her life to creating and offering, communicates a pleasure of a lifelong commitment to education supporting all children, young people and adults to develop their talents and to create, value, and freely offer their gifts.

A Story of Love, Joy and Success – a Pedagogy of Hope
Belle Wallace

This is an edited extract from *A Tribute to Paulo Freire*. 2008 (working title) (with permission)

This personal narrative looks reflectively at the development of my life as an educator, analysing how I, together with my students, have tried to develop a process of learning and teaching that is both liberating and developmental. My journey has been an international one, but this particular reflection highlights the development of a Project called TASC: Thinking Actively in a Social Context. The Project was initially developed in KwaZulu/Natal, (literally meaning "the place of the Zulus"), an enforced "homeland" under apartheid rule in South Africa. The case study highlights the resilience and determination of a group of students who were determined to overcome the denial and repression of opportunities for Black students. It is a story of love, joy and success – a pedagogy of hope.

"We are sentient, dynamic beings capable of change: but we can be trapped not only in the learned sense of what we are not, but also in a powerful negative mirror image of ourselves that we perceive emanating from others. Yet, we can be released through enabling interactions with those special mentors who offer constant and strong scaffolding that each of us has great worth and significance as individuals with multiple and diverse potential." (Wallace, 2006, p. 9)

I have reflected for some time about the influences that have infused my professional and personal life; and I decided to share with you as honestly and as clearly as I can those influences that have impacted on the decisions and consequent actions I have taken over the last 40 years as a school teacher, university lecturer, researcher and national and international education consultant. This personal narrative is outspokenly direct and linked to real life learning. I have tried to follow in Paulo Freire's footsteps of being open and grounded in the process of linking action and reflection (Freire, 1998a, 1998b). Quite intuitively, I was working within the paradigm of Living Theory in that everything I have learned primarily began with open interaction with learners and their teachers.

When my career first began in education, although I was not aware of Freire's Philosophy, nor of Living Theory, I was deeply concerned with the ethics of ensuring equality of opportunity for all learners. I was intuitively aware that learners needed to feel motivated and enthused by the topics they were investigating. I was equally aware that I needed to build rapport and trust that learners need in order to risk the sharing of their ideas and questions. This seemed to me to be the basic requisites for communication and understanding. How can young people learn if they do not feel emotionally and cognitively engaged, and if they are not highly valued and praised?

As a naïve, inexperienced, but enthusiastic young educator, my first encounter with the philosophy of Paulo Freire crystallized for me what was, until then, only half formulated in my mind, and clarified what I was trying to achieve, broadly:

- The development of learners' ownership of their learning through the negotiation of relevant problems to be solved in relation to real life understanding;
- The development of dialogue and interaction in the learning/teaching dynamic with reciprocity and equality of teachers and learners as jointly negotiating and constructing meaning;
- The development of learners' self-confidence and independence in decision-making and actions leading to their self-actualisation;
- The mutual respect derived from active listening and talking (Freire, 1998a; Freire, 1998b; Fraser, 1997; McLaren, 1993, 1998; Apple & King, 1977; Ramos, 1974).

Although my personal life path has led me to work in many countries for short periods of time, I spent an intensive and extensive period in KwaZulu/Natal (South Africa), and my narrative will trace this particular journey. In writing about South Africa, however, I have both philosophical and emotional reservations in referring to any country as either a "third" or "developing" world, or a "first" or "developed" world: so I will use the terms SA and KwaZulu, (later called KwaZulu/Natal). In addition, I acknowledge that this is a personal narrative, shared with you from my own perspectives and system of values. I hope, however, that I can provide a rich case-study based on real life experiences milled and refined both cognitively and emotionally through many processes of analysis and reflection, as an individual engaged in quiet contemplation: and also as an interactive member of the communities I have worked with in partnership, joy and love. Walking in Paolo Freire's shoes, and seeing with his understanding, I have tried:

- to share in the humanity and reality of the community as an equal member of the group, sometimes a mentor, always a learner, but never, I hope, the benevolent imposer of "liberation" on the "oppressed";
- to allow the students the ownership of the creation of their own concepts of freedom, autonomy and possible life journeys;
- to develop students' awareness of their own powers of reflective participation in their affairs (Freire, 1998a, 1998b; Ramos, 1974).

It is necessary, at this stage, to share with you just a little of my early background so that you can understand the lens through which I learned to view the world as a child and young adult. This early world view has obviously impacted on my adult perception of how I view education principles and practice; endeavouring to influence both by emphasising the indivisible nature of emotion and cognition; the interdependence and reciprocity of teaching and learning; the essential need for relevance and real life experiential learning, and the vital importance of motivation and understanding.

I grew up in an impoverished district in South Wales (UK) in a large family familiar with hunger and poverty, always short of money for even basic necessities: and I won a free scholarship to the town's grammar school[1] at eleven years of age. Thrust into a "middle-class" professional, articulate milieu, I was one of a minority of learners submerged in "the culture of silence"; I had no voice in the social milieu of the daughters of doctors, teachers, lawyers and the like. I had neither personal identity nor social significance within their conversations and life-styles.

My education fell neatly and very aptly within the framework of the Freire's "banking" concept, it was a series of acts of, "depositing, in which the students are the depositories and the teacher is the depositor. Instead of communicating, the teacher issues communiqués and makes deposits which the students patiently receive, memorise and repeat" (Freire, 1998b, p72). I was a disengaged observer of happenings and incidents that had no relation to my own life; I was not a participant in an interactive learning-teaching process, I was an object to be processed in the ritualistic practice of listening and memorising towards levels of "academic" achievement. I was denied access to any form of enquiring, questioning, or real life experiential learning, and was disabled "from learning rather than enabled to learn" (McLaren, 1993).

I survived due to the influence of a singular and wonderful teacher who recognised that I had a talent for writing – with her I received the acknowledgement that I had personal worth, that I was an emotional and thinking being, alive and searching for meaning, albeit to often ill-formulated questions. I experienced the glow of excitement that comes from the reciprocal respect derived from active listening and talking: she was in every sense a mentor, the barrier between teacher and learner invisible; the relationship one of loving respect and smiling

---

[1] The scholarship to a grammar school was the result of an intelligence test administered at the age of 11+ years. This meant that the "top" 10 to 15 percent of children went to a special school supposedly for academic high fliers.

understanding. It is to this living learning experience that I attribute the formulation of the direction that my life has broadly followed – to understand and to promote the dynamic processes that bring life, reality and vitality to any learning-teaching interaction (Fraser, 1997, Freire, 1997).

The impact of South Africa on my life and educational vision has been paramount in formulating and refining my personal life path, my aims for education and my practice. Finding myself in a totally different cultural context from that of the UK, the impact of KwaZulu/Natal (SA) was raw, stark and overwhelming: brilliantly vibrant and colourful, socially, emotionally and politically complex and convoluted; a mixture of resilience and submission; a kaleidoscope of despair and hope; and profoundly challenging in its need for change.

This personal life change was almost accidental in that it was not planned, but evolved in response to an overwhelming sense of the need to work with the nation of Zulu people who were excluded within their own country and forcibly segregated in an impoverished, infertile mountainous area euphemistically called their "homeland". So an intended stay of one year's Sabbatical leave became fifteen years of personal commitment from 1984 to 1998: these fifteen years witnessing the crumbling of the apartheid regime. The beginning of this period was characterised by an intense civil war in KwaZulu/Natal, the contest involving members within the system of government of the traditional Zulu king and tribal chiefs; the rising African National Congress (ANC), and the South African National Government; culminating in the release of Nelson Mandela in 1990. The latter part of this time was characterised by a turmoil of instability and change brought about by the new fledgling government, the Government of National Unity, as it endeavoured to establish a new social system: the struggle fraught with considerable contention for political and financial power, and a populace desperate for rapid change and anticipated benefit.

The 15 years I lived and worked in KwaZulu/Natal taught me a great deal about joy and laughter despite crippling disadvantage; about love, friendship and sharing although there were few resources to share; about resilience and determination to succeed, surmounting all obstacles; about the rich quality of communication and striving towards a common goal.

However, I would not like to end my personal narrative without adding a postscript. Since returning to England and working as a consultant in schools nationally from 1999, I have witnessed the mechanisation of the teaching and learning processes in schools, and also in other areas of public life, brought about by the insistence of the government on "measurable" achievement targets and "universal" standards. I am certainly not against learners and teachers striving to reach goals; but not every learning goal can be quantified and measured, organised statistically and then compared and contrasted in what has come to be labelled "the shame and blame culture". Teachers generally are reporting that they are treated as mechanical technicians delivering set content, rather than as educators interacting with learners. They report that increasing numbers of pupils are de-motivated and anti-school.

My lived experience has taught me very powerfully that learners and teachers need to have ownership of their learning and teaching interactions. These interactions should be dynamic, negotiable, and relevant to life. Learning is a personal journey for everyone, and every learner needs to feel involved, significant and valued as an individual of worth and potential.

HOW HAVE I IMPROVED MY WAY TO PROFESSIONALISM IN EDUCATION? 1967–2007

Jack Whitehead, Department of Education, University of Bath.

A paper to celebrate the 2007 graduations and knowledge-creation of Barry Hymer from Newcastle University, Eden Charles from the University of Bath and Margaret Follows from the University of Plymouth as a gift of ideas about educational theory from 40 years professional engagement in education.

A gift for the Department of Education of Newcastle University on the 13 July 2007 in memory of the creative educational space offered to this student of education in 1966/7.

Forty years ago, in July 1967, I was a student here in the Department of Education of Newcastle University. I had enjoyed myself writing a special study on 'The Way To Professionalism in Education?' The study included insights from my readings during the year and included the works of John Dewey, Erich Fromm, Richard Peters and Anna Freud. I look back on the study with both pleasure and embarrassment. There is the embarrassment of seeing the naivety of the writing with its belief that producing a good idea about enhancing professionalism in education was sufficient to move a social order in the desired direction. If only the world were that simple! Then there is the pleasure of feeling my original passion for education and my initial engagement with ideas that have continued to influence my life in education and I hope that you feel in my contribution today.

Returning to the Department of Education in July 2007, some 40 years later, is the catalyst for these reflections on the growth of my educational knowledge about enhancing professionalism in education. The stimulus to return was Barry Hymer's graduation later today for his Doctor of Educational

Gifts, Talents and Education By Barry Hymer, Jack Whitehead and Marie Huxtable
© 2008 Wiley-Blackwell

Psychology Thesis on, 'How do I understand and communicate my values and beliefs in my work as an educator in the field of giftedness?' (Hymer 2007a). Barry's research programme was successfully completed with the supervision of Liz Todd and I know something of the delight in seeing doctoral researchers graduating after years of supervision. Two weeks ago I felt this pleasure myself in celebrating with Eden Charles his graduation from the University of Bath, for his doctoral thesis on 'How can I bring Ubuntu as a living standard of judgment into the Academy? Moving beyond decolonisation through societal reidentification and guiltless recognition' (Charles, 2007). Also today, at the graduation ceremony of the University of Plymouth, Margaret Follows is celebrating her doctoral success for her thesis on 'Looking for a fairer assessment of children's learning, development and attainment in the infant years: an educational action research case study' (Follows, 2007).

Looking at the titles of these three doctoral theses gives an indication of the uniqueness and originality of these contributions to educational knowledge. What they also have in common is that they have researched the embodied knowledge in their professional lives and gained academic legitimacy for their stories of their educational influence in their own learning and in the learning of others. They have affirmed the value for their research of the idea of creating their own living educational theories. This is the idea that individuals can create their own living theories as explanations for their educational influences in their own learning and in the learning of others as they ask, research and answer questions of the kind, 'How do I improve what I am doing?' (Whitehead 1989a, 2006). I identify the affirmation I feel, when other individuals recognise the value and affirm the use of ideas that have emerged from my educational research, with what Marx said about producing something as a human being:

> Suppose we had produced things as human beings: in his production each of us would have twice affirmed himself and the other.
>
> In my production I would have objectified my individuality and its particularity, and in the course of the activity I would have enjoyed an individual life, in viewing the object I would have experienced the individual joy of knowing my personality as an objective, sensuously perceptible, and indubitable power.
>
> In your satisfaction and your use of my product I would have had the direct and conscious satisfaction that my work satisfied a human need, that it objectified human nature, and that it created an object appropriate to the need of another human being.
>
> I would have been the mediator between you and the species and you would have experienced me as a redintegration of your own nature and a necessary part of yourself; I would have been affirmed in your thought as well as your love.

In my individual life I would have directly created your life, in my individual activity I would have immediately confirmed and realized my true human nature. (Bernstein, 1971)

What I have gained from Barry's thesis is the idea of an inclusional approach to gifts and talents in education. I particularly like his idea of the creation of gifts and talents to counteract the prevailing emphasis on identification. Barry's focus on the emergence of the meanings of his ontological values as living standards of judgment through his self-study, and the originality of his idea of gift and talent creation can be appreciated in the Abstract to his thesis:

> I articulate in narrative form the meanings of my embodied ontological values through their emergence in my practice – specifically in my practice of philosophy with children, in creating webs of meaning through dilemma-based learning, and in seeking to unmask (Foucault, in Rabinow, 1984) the concept of giftedness – by asking whose interests the concept serves. In the process of living, clarifying and communicating the meanings of these practices are formed, I argue, living epistemological standards of judgment for a new, relationally dynamic epistemology of educational enquiry. . . . I make a claim to originality in scholarship in articulating the emergence of the value-laden concept of generative-transformational giftedness and its latent fecundity in and relevance to the field of gifted and talented education. To this end, I suggest an inclusional, non-dualistic alternative to the identification or discovery of an individual's gifts and talents by arguing that activity- and development-centred (not knowing-centred) learning-leading-development (Vygotsky, ibid.) environments lead not to the identification of gifts and talents but to their creation. (Hymer, 2007a)

Inspired by Barry's idea of gift creation I set to work on this paper with the idea of producing a gift of ideas about educational theory for the Department of Education of Newcastle University to celebrate both Barry's accomplishment and the creative space offered to me by the Department in my Dip.Ed. Year as I began my lifetime's vocation in education.

Researching with a different question, Eden Charles also focuses attention in his Abstract on inclusional qualities in the African way of being, enquiring and knowing of Ubuntu:

> This is a living theory thesis which traces my engagement in seeking answers to my question that focuses on how I can improve my practice as someone seeking to make a transformational contribution to the position of people of African origin. In the course of my enquiry I have recognised and embraced Ubuntu, as part of an African cosmology, both as my living practice and as a living standard of judgment for this thesis. It is through my Ubuntu way of being, enquiring and knowing that my original contribution to knowledge has emerged. (Charles, 2007)

The examiner's commented:

> We found the thesis to be an important, discerning and highly original piece of work, containing much publishable material about the new approaches necessary to address and alleviate oppressive practices of all kinds, especially those associated with colonialism and post-colonialism. Two key approaches are identified and described in depth: 'guiltless recognition' and 'societal re-identification'. These emerge from a perception of selfhood that is distinct within but not isolated from natural neighbourhood. The relationship between this perception, the African cosmology of Ubuntu and the recently described philosophical awareness of 'inclusionality' is brought out in a clear, insightful and well-rounded way, through the artful use of personal narrative. (Email of 18 June 2007 from Director of Studies with congratulations on Eden's success.)

Inspired by Eden's Ubuntu way of being and his ideas on 'guiltless recognition' and 'societal reidentification', I am seeking to produce an inclusional communication informed by an Ubuntu way of being that stresses the importance of recognising 'I am because we are'.

In the Abstract to her thesis Margaret Follows explains that:

> This thesis tells the story of an infant head teacher researcher's journey into the heart of a living educational assessment landscape. She embarks on this journey to search for a fairer assessment of young children's learning, development and attainment. It is a journey that forces her to question everything about the professional world in which she works and lives . . . The research offers an original contribution to educational knowledge in that it clarifies meanings of the researcher's ontological value of a fairer assessment of children's learning, development and attainment and transforms that value into a living epistemological standard of critical judgement.

So, my intention today is to celebrate Barry Hymer's, Eden Charles' and Margaret Follows' accomplishments by offering this paper in the spirit of Barry's gift creation, Eden's Ubuntu way of being and knowledge-creation and Margaret's commitment to fairer assessment. In producing the gift I can see that it also offers me the opportunity of accounting for what I have been doing to live a productive life in education since leaving Newcastle those 40 years ago!

The gift is created with talents that had their genesis in the Library of the Department of Education here in Newcastle. I am thinking of the talents I bring to my work as an educational researcher who is generating living educational theories with an understanding of an action research approach to clarifying the meanings of ontological values, living logics and living standards of judgment in claims to educational knowledge. I am thinking of the expression of these talents in the living theory research programmes with their completed theses at http://people.bath.ac.uk/edsajw/living.shtml.

Each thesis has been given as a gift by the researcher to flow freely through web-space and accessible to all with the appropriate technology. From each researcher I have learnt much from the expression of their original contributions and critical judgment.

I am showing you these living theories to emphasise the importance of our collective contributions to educational knowledge and to stress the importance of amplifying the influence of each others' good ideas in our own work. In the collection of living theories flowing through web-space, each individual's contribution can be recognised and affirmed within the flow of their collective contribution.

These living theories are still being informed by the ideas I first encountered in the Library of the Department of Education of Newcastle University during 1966/7. The Department of Education provided me with a creative space in which to read, think and write. The Department also provided me with my first encounter with video-technology. I can still see the new equipment in 1966 with cameras and recorders an individual could hardly carry, with wires running everywhere that nobody had a clue how to use! We had a great deal of enjoyment learning how to use it in what was a new building with the most advanced technology of the day. This pleasure in exploring the educational potential of advances in technology is still with me as I hope to show in the development of visual narratives of educational influences in learning with the most advanced technology of today.

What I want to do is to draw your attention to, and captivate your imaginations with, the evolution of thinking about the nature of educational theory since leaving Newcastle for the past 40 years of professional engagement in education. I know that I might be mistaken in believing that enhancing professionalism in education is dependent on the quality of the professional knowledge-base of education. I might also be mistaken, in believing that the quality of this knowledge-base is dependent on the validity of the educational theories that can explain the educational influences of individuals in their own learning, in the learning of others and in the learning of the social formations in which we live and work. However, until I am shown to be mistaken, I intend to hold these beliefs with a passion that flows with a life-affirming energy.

As you reflect on our conversation today I hope that you find something of significance for your own educational research in the creation and legitimation of living educational theories in the University.

I am thinking in particular of the significance of focusing on including the flows of life-affirming energy with values in research that is educational.

I am thinking of an inclusional approach to the generation of living educational theories that requires a living logic.

I am thinking of the new ways, enabled by digital technology, of communicating the embodied meanings of ontological values in the process of their clarification as they emerge in the practice of enquiries of the kind, 'how do I improve what I am doing?'

I am thinking of a living theory action research approach to professional development that uses new technologies in producing these theories in visual narratives with living standards of judgment.

So, what I want to do is to show the evolution in this thinking about educational theory that had its genesis in my responses to my readings in the Library of the Department of Education of Newcastle University some 40 years ago.

CREATING LIVING EDUCATIONAL THEORIES

Original ideas from my educational research at the University of Bath began to emerge in my first presentation to BERA in 1977 where I outlined the action reflection cycles used by a group of six teachers I worked with in one of the first Schools Council local curriculum projects (Whitehead, 1976). Initially my ideas focused on a methodological concern to find an appropriate approach for exploring the implications of the question, 'how do I improve my practice?' The ideas evolved from methodology to theory in a new understanding of living educational theories and research-based professionalism in education (Follows, 2007; Whitehead, 1989b). The ideas focused on the inclusion of 'I' as a living contradiction in questions of the form, 'How do I improve what I am doing?' and on the inclusion of 'I' as a living contradiction in the knowledge-claims to know one's educational influence in learning. They included the use of action reflection cycles, through which the meanings of embodied values could be clarified in the course of their emergence in practice and form living standards of judgement. I am thinking here of action reflection cycles in which individuals express concerns when their values are not being lived as fully as they could be. They imagine ways forward and choose one in an action plan, they act, gather data and evaluate the influence of their actions.

Their ideas also included the living logics for engaging in educational enquiries. They included ideas about the significance of making public the living educational theories of practitioner researchers as a contribution to the education of social formations and to the development of research-based professionalism in education.

One publication I would like to draw your attention to is 'Educative relations in a new era' a paper published in *Pedagogy, Culture & Society* (Whitehead,

1999). In this paper I stress the importance of judging an educator's educational influence in their educational relationships in terms of the student's own voice and learning. In the section on claiming to know my own educative influence with Kevin Eames, a doctoral researcher, I draw evidence from Kevin's learning in his doctoral thesis. The importance for me, of drawing on a student's own living theory of their educational influence in their own learning, is that I cannot claim to have educated anyone through what I do. I mean this in the sense of a causal relationship between what I do and the educational influence an individual expresses in their own learning. This is because of the role I give to creativity in each learner. I believe that an individual's creativity mediates between what I do and their educational influence in their own learning. I take responsibility for my educational influences in my own learning and hence will accept the responsibility for claiming to know my educational influences in my own learning, while recognising the influences of others in this learning. I cannot overemphasise the importance of Eames' research (1990, 1995b), especially in his researching the development of a school-based teacher-researcher group in partnership with the masters programme at the University of Bath. Linda Grant came over from the Ontario College of Teachers to see this work in the mid 1990s and initiated similar developments in Ontario with Jacqueline Delong of the Grand Erie District School Board. You can appreciate Jacqueline's integration of these ideas in her research into the development of a culture of inquiry with teacher–researchers in her doctorate (Delong, 2002) and access the publications from 5 volumes of Passion in Professional Practice from the front page of http://www.actionresearch.net.

Working with the idea that educators, who are researching their educational influences in learning with their pupils and students, can judge their educational influences through the narratives of learning produced by pupils and students, continues to inform my tutoring of educational enquiries in masters programmes and my supervision of research degrees. One account of a master's enquiry that particularly pleases me is that of Joy Mounter (2007a) with her 6 year old pupils. The narrative and video evidence in Appendix 2 of this enquiry show the 6 year olds responding to Joy's enquiries with a creative reformation of the action research cycle known as the TASC wheel (Thinking Actively in a Social Context) developed by Belle Wallace (2000). Joy can show her educational influences, in opening and sustaining a creative space with her pupils in school, and I can show my educational influence in helping to make public Joy's account through sustaining a creative space with the masters group in the Department of Education of the University of Bath.

In the evolution of my thinking about the nature of educational theory I have become increasingly aware of the significance of finding appropriate ways of representing the educational influence of flows of life-affirming energy with values in educational relationships.

FLOWS OF LIFE-AFFIRMING ENERGY WITH VALUES

In relation to the significance in educational research of acknowledging the importance of a flow of life-affirming energy I recall an experience while sunbathing in the park a couple of hundred yards from this Department of Education, before registering here for my Diploma of Education in 1966. I use the words of Paul Tillich (1973) to describe this experience as the state of being affirmed by the power of being itself. I experience this power as a flow of life-affirming energy with values. Through my introduction, here in the Departmental Library, to the writings of Richard Peters (1966) in his *Ethics and education* I felt this energy flowing with the values of freedom, justice, consideration of interest, respect for persons, worth-while activities and a procedural principle of democracy. It was this flow of energy with values that led me to apply for and accept a first teaching post at Langdon Park School in London's Tower Hamlets in 1967.

I also felt this life-affirming energy with values in the writings of Erich Fromm where he focused his analysis on living a loving and productive life while working within and resisting the alienating influences of capitalist social formations. As I read his *Fear of freedom* (1960), I was inspired by his idea that if an individual could face the truth without panic then they will realise that they are faced with the choice of uniting with the world in the spontaneity of love and productive work or of seeking a kind of security that destroys integrity and freedom. I still live with the tension in this recognition and continue to be inspired by a desire to enhance the quality of my loving relationships and productive work. The writings of Anna Freud (1965) helped me to understand what can happen in relation to normality and pathology when the development of a healthy expression of sexuality in relation to love and productive work is blocked. Her psycho-analysis of some 13 defence mechanisms resonated with my own experience and her ideas about projection continue to be helpful in resisting inappropriate interpretations of the behaviour of others. My psychoanalytic insights have continued to grow and the most recent influence is Daniel Cho's (2005) analysis in *Educational Theory* where he draws on the work of Jacques Lacan:

> ... knowledge is by definition the inquiry we make into the world, which is a pursuit inaugurated by a loving encounter with a teacher. With love, education becomes an open space for thought from which emerges knowledge. (Cho, 2005, p. 37)

My reading of Fromm's *Man for himself* (1947) introduced me to Marxist theory with his distinction between the marketing and productive personalities. I felt the validity of his analysis of the workings of capitalist forms of social order with their pressure to conform to the characteristics of the marketing personality. That is, to conform to the imperatives of the movement of capital to maximise profit. While recognising the necessity of being paid for working, I felt that my vocation for education would permit me to evolve a loving and productive form of life while working with the socio-historical and socio-cultural influences of capitalism. Some 40 years later I think this feeling has been vindicated as I look back on a productive life in education. Part of this productive life has been concerned with understanding the living logics in educational enquiries.

LIVING LOGICS IN EDUCATIONAL ENQUIRIES

In the library of the Department of Education of Newcastle University I devoured the works of John Dewey on *Democracy and education* (1916) and on *Logic: the theory of inquiry* (1938). What I felt in Dewey's *Logic: the theory of inquiry* was a form of scientific living in which the individual experiences a problem, imagines a solution, acts, evaluates and modifies the problem, imagined solution and action in the light of the evaluation. This logic can still be distinguished in my recent visual narratives on living inclusional values (Whitehead, 1989a, 2007b). The importance of the logics of educational theories and educational enquiries was brought home to me through Marcuse's writings when he pointed out that logic is a mode of thought that is appropriate for comprehending the real as rational (Marcuse, 1964).

The evolution of my understanding of the logics of educational enquiries and educational theories has included an understanding of the 2500 year old battle between dialectical and propositional logicians where each denies the rationality of the other (Popper 1963; Fromm 1947). Since 2002 I have engaged with the ideas of Alan Rayner (2007b) on inclusionality and can see the benefits of developing a living logic from a relationally dynamic awareness of space and boundaries as connective, reflexive and co-creative. What I like about Rayner's living logic of inclusionality is that it can include insights from theories that are structured through dialectical or propositional logics without denying the rationality of either logic. I think the need for a living logic can be understood in relation to Ilyenkov's (1977) question from his work on *Dialectical logic*, 'If an object exists as a living contradiction, what must the thought be (statement about the object) that expresses it?'

The reason I stress the importance of a living, inclusional logic is because I think that Ilyenkov could not answer his question without engaging in an examination of the living logic in his own form of life. His decision to 'write' Logic, and not to engage in a self-study of his own life of enquiry (Marshall, 1999) seems to me to have brought Ilyenkov back into the conflict with propositional logicians:

> The concretisation of the general definition of Logic presented above must obviously consist in disclosing the concepts composing it, above the concept of thought (thinking). Here again a purely dialectical difficulty arises, Namely, that to define this concept fully, i.e. concretely, also means to 'write' Logic, because a full definition cannot by any means be given by a 'definition' but only by 'developing the essence of the matter'.

A decision to develop one's own living educational theory may rest on an understanding of the significance of exploring the implications of asking, researching and answering questions of the kind, 'How do I improve what I am doing?' and of the kind that Rayner prefers to ask, 'How may we respond receptively in this situation so as to sustain our natural co-creative neighbourhood?'. It includes resisting a colonisation of mind, such as the one I permitted below, through allowing the conceptual frameworks of propositional theories to dominate the generation of one's own living theory. I think that this resistance can be accomplished while acknowledging the value of insights from propositional theories in the generation of a living theory in one's educational enquiry.

EDUCATIONAL ENQUIRY AND ACKNOWLEDGING A MISTAKE IN MY EARLY EDUCATIONAL THEORY

The ideas of Richard Peters in his Ethics and Education (1966) fascinated me through their focus on exploring the implications for a person who is exploring the implications of seriously asking themselves a question of the kind, 'What ought I to do?'. In my first lesson at Langdon Park School in 1967 I found myself feeling very concerned that I wasn't doing as good a job as I could do with my pupils and found myself saying, 'I must do this better', 'how do I improve what I am doing?' and 'how do I help my pupils to improve their learning?' These kinds of questions continue to inform my research and educational enquiries. Perhaps the most significant transformation in my thinking came with the recognition that I was making the following mistake in my thinking about the nature of educational theory.

At the start of my second year's teaching in 1968 I registered for the Academic Diploma programme at the Institute of Education of the University of London and studied the philosophy of education component with a team of philosophers of education led by Richard Peters. I initially accepted the idea that educational theory was constituted by the disciplines of education of the philosophy, psychology, sociology and history of education. By 1971 I felt that I was mistaken in accepting this idea because I could not see that any of the propositional theories of the disciplines approach, either individually or in any combination could produce a valid explanation for my educational influence in my own learning, in the learning of others or in the learning of a social formation. My decision in 1973 to apply for and accept the post of Lecturer in Education at the University of Bath was based on a change in my vocation from educator to educational researcher. From the belief that the dominant view of educational theory in the profession was mistaken, I decided to see if I could help to generate a form of educational theory that could explain an individual's educational influence in learning. I like the way Paul Hirst acknowledged the following mistake in the disciplines approach to educational theory. Its clear articulation is consistent with the intuitions that moved me to reject the approach. Hirst explained that much understanding of educational theory will be developed:

> ... in the context of immediate practical experience and will be co-terminous with everyday understanding. In particular, many of its operational principles, both explicit and implicit, will be of their nature generalisations from practical experience and have as their justification the results of individual activities and practices.
>
> In many characterisations of educational theory, my own included, principles justified in this way have until recently been regarded as at best pragmatic maxims having a first crude and superficial justification in practice that in any rationally developed theory would be replaced by principles with more fundamental, theoretical justification. That now seems to me to be a mistake. Rationally defensible practical principles, I suggest, must of their nature stand up to such practical tests and without that are necessarily inadequate. (Hirst, 1983)

It was the recognition of this mistake in 1971 that moved my sense of vocation from being a science teacher in comprehensive education to becoming an educational researcher in 1973 at the University of Bath, with a commitment to contribute to the generation of valid educational theories. In taking up the appointment I brought with me the enthusiasm for experimenting with the educational implications of new technologies that was first evoked in Newcastle in 1966. This enthusiasm for experimenting with new technology was heightened in 1971/2 by being provided with a video-camera and recorder, while Head of the Science Department of Erkenwald Comprehensive School in Barking. I was asked by the Headteacher and Inspectorate to explore its educational potential. Turning the camera on myself while teaching, and then viewing the results, gave me my first evidence of my existence as a living contradiction. I could see that what I was mistaken in my belief that I had established enquiry learning with my pupils. I could see that I was actually stifling enquiry learning because of the way I was questioning and structuring the learning resources. Hence my continuing emphasis on the importance of recognising the 'I' as a living contradiction in questions of the kind, 'How do I improve what I am doing?' Having now worked with hundreds of teachers who have used video I know that many have born witness to a similar experience of recognising themselves as living contradictions. They have also acknowledged an enhanced motivation to improve their practice from this recognition.

My interest in the educational influences of new technologies continues with the ease of access to streamed servers that are now making it possible to include video-data in visual narratives of educational influences in learning. These narratives (Charles, 2007) can communicate some of the meanings being expressed through the body, ie, non-verbally, in a way that written communications of print on pages of text cannot do. As I show you the visual narrative in a 2007 presentation to AERA (Cho, 2005), I hope that you can see and feel the power of the digital technologies for communicating the meanings of flows of life-affirming energy with values. I hope that you can see the potential of such narratives for showing how the expression of ontological values that are expressed in the practice of enquiry can be formed into the living standards of judgment (Laidlaw, 1996) of educational knowledge.

USING NEW TECHNOLOGIES IN PRODUCING VISUAL NARRATIVES WITH LIVING STANDARDS OF JUDGMENT

To close this celebration of accomplishment in the knowledge-creation of Barry Hymer, Eden Charles and Margaret Follows and to finish the wrapping of my present to the Department, I want to return to the image of the new video technology of the day in the Department in 1967. I want to move the image to the present day use of digital technologies with the use of video-narratives and streaming servers. Using video in the Department of Education of the University of Newcastle in 1967 helped me to get over the embarrassment that still puts many people off researching their own practices with video. The use of digital technology today, especially the use of Quicktime as a video-player, with its facility of moving the images at speed with a cursor, has helped to extend my understandings into the relationally dynamic awareness of space and boundaries known as inclusionality (Whitehead, 1989a). Visual narratives, using the new technology can integrate accounts of knowing oneself as a living contradiction (the dialectical accounts) and the insights from propositional theories including the disciplines of education, in the generation of living educational theories (McNiff, 2007).

What I am hoping is that my gift of ideas about educational theory to the Department of Education at the University is consistent with the originality of Barry Hymer's ideas on gift and talent creation, Eden Charles's Ubuntu way of being and knowing with guiltless recognition and societal reidentification, and Margaret Follows' understanding and commitment to fairer assessment.

The creation of this gift was catalysed by Barry Hymer's invitation to celebrate his graduation day here in Newcastle. This evoked memories of my educational response to the creative space opened up by staff, students, video and books in the Library in the Department of Education of Newcastle University in 1966/7. I am hoping that the gift is useful in the spirit of the early writings of Marx and of Barry's idea of gift creation from our talents as we affirm each other in enhancing our loving and productive lives. I am thinking of this affirmation in the expression of our talents and gifts in the generation and evaluation of our living educational theories in contributing to the creation of a world of educational quality.

Given that there is a forty year gap between the presentation of my first special study on 'The way to professionalism in education?' and 'How have I improved my way to professionalism in education? 1967–2007', if we leave it this long again, you will only have the virtual records to refer to!!

I usually end my e-mails with Love Jack in recognition of the loving warmth of humanity of Martin Dobson, a colleague I worked with in the Department of Education of the University of Bath. Here is the signature message that seems appropriate in affirming the value of the creative space offered by the Department of Education of Newcastle University to this new recruit to the profession of education in 1967:

Love Jack.

When Martin Dobson, a colleague, died in 2002 the last thing he said to me was 'Give my Love to the Department'. In the 20 years I'd worked with Martin it was his loving warmth of humanity that I recall with great life affirming pleasure and I'm hoping that in Love Jack we can share this value of common humanity.

Here is a copy of my latest book with Jean McNiff on *Action research living theory* (Whitehead & McNiff, 2006) for your library, given with the enthusiasm, creative spirit and love of educational enquiry I have shared with Jean over the last 25 years, and that I discovered in the Department of Education of the University of Newcastle those 40 years ago. Thank You.

REFERENCES

Abbott J & Ryan T (2000). *The unfinished revolution: learning, human behaviour, community and political paradox.* Stafford, Network Educational Press.

Adams P (2003). Thinking skills and constructivism. *Teaching Thinking*, **10**, 50–54.

Adey P, Csapo B, Demetriou A, Hautmaki J & Shayer M (2007). Can we be intelligent about intelligence? Why education needs the concept of plastic general ability. *Educational Research Review*, **2**(2), 75–97.

Albom M (1997). *Tuesdays with Morrie.* London, Times Warner.

Apple MW & King NR (1977). What do schools teach? In A Molnar & JA Zahorik (eds), *Curriculum theory.* Washington, DC, The Association for Supervision and Curriculum Development, pp. 108–126.

Arendt H (1978). *Life of the mind.* London, Secker and Warburg.

Ashby H (dir.) (1971). *Harold and Maude.* Paramount Pictures.

Balchin T, Hymer BJ & Matthews DJ (2008). *The Routledge-Falmer International Companion to Gifted Education.* London and Abingdon, Routledge-Falmer.

Bernstein R (1971). *Praxis and action, about some of Marx's unpublished notes written in 1944.* London, Duckworth.

Best B, Blake A & Varney J (2005). *Making meaning – learning through logovisual thinking.* Cambridge, Chris Kington.

Biesta GJJ (2006). *Beyond learning; democratic education for a human future.* Boulder, Paradigm Publishers.

Black P & Wiliam D (1998). *Inside the Black Box – Raising standards through classroom assessment.* London, King's College School of Education.

Bognar B (2006). *Branko Bognar on action research with children in Croatia.* Retrieved 10 March 2008 from http://www.youtube.com/watch?v=bw0l3WJxbdM

Borland JH (1997). The construct of giftedness. *Peabody Journal of Education*, **72**, 3–4, Charting a New Course in Gifted Education, Parts 1 & 2, pp. 6–20.

Borland JH (2003). The death of giftedness: gifted education without gifted children. In JH Borland (ed.), *Rethinking gifted education.* New York and London, Teachers College Press pp. 105–124.

Boyer EL (1990). *Scholaship reconsidered, priorities of the prfessoriate.* San Francisco, Josely-Bass, Inc.

Broks P (2003). *Into the silent land.* London, Atlantic Books.

Bruner JS (1966). *Toward a theory of instruction*. Cambridge, MA, Harvard University Press.

Buber M (1947). *Between man and man*. London, Kegan Paul, Trench, Trubner & Co. Ltd.

Buber M (1958). *I and thou*. New York, Charles Scribner.

Buber M (1961). *Between man and man*. London and Glasgow, Fontana.

Buber M (2002). *Between man and man*. London, Routledge Classics.

Buckingham M & Coffman CW (1999). *First, break all the rules*. New York, Simon & Schuster.

Bullough R & Pinnegar S (2004). Thinking about the thinking about self-study: an analysis of eight chapters. In JJ Loughran, ML Hamilton, VK LaBoskey & T Russell (eds), *International handbook of self-study of teaching and teacher-education practices*. Dordrecht, Kluwer Academic Publishers pp. 105–124.

Ceci S (1990). *On intelligence . . . more or less: a bio-ecological treatise on intellectual development*. Englewood Cliffs, NJ, Prentice Hall.

Ceci S (1996). *On intelligence*. Cambridge, MA, Harvard University Press.

Chaffey GW & Bailey SB (2003). The use of dynamic testing to reveal high academic potential and underachievement in a culturally different population. *Gifted Education International*, **18**(2), 124–138.

Charles E (2007). How can I bring Ubuntu as a living standard of judgment into the academy? Moving beyond decolonisation through societal reidentification and guiltless recognition. PhD Thesis, University of Bath. Retrieved 17 March 2008 from http://www.actionresearch.net/edenphd.shtml

Cho D (2005). Lessons of love. *Educational Theory*, **55**(1), 94, 95.

Claxton G (1997). *Hare brain, tortoise mind: how intelligence increases when you think less*. New York, HarperCollins.

Claxton G (1999). *Wise up – learning to live the learning life*. Stafford, Network Educational Press.

Claxton G (2002). *Building learning power: helping young people become better learners*. London, TLO.

Claxton G & Lucas B (2004). *Be creative: essential steps to revitalise your work and life*. London, BBC Books.

Costa A (ed.) (2001). *Developing minds. A resource book for teaching thinking*. Alexandria, VA, Association for Supervision and Curriculum Development.

Covey S (2004). *The 8th habit: from effectiveness to greatness*. London, Simon & Shuster.

Cripps L (2007). How do I improve my educational relationship with the learners I work with, both adults and children? Educational Enquiry. Master's Module, University of Bath. Retrieved 20 December 2007 from http://www.jackwhitehead.com/tuesdayma/louiseeenov07.htm

Crocket K (2004). From narrative practice in counselling to narrative practice in research. *International Journal of Narrative Therapy and Community Work*, **2**, 63–67.

Csikszentmihalyi M (1998). *Finding flow: the psychology of engagement with everyday life*. New York, Basic Books.

Csikszentmihalyi M, Rathunde K & Whalen S (1997). *Talented teenagers – the roots of success and failure*. Cambridge, Cambridge University Press.

Davies P, Hymer BJ & Lawson H (2005). Developing 'learning to learn' skills through experiential challenges. *Gifted Education International*, **20**(1), 80–87.

Delong J (2002). How can I improve my practice as a superintendent of schools and create my own living educational theory? PhD Thesis, University of Bath. Retrieved 17 January 2008 from http://people.bath.ac.uk/edsajw/delong.shtml

Delong J, Black C & Knill-Griesser H (2001–2007). *Passion in professional practice: action research in Grand Erie*. Brantford, Grand Erie District School Board.

Delong J, Black C & Wideman R (2005). *Action research for teaching excellence*. Barrie, DataBased Directions.

Denton C & Postlethwaite K (1984). The incidence and effective identification of pupils with high ability in comprehensive schools. *Oxford Review of Education*, **10**(1), 99–113.

Dewey J (1902). *The child and the curriculum*. Chicago, The University of Chicago Press.

Dewey J (1916). *Democracy and education*. London, The Macmillan Company.

Dewey J (1938). *Logic: the theory of inquiry*. New York, Henry Holt & Co.

Dewey J (1958). *Experience and nature*. New York, Dover Publications.

DfEE (1999). *Supporting documents for Excellence in Cities Initiative*. London, Her Majesty's Stationery Office.

DfES (2005). *The standards site, gifted and talented strand 'non-negotiables'*. Website for the Department for Education and Skills.

Donmoyer R (1996). Educational research in an era of paradigm proliferation: what's a journal editor to do? *Educational Researcher*, **25**(2), 19–25.

Dweck C (1999). *Self-theories: their role in motivation, personality and development*. Florence, Psychology Press.

Dweck C (2006). *Mindset: the new psychology of success*. New York, Random House.

Eagleton T (2008). Coruscating on thin ice. *London Review of Books*, 24 January, pp. 19–20.

Eames K (1990). Growing your own: the development of action researchers within an action-research approach to whole-school development. *British Journal of In-Service Education*, **16**(2), 123–127.

Eames K (1995a). How do I, as a teacher and educational action-researcher, describe and explain the nature of my professional knowledge? PhD Thesis, University of Bath. Retrieved 17 March 2008 from http://www.actionresearch.net/kevin.shtml

Eames K (1995b). Action research, dialectics and an epistemology of practically-based professional knowledge for education. Retrieved 18 June 2008 from http://people.bath.ac.uk/edsajw/kevin.shtml. See Chapter 6, Action research as a form of professional knowledge in a whole-school setting (pp. 193–224) Retrieved 18 June 2007 from http://people.bath.ac.uk/edsajw/KEVINPHD/kechap6.pdf

Eisner E (1988). The primacy of experience and the politics of method. *Educational Researcher*, **17**(5), 15–20.

Eisner E (1993). Forms of understanding and the future of educational research. *Educational Researcher*, **22**(7), 5–11.

Elliot CD (1997). British Ability Scales, 2nd edn. Windsor, NFER-Nelson.

Eyre D (1997). *Able children in ordinary schools*. London, David Fulton.

Farren M (2006). How can I create a pedagogy of the unique through a web of betweenness? PhD Submission to the University of Bath. Retrieved 30 January 2008 from http://www.actionresearch.net/farren.shtml

Feldhusen JF, Asher JW & Hoover SM (2004). Problems in the identification of giftedness, talent or ability. In J Renzulli (eds.), *Essential readings in gifted education*, vol. 2: *Identification of students for gifted and talented programs*. London, Sage.

Feldman A (2007). Teachers responsibility and action research. *Educational Action Research*, **15**(2), 239–252.

Fisher R (2003). *Teaching thinking*, 2nd edn. London, Continuum.

Flavell JH (1979). Metacognitions and cognitive monitoring: a new area of child developmental inquiry. *Applied Psychology*, **34**, 906–911.

Fogarty R (1994). *The mindful school – teach for metacognitive reflection*. Arlington Heights, Skylight.

Follows M (2007). Looking for a fairer assessment of children's learning, development and attainment in the infant years: an educational action research case study. Ph.D. Thesis, University of Plymouth. Chapter 7 on Creating living educational theory about assessment in the infant years. Retrieved 3 July 2007 from http://www.jackwhitehead.com/followsphd/followsphd7livth.pdf

Formby C (2007). How do I sustain a loving, receptively responsive educational relationship with my pupils which will motivate them in their learning and encourage me in my teaching? Educational Enquiry Master's Module, University of Bath, September. Retrieved 10 March 2008 from http://www.jackwhitehead.com/tuesdayma/formbyee.htm

Fraser JW (1997). Love and history in the work of Paulo Freire. In P Freire, JW Fraser, D Macedo, T McKinnon & WT Stokes (eds), *Mentoring the mentor: a critical dialogue with Paulo Freire*. New York, Peter Lang Publishing, Inc., pp. 175–199.

Freeman J (1980). *Gifted children – their identification and development in a social context*. Lancaster, MTP Press Ltd.

Freeman J (1991). *Gifted children growing up*. London, Cassell.

Freeman J (1998). *Educating the very able – current international research*. London, The Stationery Office.

Freeman J (2001). *Gifted children grown up*. London, NACE/Fulton.

Freeman J (2002). *Out-of-school educational provision for the gifted and talented around the world': a report to the DfES*. Retrieved 22 April 2007 from http://www.joanfreeman.com/mainpages/freepapers.htm

Freire P (1993). *Pedagogy of the oppressed*. London, Penguin Books.

Freire P (1997). A response. In P Freire, JW Fraser, D Macedo, T McKinnon & WT Stokes (eds), *Mentoring the mentor: a critical dialogue with Paulo Freire*. New York, Peter Lang Publishing, Inc., pp. 175–199.

Freire P (1998a). *Pedagogy of hope*. New York, Continuum.

Freire P (1998b). *Pedagogy of the oppressed*, New Revised 20th Anniversary edn. New York, Continuum Publishing Co.

Freud A (1965). *Normality and pathology in childhood. assessments of development*. New York, International Universities Press, Inc.

Fromm E (1947). *Man for himself. an inquiry into the psychology of ethics*, 1969 edn. Greenwich, CT, Fawcett Premier.

Fromm E (1957). *The art of loving*. London, HarperCollins Publishers.

Fromm E (1960). *The fear of freedom*. London, Routledge & Kegan Paul.

Fromm E (1979). *To have or to be*. London, Abacus.

Fukuyama F (1992). *The end of history and the last man*. London, Penguin.

Gallagher JJ (1996). A critique of critiques of gifted education. *Journal for the Education of the Gifted*, **19**, 234–249.

Gatton F (1865). *Hereditory talent and character*, Macmillan's Magazine **12**, pp. 157–166.

Gardner H (1983). *Frames of mind*. London, Fontana Press.

Gardner H (1993). *Multiple intelligences – the theory in practice*. New York, Basic Books.

Gardner H (1999). *Intelligence reframed – multiple intelligences for the 21st century*. New York, Basic Books.

Geake JG (2002). Knock down the fences: implications of brain science for education. In *National Association for Able Children in Education (NACE) Newsletter*, Spring 2002, pp. 4–7, reprinted from Primary Matters, April 2000, pp. 41–43.

Ginott H (1993). *Teacher and child: a book for parents and teachers*. New York, Collier Books.

Haddon M (2004). My best teacher. *Times Educational Supplement*, 13 February, p. 5.

Hannaford C (2005). *Fairer schools: fairer society*. Utbildung and Demokrati, Örebro University.

Hart S, Dixon A, Drummond MJ & McIntyre D (2004). *Learning without limits*. Maidenhead, Open University Press.

Higgins S, Hall E, Baumfield V & Moseley D (2005). *A meta-analysis of the impact of the implementation of thinking skills approaches on pupils*. EPPI Review (Social Science Research Unit, Institute of Education, University of London).

Hirst P (ed.) (1983). *Educational theory and its foundation disciplines*. London, Routledge Kegan Paul, p. 18.

Holley E (1997). How do I as a teacher-researcher contribute to the development of a living educational theory through an exploration of my values in my professional practice? MPhil, University of Bath. Retrieved 17 March 2008 from http://www.actionresearch.net/erica.shtml

Holzman L (1997). *Schools for growth – radical alternatives to current educational models*. New Jersey, Lawrence Erlbaum Associates.

Horowitz A (2001). *Times Educational Supplement*, 5 October 2001, p. 7.

House of Commons (1999). *Education and Employment Committee Third Report, highly able children, vol. 2: Minutes of evidence and appendices*. London, The Stationery Office.

Howe MJA (1990). *Sense and nonsense about hothouse children*. Leicester, British Psychological Society.

Hurford R (2007). How does the writing of a new gifted and talented policy enable me to reflect upon and evaluate my personal values about gifts and talents? In what ways am I living my values in this area? Educational Enquiry Master's Module, University of Bath, Retrieved 17 March 2008 from http://www.jackwhitehead.com/tuesdayma/roshurfordee2.htm

Huxtable M (2005). How can I improve my practice through 'walking the talk' and 'dealing with doorsteps? Educational Enquiry Master's Module, University of Bath. Retrieved 17 July 2008 http://www.jackwhitehead.com/jack/mhjwwcg&t.pdf

Huxtable M & Whitehead J (2007). *How can inclusive and inclusional understandings of gifts/talents be developed educationally?* Paper presented at The World Conference

For Gifted and Talented Children on from Local Worlds of Giftedness to Global, 5–10 August 2007, University of Warwick.

Hymer BJ (1998). *Rapid checklist for identifying more able pupils*. Unpublished.

Hymer BJ (2000). Understanding and overcoming underachievement in boys. In D Montgomery (ed.), *Able underachievers*, Chapter 5. London, Whurr, pp. 62–75.

Hymer BJ (2001a). BarroWise: nurturing the gift of wisdom. *NACE Newsletter*, Summer, 2001, pp. 1–2.

Hymer BJ (2001b). *Parents' Questionnaire: multiple intelligences profile of child*. Unpublished.

Hymer BJ (2002). Test that insults the nation – open minds to see that everyone is gifted and a richer world unfolds. *Times Educational Supplement*, 24 May, p. 23.

Hymer BJ (2003a). If you think of the world as a piece of custard . . . : gifted children's use of metaphor as a tool for conceptual reasoning. *Gifted Education International*, **17**(2), 151–164.

Hymer BJ (2003b). Included not isolated: meeting the needs of gifted and talented learners in mainstream schools. *Curriculum Briefing*, **1**(2), 31–34.

Hymer BJ (2004). The philosopher's moan – is it not time we taught children to think properly? In an open letter to the schools minister, Barry Hymer puts the case for philosophy. *Times Educational Supplement*, 3 September, p. 23.

Hymer BJ (2005). Gifted and talented – time for a rethink? *G&T Update*, (30), 6–7 December 2005, republished in *Teaching Thinking and Creativity*, Summer 2006, **20**, 28–31.

Hymer BJ (2006). Unpublished letter, dated 14 July 2006.

Hymer BJ (2007a). How do I understand and communicate my values and beliefs in my work as an educator in the field of giftedness? DEdPsy Thesis, University of Newcastle. Retrieved 20 December 2007 from http://people.bath.ac.uk/edsajw/hymer.shtml

Hymer BJ (ed.) (2007b). Special philosophy for children. *Gifted Education International*, **22**, 2–3.

Hymer BJ & Harbron N (1998). Early transfer: a good move? *Educating Able Children*, **2**, 38–47.

Hymer BJ & Jenkins P (2005). 'The fruits of age': cross-generational learning through all-age philosophical enquiry. *G&T Update*, **21**, 3–5.

Hymer BJ, Michel D & Todd E (2002). Dynamic consultation: towards process and challenge. *Educational Psychology in Practice*, **18**(1), 47–62.

Hymer BJ & Michel D (2002). *Gifted and talented learners – creating a policy for inclusion*. London, NACE/David Fulton.

Illich I (1976). *Medical nemesis*. New York, Pantheon Books.

Ilyenkov E (1977). *Dialectical logic*. Moscow, Progress Publishers.

Ingram C & Perlesz A (2004). The getting of wisdoms. *International Journal of Narrative Therapy and Community Work*, **2**, pp. 49–56.

Jeffrey B & Woods P (2003). *The creative school – a framework for success, quality and effectiveness*. London, Routledge-Falmer.

Jesson D (2000). *The comparative evaluation of GCSE value-added performance by type of school and LEA*. Discussion Papers 00/52, Department of Economics, University of York. Retrieved 24 March 2008 from http://www.york.ac.uk/depts/econ/documents/dp/0052.pdf

Kelemen L (2001). *To kindle a soul*. Southfield, MI, Targum Press.

Kellett M (2005). *How to develop children as researchers: a step-by-step guide to teaching the research process.* London, Paul Chapman Publishing.

Laidlaw M (1996). *How can I create my own living educational theory as I offer you an account of my educational development?* PhD Thesis, University of Bath. Retrieved 14 March 2008 from http://www.actionresearch.net/moira2.shtml

Larter A (1987). An action research approach to classroom discussion in the examination years. MPhil Dissertation, University of Bath. Retrieved 16 March 2008 from http://www.actionresearch.net/andy.shtml

Lewis CS (1960). *The four loves.* Glasgow, William Collins Sons & Co. Ltd.

Leyden S (1990). *Helping the child of exceptional ability.* London, Routledge.

Leyden S (2000). *Keynote presentation to Annual Conference of the National Association for Able Children in Education (NACE),* Cardiff.

LGT (2007). *Realising potential: challenging learners and supporting teachers* (DVD). London, London Grifted & Talented.

Lidz C & Elliott J (2006). Use of dynamic assessment with gifted students. *Gifted Education International,* **21**(2/3), 151–161.

Lidz C & Macrine S (2001). Identification of minority and immigrant students for gifted education: the contribution of dynamic assessment. *School Psychology International,* **22**(1), 74–96.

Light P & Littleton K (1999). *Social processes in children's learning. Cambridge studies in cognitive and perceptual development.* Cambridge, Cambridge University Press.

Lipman M (ed.) (1993). *Thinking children and education.* Iowa, Kendall-Hunt.

Lipman M (2003). *Thinking in education.* Cambridge, Cambridge University Press.

Lipman M, Sharp AM & Oscanyan FS (1980). *Philosophy in the classroom,* 2nd edn. Philadelphia, Temple University Press.

Lublin J (2003). *Deep, surface and strategic approaches to learning.* UCD Dublin: Centre for Teaching and Learning: Good Practice in Teaching and Learning. Retrieved 20 March 2008 from http://www.ucd.ie/teaching/printableDocs/GoodPracticesinT&L/deepsurface&stragticapproachestolearning.pdf

MacBeath J (2006). *Study support: a national framework for extending learning opportunities.* Retrieved 10 March 2008 from http://www.standards.dfes.gov.uk/studysupport/816987/817959/study_support_framework.pdf

Mai Li J (2005). *How can I attract my students' attention educationally?* CECEARFLT, Ningxia Teachers University, Guyuan 756000 Draft, May 2006. Retrieved 18 September 2007 from http://www.jackwhitehead.com/china/malijuanar3.htm

Marcuse H (1964). *One dimensional man.* London, Routledge and Kegan Paul, p. 105.

Maree K (ed.) (2007). *Shaping the story: a guide to facilitating narrative counselling.* Pretoria, Van Schaik Publishers.

Marshall J (1999). Living life as inquiry. *Systemic Practice and Action Research* **12**(2), 155–171.

Matthews DJ & Foster JF (2006). Mystery to mastery: shifting paradigms in gifted education. *Roeper Review,* **28**(2), 64–69.

McBarnett D (2006). *Controlling creative compliance: new sources of leverage.* Paper presented at the annual meeting of the American Society of Criminology 2006-10-05. Retrieved 10 January 2008 from http://www.allacademic.com/meta/p126846_index.html

McBeath J (2006). *Personalised learning, in study support: a national framework for extending learning opportunities.* Retrieved 3 August 2007 from http://www.standards.dfes.gov.uk/studysupport/816987/817959/study_support_framework.pdf

McLaren P (1993). *Schooling as a ritual performance.* London, Routledge.

McLaren P (1998). *Life in schools: an introduction to critical pedagogy in the foundations of education.* New York, Longman.

McLure M (1996). Telling transitions: boundary work in narratives of becoming. *British Educational Research Journal,* **22**(5), 273–286.

McNiff J, Whitehead J & Laidlaw M (1992). *Creating a good social order through action research.* Bournemouth, Hyde.

McNiff J (2007). *My story is my living educational theory.* New York, Thousand Island, Sage.

Mead GH (1972). *Mind, self and society.* Chicago, IL, The University of Chicago Press.

Medawar PB (1969). *Induction and intuition in scientific thought.* London, Methuen & Co. Ltd.

Meier D (2005). Creating democratic schools. *ReThinking School Online,* **19,** 4. Retrieved 28 December 2007 from http://www.rethinkingschools.org/archive/19_04/demo194.shtml

Miles MB & Huberman AM (1994). *Qualitative data analysis: an expanded sourcebook,* 2nd edn. Thousand Oaks, Sage.

Montgomery D (ed.) (2000). *Able underachievers.* London, Whurr.

Mounter J (2007a). Can children carry out action research about learning, creating their own learning theory? Learning and Learners Master's Module, University of Bath. Retrieved 25 November 2007 from http://www.jackwhitehead.com/tuesdayma/joymounterull.htm

Mounter J (2007b). If I want the children in my class to extend their thinking and develop their own values and learning theories, how can I show the development of their learning? How do I research this in my classroom? Research Methods Master's Module, University of Bath. Retrieved 30 October 07 from http://www.jackwhitehead.com/tuesdayma/joymounterrme.htm.

Mounter J (2008). *Pathfinder: wisdom begins with wonder.* Unpublished.

Munno A (2006). A complaint which changed my practice. *British Medical Journal,* **332,** 1092.

OfSTED (2001). *Providing for gifted and talented pupils: an evaluation of Excellence in Cities and other grant-funded programmes.* London, Office for Standards in Education.

Okri B (1996). *Birds of heaven.* London, Phoenix.

Passow AH (1979). Educational policies, programs and practices for the gifted and talented. In AH Passow (ed.), *The gifted and the talented: their education and development, the 78th Yearbook of the National Society for the Study of Education, part 1.* Chicago, The University of Chicago Press.

Polanyi M (1958). *Personal Knowledge.* Chicago, The University of Chicago Press.

Perkins D (1995). *Outsmarting IQ: the emerging science of learnable intelligence.* New York, The Free Press.

Perkins D, Jay E & Tishman S (1993). Beyond abilities: a dispositional theory of thinking. *Merrill-Palmer Quarterly,* **39**(1), 1–21.

Peters RS (1966). *Ethics and education.* London, Allen and Unwin.

Popper K (1963). *Conjectures and refutations*. Oxford, Oxford University Press.

Potts M (2004). How can I improve my practice by communicating more effectively with others in my role as a professional educator? MA Dissertation, University of Bath. Retrieved 17 March 2008 from http://www.jackwhitehead.com/monday/mpmadis.pdf

Rabinov P (ed.) (1984). *The Foucault Reader*. London, Random House.

Ramos MB (1974). *Paulo Freire's pedagogy of the oppressed*. New York, Seabury.

Rayner A (2004). Inclusionality: the science, art and spirituality of place, space and evolution, Retrieved 2 July 2008 from http://people.bath.ac.uk/bssadmr/inclusionality/placespaceevolution.html

Rayner A (2005). *Why I need my space – I'd rather be a channel than a node*. Retrieved 31 July 2006 from http://www.scimednet.org/Leadarts/Rayner_space.htm

Rayner A (2007a). *My Achilles heel: testimony of a 'gifted' child*. Retrieved 14 February 2008 from http://people.bath.ac.uk/bssadmr/inclusionality/AchillesHeel.html

Rayner A (2007b). Essays and talks about inclusionality by Alan Rayner. Retrieved on 18 June 2007 from http://people.bath.ac.uk/bssadmr/inclusionality/

Reis SM (2004). *Series introduction to essential readings in gifted education*, vols. 1–12. London, Sage.

Reis SM, Burns DE & Renzulli JS (1992). *Curriculum compacting*. Conneticut, Creative Learning Press.

Renzulli JS (2004). Introduction to identification of students for gifted and talented programs. In *Essential readings in gifted education*, vol. 2: *Identification of students for gifted and talented programs*. London, Sage, pp. xxiii–xxxiv.

Richardson R (2002). *In praise of teachers – identity, equality and education*. Stoke-on-Trent, Trentham Books.

Riding S (2003). Living myself through others. How can I account for my claims and understanding of a teacher-research group at Westwood St Thomas School? MA Dissertation, University of Bath. Retrieved 17 March 2008 from http://www.actionresearch.net/module/srmadis.pdf

Ross P (1993). *National excellence: a case for developing America's talent*. Washington, DC, U.S. Department of Education, Government Printing Office.

Sapon-Shevin M (2003). Equity, excellence and school reform: why is finding common ground so hard? In JH Borland (ed.), *Rethinking gifted education*. New York and London, Teachers College Press, pp. 127–142.

Sasso SE (1998). *God in between*. Woodstock, VT: Jewish Lights.

Scardamalia M & Bereiter C (1994). Computer support for knowledge-building communities. *Journal of the Learning Sciences*, **3**(3), 265–283.

Scharmer CO (2000). Organizing around not-yet-embodied knowledge. In G von Krogh, I Nonaka & T Nishiguchi (eds), *Knowledge creation, a source of value*. London, Macmillan Press, pp. 36–60.

Sharp AM (2007). Education of the emotions in the classroom community of enquiry. In BJ Hymer (ed.), *Special philosophy for children double-issue of Gifted Education International*, **22**, 2–3.

Sharron H (1996). *Changing children's minds – Feuerstein's revolution in the teaching of intelligence*. Birmingham, Imaginative Minds.

Shekerjian D (1991). *Uncommon genius*. London, Penguin.

Shore BM & Dover AC (2004). Metacognition, intelligence and giftedness. In RJ Sternberg (ed.), *Essential readings in gifted education*, vol. 1: *Definitions and conceptions of giftedness*. London, Sage, pp. 39–45.

Simonton DK (2008). Giftedness: the gift that keeps on giving. In T Balchin, BJ Hymer & DJ Matthews (eds), *The Routledge-Falmer international companion to gifted education*. London and Abingdon, Routledge-Falmer, pp. 26–31.

Spark M (1961). *The prime of Miss Jean Brodie*. London, Macmillan.

Sternberg RJ (2004a). Introduction to definitions and conceptions of giftedness. In RJ Sternberg (ed.), *Essential readings in gifted education*, vol. 1: *Definitions and conceptions of giftedness*. London, Sage, pp. xxiii–xxvi.

Sternberg RJ (2004b). Lies we live by: misapplication of tests in identifying the gifted. In J Renzulli (ed.), *Essential readings in gifted education*, vol. 2: *Identification of students for gifted and talented programs*. London, Sage, pp. 53–62.

Sternberg RJ (2004c). Wisdom as a form of giftedness. In RJ Sternberg (ed.), *Essential readings in gifted education*, vol. 1: *Definitions and conceptions of giftedness*. London, Sage, pp. 63–77.

Sternberg RJ (2007). Turning lemons to lemonade. In K Maree (ed.), *Shaping the story: a guide to facilitating narrative career counselling*. Pretoria, Van Schaik Publishers, pp. 210–213.

Sternberg RJ (2008). Wisdom, intelligence, creativity, synthesised: a model of giftedness. In T Balchin, BJ Hymer & DJ Matthews (eds), *The Routledge-Falmer international companion to gifted education*. London and Abingdon, Routledge-Falmer.

Sternberg RJ & Davidson JE (1986). *Conceptions of giftedness*. Cambridge, Cambridge University Press, pp. 255–264.

Stevens A (1980). *Clever children in comprehensive schools*. London: Penguin.

Stevens SS (1968). Measurement, statistics and the schemapiric view. *Science*, **161**, 845–856.

Stopper MJ (2000). *Meeting the social and emotional needs of gifted and talented children*. London, David Fulton.

Tannenbaum AJ (1979). Pre-Sputnik to post-Watergate concern about the gifted. In AH Passow (ed.), *The gifted and the talented: their education and development, the 78th Yearbook of the National Society for the Study of Education, part 1*. Chicago, The University of Chicago Press.

Terman LM (1925). *Mental and physical traits of a thousand gifted children*, vol. 1, *Genetic studies of genius*. Stanford, Stanford University Press.

Thayer-Bacon B (2003). *Relational (e)pistemologies*. Oxford, Peter Lang.

Tian F & Laidlaw M (2006). *Action research and the foreign languages teaching*. Shaanixi, Shaanxi Tourism Publishing House.

Tillich P (1973). *The courage to be*. London, Fontana, p. 168.

Tomm K (1990). Foreword to White M & Epston D (1990) *Narrative means to therapeutic ends*. New York, Norton & Co.

Trickey S (2007). An evaluation of philosophical enquiry: a process for achieving the future curriculum? *Gifted Education International*, **22**, 2–3.

Trickey S & Topping KJ (2004). 'Philosophy for children': a systematic review. *Research Papers in Education*, **19**(3), 365–380.

Vygotsky L (1978). In M Cole, V John-Steiner, S Scribner & E Souberman (eds), *Mind in society*. Cambridge, MA, Harvard University Press.

Walberg HJ, Tsai S, Weinstein T *et al.* (2004). Childhood traits and environmental conditions of highly eminent adults. In RJ Sternberg (ed.), *Essential readings in gifted education,* vol. 1: *Definitions and conceptions of giftedness.* London, Sage.

Wallace B & Eriksson G (eds) (2006). *Diversity in Gifted Education: International Perspecting on Global Issues.* London & New York: Routledge, p. 9.

Wallace B (2000). The TASC wheel. See: Welcome to TASC – developing problem-solving and thinking skills across the curriculum. Retrieved 19 June 2007 from http://www.nace.co.uk/tasc/tasc_home.htm

Wallace B (ed.) (2001). *Teaching thinking skills across the primary curriculum.* London, David Fulton.

Warwick I & Matthews DJ (2008). Fostering giftedness in urban and diverse communities: context-sensitive solutions. In T Balchin, BJ Hymer & DJ Matthews (eds), *The Routledge-Falmer international companion to gifted education.* London and Abingdon, Routledge-Falmer.

Watkins C (2001). Learning about learning enhances performance. In *NSIN (National School Improvement Network) Research Matters,* no. 13. London, Institute of Education.

Watkins C (2005). *Classrooms as learning communities – what's in it for schools?* London, Routledge.

Watkins C, Carnell E & Lodge C (2007). *Effective learning in classrooms.* London, Paul Chapman Publishing.

West-Burnham (2003). *Learning to lead. National College of School Leadership.* Retrieved 12 March 2008 from http://www.ncsl.org.uk/media/F7B/52/kpool-evidence-west-burnham.pdf

White J (2006). *Intelligence, destiny and education: the ideological roots of intelligence testing.* London, Routledge.

White M & Epston D (1990). *Narrative means to therapeutic ends.* New York, Norton & Co.

White K, Fletcher-Campbell F & Ridley K (2003). *What works for gifted and talented pupils: a review of recent research; LGA Research account 51.* Slough, NFER.

Whitehead J (1976). *Improving learning for 11–14 year olds in mixed ability science groups.* Wiltshire Curriculum Development Centre; Swindon. Retrieved 15 March 2008 from http://www.jackwhitehead.com/ilmagallfin.pdf

Whitehead J (1989a). Creating a living educational theory from questions of the kind, 'how do i improve my practice?' *Cambridge Journal of Education,* **19**(1), 41–52.

Whitehead J (1989b). How do we improve research-based professionalism in education? A question which includes action research, educational theory and the politics of educational knowledge. 1988 Presidential Address to the British Educational Research Association. *British Educational Research Journal* **15**(1), 3–17.

Whitehead J (1993). *The growth of educational knowledge – creating your own living educational theories.* Bournemouth, Hyde.

Whitehead J (1999). Educative relations in a new era. *Pedagogy, Culture and Society,* **7**(1), 73–90.

Whitehead J (2003). Creating our living educational theories in teaching and learning to care: using multi-media to communicate the meanings and influence of our embodied educational values. *Teaching Today for Tomorrow,* **19**, 17–20.

Whitehead J (2006). Living inclusional values in educational standards of practice and judgment. *Ontario Action Researcher* Vol. 8.2.1. Retrieved 18 June 2007 from http://www.nipissingu.ca/oar/new_issue-V821E.htm

Whitehead J (2007a). Action Planning in Creating your own Living Educational Theory. Retrieved 30 October 2007 from http://www.jackwhitehead.com/jack/arplanner.htm

Whitehead J (2007b). Creating a world of educational quality through living educational theories. Paper presented to AERA 2007 in Chicago on the 13 April. Retrieved 18 June 2007 from http://www.jackwhitehead.com/aera07/jwaera07.htm

Whitehead J & Huxtable M (2006). *How do I~we explain the educational influences of our values in our own learning and in the learning of others?* Draft document, Retrieved 15 February 2006 from http://www.jackwhitehead.com/marie/mhjwvalues5.htm

Whitehead J & McNiff J (2006). *Action research living theory.* London, Sage.

Williamson M (1992). *A return to Love: reflections on the principles of* a course in miracles. New York, Harper Willins.

Winner E (1996). *Gifted children – myths and realities.* New York, Basic Books.

Winslade J (2007). Chapter 4 Constructing a career narrative through the care of self. In K Maree (ed.), *Shaping the story: a guide to facilitating narrative counselling.* Pretoria, Van Schaik Publishers, pp. 52–62.

Winstanley C (2004). *Too clever by half: a fair deal for gifted children.* Stoke-on-Trent, Trentham Books.

Wood P, Hymer BJ & Michel D (2007). *Dilemma based learning in the humanities. Integrating social, emotional and thimking skills.* London, Chris Kington.

Yeats WB (1974) (1899). He wishes for the embroidered cloths of heaven. In *Selected poetry.* London, Macmillan, p. 35.

Yurkevitch VS & Davidoff BM (2008). Russian strategies for talent development – stimulating comfort and discomfort. In T Balchin, BJ Hymer & DJ Matthews (eds), *The Routledge-Falmer international companion to gifted education.* London and Abingdon, Routledge-Falmer.

INDEX